DAILY GUIDEPOSTS

2017

Guideposts
New York

ZONDERVAN®

ZONDERVAN

Daily Guideposts 2017
Copyright © 2016 by Guideposts. All rights reserved.

Requests for information should be addressed to:
Zondervan, 3900 *Sparks Dr. SE, Grand Rapids, Michigan 49546*

ISBN: 978-0-310-34644-9 (large print)

Acknowledgments: Every attempt has been made to credit the sources of copyrighted material used in this book. If any such acknowledgment has been inadvertently omitted or miscredited, receipt of such information would be appreciated.

Scripture quotations marked (CEB) are taken from the *Common English Bible.* Copyright © 2011 by Common English Bible. Scripture quotations marked (CEV) are taken from *Holy Bible: Contemporary English Version.* Copyright © 1995 American Bible Society. Scripture quotations marked (ESV) are taken from the *Holy Bible, English Standard Version,* copyright © 2001 by Crossway Bibles, a division of Good News Publishers. Used by permission. All rights reserved. Scripture quotations marked (GNT) are taken from the *Holy Bible, Good News Translation.* Copyright © 1992 by American Bible Society. Scripture quotations marked (ISV) are taken from the *Holy Bible, International Standard Version.* Copyright © 1995-2014 by ISV Foundation. All rights reserved internationally. Used by permission of Davidson Press, LLC. Scripture quotations marked (JPS) are taken from *Tanakh: A New Translation of the Holy Scriptures according to the Traditional Hebrew Text.* Copyright © 1985 by the Jewish Publication Society. All rights reserved. Scripture quotations marked (KJV) are taken from the *King James Version of the Bible.* Scripture quotations marked (MSG) are taken from *The Message.* Copyright © 1993, 1994, 1995, 1996, 2000, 2001, 2002 by Eugene H. Peterson. Scripture quotations marked (NAS) are taken from the *New American Standard Bible,* copyright © 1960, 1962, 1963, 1968, 1971, 1972, 1973, 1975, 1977, 1995 by the Lockman Foundation. Used by permission. Scripture quotations marked (NCV) are taken from *The Holy Bible, New Century Version.* Copyright © 2005 by Thomas Nelson, Inc. Scripture quotations marked (NIrV) are taken from *New International Reader's Version.* Copyright © 1995, 1996, 1998, 2014 by Biblica, Inc.® Used by permission. All rights reserved worldwide. Scripture quotations marked (NIV) are taken from *The Holy Bible, New International Version.* Copyright © 1973, 1978, 1984, 2011 by Biblica, Inc.® Used by permission of Zondervan. All rights reserved worldwide. www.Zondervan.com. Scripture quotations marked (NKJV) are taken from *The Holy Bible, New King James Version.* Copyright © 1982 by Thomas Nelson, Inc. Scripture quotations marked (NLT) are from the *Holy Bible, New Living Translation.* Copyright © 1996, 2004, 2007 by Tyndale House Foundation. Used by permission of Tyndale House Publishers Inc., Carol Stream, Illinois 60188. All rights reserved. Scripture quotations marked (NRSV) are taken from the *New Revised Standard Version Bible.* Copyright © 1989 by the Division of Christian Education of the National Council of the Churches of Christ in the United States of America. Used by permission. All rights reserved. Scripture quotations marked (RSV) are taken from the *Revised Standard Version of the Bible.* Copyright © 1946, 1952, 1971 by Division of Christian Education of the National Council of Churches of Christ in the United States of America. Used by permission. Scripture quotations marked (TLB) are taken from *The Living Bible.* Copyright © 1971 by Tyndale House Publishers, Wheaton, Illinois 60188. All rights reserved.

Fellowship Corner photos: Lisa Bogart photo by Lisa Vosper; Mark Collins photo by Kathryn Hyslop; Brian Doyle photo by Jerry Hart; Katie Ganshert photo by Kinsey Christin; Julie Garmon photo by Brad Newton; Edward Grinnan photo by Amy Etra; Rick Hamlin photo by Julie Brown; Jim Hinch photo by Martin Klimek; Debbie Macomber photo by Deborah Feingold; Erin MacPherson photo by Bloom Austin; Roberta Messner photo by Craig Cunningham; Rebecca Ondov photo by Deborah K. Hamilton; Natalie Perkins photo by Kris Rogers Photography; Ginger Rue photo by Patrick Jacks; Daniel Schantz photo by Sherry Wallis; Gail Thorell Schilling photo by Doug Schwarz; Melody Bonnette Swang photo by Crystal Logiudice; Jon Sweeney photo by Pamela Jordan; Marilyn Turk photo by Sarah Clauson; Marion Bond West photo by Michael Schwarz.

Monthly page opener photos: January by Anastacia-azzzya/Shutterstock.com; February by StevenRussell SmithPhotos/Shutterstock.com; March by VICUSCHKA/Shutterstock.com; April by Sailorr/Shutterstock.com; May by aceshot1/Shutterstock.com; June by Gelner Tivadar/ Shutterstock.com; July by Sandra Cunningham/ Shutterstock.com; August by LittleStocker/Shutterstock.com; September by Sunny studio/ Shutterstock.com; October by iravgustin/Shutterstock.com; November by Maya Kruchankova/Shutterstock.com; December by fotohunter/Shutterstock.com

Cover and interior design by Müllerhaus; Cover photo of Neerijse, Belgium, by Lars van de Goor/Trevillion Images; Indexed by Patricia Woodruff; Typeset by Aptara

First printing August 2016 / Printed in the United States of America

Hello, friend.

Welcome to a new year for experiencing God's great love in personal ways. If you are already a part of the *Daily Guideposts* family, then you know that these devotions—365 vibrant reflections on living with faith—will deepen your understanding of being a cherished child of God. If you are new to the community, we're glad you've joined us. You'll find that through the year, you'll develop a bond with our writers and other readers, who are praying along with you each day.

This year marks the forty-first edition of *Daily Guideposts*! It is published by Guideposts, the organization that shares true stories of hope and inspiration and is home to OurPrayer ministry. Each day's reading includes a Scripture verse, a story of finding God in the everyday moments, a prayer, and Bible references for "Digging Deeper." This year's overarching theme is "In God's Hands": "Don't be afraid, for I am with you. Don't be discouraged, for I am your God. I will strengthen you and help you. I will hold you up with my victorious right hand" (Isaiah 41:10, NLT).

It's been our pleasure to work alongside the writers of *Daily Guideposts*, each imparting discoveries on how to joyfully remain in God's hands. This year, catch up with longtime friends Carol Kuykendall, Patricia Lorenz, Elizabeth Sherrill, Brian Doyle, and Scott Walker. Connect with younger folks Natalie Perkins and Logan Eliasen. And embrace newcomers Marilyn Turk and John Dilworth.

Daily Guideposts 2017 includes seven special series. Discover the rewards of giving something away with Erin MacPherson in "An Outward Lent." During Advent, revel with Rick Hamlin in "The Word among Us." Every month, find out how Rhoda Blecker deals with grief in "Overcoming Loss."

Many more heartfelt moments such as these await you in *Daily Guideposts 2017*, where you'll experience love in God's hands.

Faithfully yours,
Editors of Guideposts

P.S. We love hearing from you! Let us know what *Daily Guideposts* means to you by e-mailing DailyGPEditors@guideposts.org or writing to Guideposts Books & Inspirational Media, 110 William Street, New York, New York 10038. You can also keep up with your *Daily Guideposts* friends on Facebook.com/dailyguideposts.

Especially for You!

Get one-year instant access to the digital edition of *Daily Guideposts* delivered straight to your e-mail. You'll enjoy its daily inspiration and Scripture anytime, anywhere, on your computer, phone, or tablet. Visit DailyGuideposts.org/DG2017 and enter this code: hope.

JANUARY

*"Do not fear, for I am with you;
do not be dismayed, for I am your God. . . ."*

—Isaiah 41:10 (NIV)

Sunday, January 1

Pleasant words are like a honeycomb, sweetness to the soul and health to the body. —Proverbs 16:24 (NRSV)

What could this be? I pulled the padded envelope from the mailbox. *A surprise from Wanda!* Even though I hadn't seen my friend in years, we often e-mailed.

Each year we shared our resolutions, prayed for their achievement, and checked in regularly to assess each other's progress. On January 2, I'd typed out last year's goals: "Lost the weight, but gained a few pounds back over the holidays. Removed clutter from my home, but still have more to do. Speak encouraging words of love and kindness; still falling short."

I'd had the "kind words goal" on my list since 2010. I'd even taped "Pleasant words are like a honeycomb, sweetness to the soul (Proverbs 16:24)" to my computer monitor as a reminder. But I was deeply dissatisfied by the lack of headway I'd made.

I ripped open the package. Inside was a book, *Silver Boxes: The Gift of Encouragement* by Florence Littauer. "Think of your words as gifts to others wrapped up as little silver boxes," Wanda had written.

Deeper inside was another package: a small silver box on a chain. *Perfect!* I could wear it around my neck as a tangible reminder to speak love.

I picked up the telephone to thank my sweet friend. "Did you look inside the necklace?" asked Wanda.

I pulled back the tiny clasp and a scroll fell out. It was the verse from Proverbs 16:24.

Now I was sure of it! This would be the year I made kind words a habit, thanks to God, Wanda, and a little silver box.

Lord, help me to speak words of kindness and love—once and for all! —Stephanie Thompson

Digging Deeper: Proverbs 31:26, Ephesians 4:29

Monday, January 2

"For the promise is to you and to your children and to all that are far off, every one whom the Lord our God calls to him." —Acts 2:39 (RSV)

When my friends John and Sarah welcomed a new baby into their family, they named him Christopher, after a grandfather. My friends Luis and Martina had a baby on the same day; they named him Jésus, also after a grandfather. Two beautiful new children, both wonders from God's hand and born into loving families.

"Will Jésus be a doctor, an athlete, an accountant?" I asked Luis the first time I visited. Thinking about young children's futures—what they'll be interested in and good at and grow up to be—is mostly an exercise in fanciful imagination, but all of us have done it. It's fun. Which is why I was surprised at Luis's hesitation.

"I just want him to have a chance," he said. When I looked puzzled, Luis began a sobering recitation of studies about the challenges for people with less traditional names like Jésus: 50 percent less likely to get an interview, for instance, in blind résumé tests.

"I didn't know," I replied. "What can we do?"

"Just be aware," Luis said. "Pay attention. We have a long way to go, but who better to work toward equality than those who believe that every child is of God."

Will you pray for me in this commitment and maybe join me too?

How might the world be different today, God, because I was important in the life of a child? Guide me to that place. —Jeff Japinga

Digging Deeper: Mark 10:13–16

Tuesday, January 3

OVERCOMING LOSS: Seeing Beauty

"I will continue to instruct you in the practice of what is good and right." —1 Samuel 12:23 (JPS)

We noticed the ramshackle shed every time traffic on Alabama Street prompted my husband to take a cutoff, and each time we saw it, Keith would remark, "Why doesn't someone take care of that old shed? It's falling down." Its sideboards were warping and splintering. The roof was crooked and sagging. It was an eyesore.

I didn't have occasion to take the cutoff for almost two years after Keith's death. I was still missing him very much—even more, it sometimes seemed, than in the immediate aftermath when I had to deal with the hundreds of details involved when a spouse dies. I hadn't had any time to fall apart because I had to be competent, so everyone would think I was doing fine. There were times when I almost thought so too.

I had believed it would get easier, but I was wrong. It got harder. Some days seemed longer and emptier. I felt damaged when I wasn't busy and as if I were just spinning my wheels.

Then, one day, I encountered traffic and turned on to the cutoff. The shed was gone and the field was covered with wildflowers. For a moment, I wondered what had happened. Then it occurred to me that it hadn't been the damaged, dilapidated shed that Keith and I were supposed to be looking at; it was the beautiful field in which that shed stood. We had concentrated on the wrong thing.

Perhaps, I thought now, *I'm doing the same.*

Please help me, Lord, to see the beauty that still exists in my life, rather than looking at what has fallen away. —Rhoda Blecker

Digging Deeper: Proverbs 4:2

Wednesday, January 4

He saved us, through the washing of regeneration and renewing of the Holy Spirit. —Titus 3:5 (NKJV)

At the beginning of the long holiday weekend, I resolved to tackle the household clutter that I perceived to be the source of my underlying unease: feeling pressed in and crowded. Upstairs and down, I'd been walking through a path flanked by books, papers, Christmas boxes, winter clothes, shoes, and more. The kitchen counters were stacked with food containers and small appliances that needed to be tucked away in their rightful place.

Without a clear plan, I sorted a pile of junk mail, uncovering a small throw rug that suddenly looked embarrassingly ragged and dingy. After trashing it, I happened to glance upward. I cringed at the sight of silky cobwebs strung along the top of a curtain no longer white. *Into the laundry!*—along with several nearby dresser scarves skimming with dust.

Moving from room to room, I opened a kitchen drawer I'd been trying to ignore. *Are those mouse tracks? Get to the bottom of it!* I emptied the drawer, scoured the utensils, replaced the liner, and installed repellant devices.

Increasingly intolerant—not of clutter as much as of grime—I soaked and removed the gunk stuck to the bottom refrigerator shelf, under the crisper, hidden from view. As I scrubbed—behind the scenes, below the surface—I found myself praying, allowing the Spirit to wash hidden layers from my encrusted heart. *Resentments, rejections, unhealthy reactions—soap them away.*

By the end of the weekend, I hadn't significantly widened the pathways through my rooms. Yet I no longer felt so pressed in. A cleaner foundation gave my new year a fresh start.

God, show me areas of my life that need to be deeply cleansed. —Evelyn Bence

Digging Deeper: Psalm 51:1–6, Jeremiah 33:6–11, Titus 3:1–8

Thursday, January 5

PARENTING ANEW
An Unexpected Answer to Prayer
Many are the plans in a person's heart, but it is the Lord's purpose that prevails. —Proverbs 19:21 (NIV)

I was worried about my grandson Logan's unstable situation at home and expressed my concern to my husband, Chuck.

"We have to keep praying for him. That's all we can do," he said. Then, trying to lift my spirits, he offered, "Maybe this summer we can get a travel trailer." Chuck had been planning this purchase since we got married as empty nesters a few years earlier. It was one of the things on our bucket list.

"Really?" We had done a lot of talking about plans, but to put a date on one was a surprise. Immediately, my mood brightened as I envisioned trips we'd take.

"Sure. We're both retired now, so we can start traveling."

Then the phone rang and everything changed. Family Services told us that Logan couldn't live with his mother anymore. His father, my son, single and working day and night, wasn't an option. We were the only choice. Otherwise, Logan would go into foster care.

The very next day, we became guardians of a three-year-old and our plans took a backseat to his welfare and schedule. It wasn't what we'd had in mind. We weren't happy about the inconvenience, nor did we like the uncertain length of Logan's stay. But we knew we were the best choice for him. We were the people who could provide the healthy environment he needed. The trailer would have to wait, our priorities newly rearranged.

Chuck turned to me. "Well, our prayers were answered. We just didn't know *we* were the answer."

Lord, thank You for answering our prayers. Help me to be willing to do my part. —Marilyn Turk

Digging Deeper: Jeremiah 29:11

**The Lord is compassionate and merciful, slow to get angry and filled with unfailing love.
—Psalm 103:8 (NLT)**

As soon as I unfolded the check, I cupped my hand over my mouth and fought back tears. The amount blew me away. I slid it across the table to my husband. Our eyes met, and I know he felt it too: humbled, awed, repentant.

You would think, as two people who have seen God show up as often as we have, that we would have learned our lesson by now. He's proven that He will provide, over and over again.

Apparently, my default setting for worrying is strong. God has brought me a remarkably long way over the past couple of years, but sometimes when stress is exceptionally high, I fall into old patterns. Bills were mounting. Adoption expenses were growing. My husband was in the process of losing a big account. Worry started to creep in; it was beginning to fester. I didn't see how we were going to make it this time.

And then my mom and stepdad gave us a late Christmas present. It was more than generous. As I sat at their table in the wake of the gift, I was overcome by their abundant love and graciousness. They were reflecting God, blessing me in the midst of my weakness, in the midst of my inadequacy and failure.

I hope, someday, my default setting will change. God's definitely not finished with me. Until then, I'm so grateful that He and my family are exceedingly patient with me.

Lord, You are so good! —Katie Ganshert

Digging Deeper: Psalm 86:5, Matthew 6:25–34

Saturday, January 7

"Are not two sparrows sold for a penny? Yet not one of them will fall to the ground outside your Father's care." —Matthew 10:29 (NIV)

The sun lit the branches of the bare trees as I took our dog Soda for his morning walk. In the distance, the caps of the Catskill Mountains were white with snow. Our neighbor's front door and windows were wide open—strange on such a cold day. So I stood in front of their house, trying to make sense of things.

My neighbor came out from the front door, holding a small blanket. "A bird," he explained. "Got in the chimney and was in our stove. I think it's injured."

His wife appeared behind him. "We don't know what to do," she said. Her brow strained, and she wrapped her arms around herself. "We put it under the tree. We opened all the doors and windows, hoping it'd fly out. It didn't. I think it has a broken wing."

They walked over to the tree, and I stayed away because I thought Soda would only make things worse. I wished them well and continued on down the road. With every step, I prayed for the bird—that it wasn't afraid, that it would make it.

On the way back, my neighbor sat on the front step, looking over at the tree. "Still alive," he said.

"What kind of bird is it?" I asked.

"A sparrow. Just a sparrow."

I was struck by his words. *Just* seemed so wrongly placed for all his concern. I thought of the Bible verse about God caring for the sparrows, so certainly He cares for us. I looked up at the sky and thought, *The same is true for us.* No creature is unworthy of our love, and by caring for God's creation, we show our love for Him.

Dear Lord, when we open our hearts to "just" sparrows, we reflect Your love on earth.
—Sabra Ciancanelli

Digging Deeper: Psalm 121:3, Matthew 6:31

Sunday, January 8

Since we are surrounded by so great a cloud of witnesses, let us lay aside every weight....
—Hebrews 12:1 (NKJV)

My church, Hillsboro Presbyterian, had formed a relationship with a local African-American church, Spruce Street Baptist, years ago. The initial goal was to bring groups reflecting different demographics within Nashville, Tennessee, to worship together. But as time passed, the exchange became something more, a gathering of family and a reunion with people we had grown to love.

As the designated Sunday approached, it was beginning to look as though the decades-old tradition might not happen. The week had brought one of the worst ice storms that our hometown had ever seen, plus I was in a mood and wanted to avoid people, stay dry, and read the newspaper without interruption. But at the last minute, Corinne and I bundled up the girls and headed for church.

The service started with an old spiritual hymn sung by Spruce Street's choir. There was something about the warmth of their smiles that began to thaw my grumpiness. Next, one of the members reported on the past week's activities. In spite of record cold and treacherous roads, the churchwomen had managed to serve 150 meals to people who were stranded. "With Jesus there with us, the weather didn't slow us down and we fed our hungry neighbors," the member said.

The ice around my heart cracked. I'd seen the bad weather as a personal inconvenience; these women had seized on it as an opportunity to help. Their spirit was contagious, and it was with anticipation that I pledged to put their lesson to work.

God, let me see my own discomfort as a reminder to comfort others. —Brock Kidd

Digging Deeper: Matthew 5:16, 6:22

LESSONS IN STONES
A Solid Foundation

"Therefore everyone who hears these words of Mine and acts on them, may be compared to a wise man who built his house on the rock." —Matthew 7:24 (NAS)

On Christmas night, 1970, a young man pulled his car onto a rock outcrop along the river, a few miles upstream from a small north Idaho town and proposed to his "steady girl." I said yes. We hoped for happily ever after, but thirty years later we nearly called it quits.

I went to California to care for my aunt, but Terry and I kept in touch. During this time, we each earnestly sought God. We prayed. Others prayed for us. We read God's Word. We made behavioral changes: Terry let go of anger patterns; I let go of disrespect. Eventually, we got back together and began a better version of ourselves.

Jesus gave His analogy of a house built either on rock or sand at the tail end of His Sermon on the Mount while sitting on a hill outside the town of Capernaum along the Sea of Galilee. Within view would have been basalt rock common to the area and sand along the seashore. He spoke of a storm assaulting each house: "The winds blew and slammed against that house" (Matthew 7:25). In Jesus's story, the house founded on the rock—His teachings—did not fall, but the house on the sand collapsed.

Terry and I moved back to our small north Idaho town along the river. We can look out of our picture window across the valley to the same rock outcrop where we agreed to marry, only there has been a change. Someone built a house there.

Your words, Your ways, Lord, are a rock I can build my life upon. —Carol Knapp

Digging Deeper: Psalm 127:1, Matthew 5–8, Luke 6:46–49

Tuesday, January 10

Lo, I am with you always, even unto the end of the world.... —Matthew 28:20 (KJV)

When I was a kid, I thought God was a huge noun, an epic He, a vast Him, an unthinkably immense and mysterious Whom. I understood the *idea* well enough to realize that God probably did not look like old Walt Whitman, cool as the poet was. But I did think God was an entity, a being of some unimaginable sort—the Dreamer, the Imagineer, the Speaker of the Word.

Later, I began to think of God as a verb, a relentless unquenchable energy, a force, a drive, a whisper that can be heard anywhere and anytime, if you made yourself available and attentive. So for years I tried most assiduously to see and hear and savor the divine music in which we swim.

Now, I begin to realize that God comes to me most and clearest and loudest through all things that are *alive*. Daughters and deer and dormice, sons and swallows and sunfish. Consider the bright red shout of a salmon headed home, the blue chord of a jay, the divine *I am here, I am with you* that is my wife's hand stealing out to find mine as we wait at the hospital for news of our child. Do not look up for God, I told my sweet, eager, headlong Sunday school students—look around at the flutter in the ferns, at your mother; consider the birds of the air, those shards of joy flung into the vault of heaven, they who are of God, who are suffused with God, for God is not a place or a person. God is love and joy and hope and grace; God is Who we sing when we are our best and truest and deepest selves.

Dear Merciful Inventor, let me be a decent, if slightly battered and cracked, vessel for delivering Your grace and love. Let me see and hear You always, even when I am deaf and selfish and blinkered. Let me do the best I can to share the song of You in my own mumbled mutter. —Brian Doyle

Digging Deeper: Genesis 1:20–24

Wednesday, January 11

Now faith is the substance of things hoped for, the evidence of things not seen. —Hebrews 11:1 (NKJV)

There is a mother with four kids getting on the escalator—none of the children older than eight or younger than five. I happen to fall in line just behind them. As the family steps on to the escalator, the littlest one hesitates while they begin the descent. He sticks out one foot and both arms, wavering. His mother looks back and says to him, "Just step. It's okay. Go ahead." This all happens in a matter of seconds as the line continues to move behind us.

I find myself right next to the boy, who promptly grabs my coat and takes his leap of faith. I hold him just under his arm and step with him. *Okay, I guess we're doing this together, Little One.* After he is safely on, he lets go of my coat and reaches for the rail instead, attempting to close the gap between his family and him.

"No, no, just wait there," his mother says after he has descended one unsure step. She smiles at me, says thank you, and turns back toward the bottom of the escalator.

I am left to marvel at the complete trust of this little one. Not once did he look up. Not once was he curious about who had grabbed him under his arm. He trusted that whatever he needed would be right there. Ah, to trust like that! In New York City where we adults trust no one, where we are holding our bags ever closer and constantly checking to see if our phones are suddenly missing, this boy reminded me very clearly about what faith is supposed to be.

God, thank You for visual reminders of Your living Word. —Natalie Perkins

Digging Deeper: Matthew 18:1–4

Thursday, January 12

But those who wait on the Lord shall renew their strength; they shall mount up with wings like eagles.... —Isaiah 40:31 (NKJV)

Yesterday, I sorted prayer concerns from a small basket on a bookshelf in the room where I pray. When a difficult problem keeps me from sleeping,

I write it down. I place the concern into this basket for God's attention and ask Him to guide me in handling it. Then I wait for His response.

I started this routine a few years ago as I struggled to apply one of Dr. Norman Vincent Peale's teachings from Ephesians 6:13 (NIV) that "after you have done everything, to stand." My shortcoming was not so much in giving up problems but in letting God keep them. My trust was not strong enough "to stand" firm—I regularly took back problems.

However, through this symbolic act of letting go of worries, I can picture the requests in God's "in basket" and out of mine. The most significant change I've noticed since using this practice is that I've become content in waiting for God. I have found that with His response also comes renewal, bringing fresh insight, energy, and confidence all in perfect timing to deal with the issue.

As I moved my concerns from the basket into a folder of answered prayers, the practice of reading the old problems that I had taken to God and reflecting with gratitude on His solutions brought a powerful realization of why my trust has grown.

Dear Lord, when my trust starts to waver, remind me again to "stand awhile." Amen.
—John Dilworth

Digging Deeper: Proverbs 16:3, 2 Corinthians 12:9

Withhold not good from them to whom it is due, when it is in the power of thine hand to do it. —Proverbs 3:27 (KJV)

It was late one Friday night, but I wasn't spending the evening partying like most college students. I sat at the small table in my friend Buck's kitchen while he made a pot of coffee. Buck and I are old souls, so it isn't uncommon for us to chat the night away about novels, good times, and God.

Buck slid a mug of coffee across the table. I thanked him, and our conversation picked up again. I lifted my mug, but before I took a sip, I noticed a dark brown ring around the inside. In fact, there were several. The rings weren't fresh and new. They were old, caked on, like the mug hadn't had a good clean scrub for far too long.

I lowered the mug back to the table and hoped that Buck hadn't seen the look on my face. One of his best qualities is hospitality. He loves to share what he has with others and would have been mortified if I'd mentioned the dirty mug. I had planned to pour my coffee down the drain the next time he left the room.

"Logan, is the coffee okay?" Buck asked.

I grimaced. He must have noticed how I'd abandoned it. I geared up to tell him why but then did something unexpected instead. I took a big gulp. "It's great!" I said.

Buck smiled, and I knew his small act of hospitality had brought him much joy.

Lord, thank You for good friends, warm coffee, and giving hearts. —Logan Eliasen

Digging Deeper: Galatians 6:10, Hebrews 13:16

Saturday, January 14

"For I am the Lord your God who takes hold of your right hand and says to you, Do not fear; I will help you." —Isaiah 41:13 (NIV)

"What are you afraid of?" the emergency room doctor asked me, her face close to mine as my tears came, tears I'd tried so hard to hold back.

It was a few minutes after midnight, and I'd gone to the ER with a painful intestinal blockage, a periodic result of my ovarian cancer surgery years ago. The doctor had ordered some tests and she'd just returned to tell my husband, daughter, and me that I was being admitted and would be taken by ambulance to the other hospital across town as soon as a bed opened up.

All I wanted to do was to go home...to my own bed...with my own husband.

"What are you afraid of?" she asked again, but I couldn't find words. So she continued talking about details and then left. I insisted that my husband and daughter go home, which they did. Soon I was alone with God, so I talked with Him.

What am I afraid of? Words came slowly. Being alone in the middle of a dark night, in a hospital that brings back painful memories of surgeries and facing so many unknowns.

Naming those fears in conversation with God took some of the power out of them, especially as I remembered His faithfulness within those painful memories. By 2:00 a.m., when I was wheeled into an ambulance, I felt less alone and less afraid.

Lord, I know that when I name my fears and lift them up to You, You reshape them and replace them with Your promises and peace.
—Carol Kuykendall

Digging Deeper: Psalm 46:1–3, 2 Thessalonians 3:16

Sunday, January 15

I heard the voice of the Lord, saying, Whom shall I send, and who will go for us? Then said I, Here am I; send me. —Isaiah 6:8 (KJV)

Church marquee messages intrigue me. In just a few words, these maxims can elicit a smile, a laugh, or at least a nugget of a larger truth.

While wintering in central Florida, I drove past a marquee remarkable not for its inspiration but for its disrepair. Several raised letters had fallen off, resulting in "urch of Go." In more prosperous times, the sign must have announced Church of God.

As I routinely drove past the sign, I began to think of it as Church of Go. Certainly, we need to nourish our souls at services with quiet prayer, music, and meditation on Scripture, but then we have to go. Ours is a faith of doing, of putting our beliefs into action. A traditional dismissal from the Episcopalian and Catholic services says it well: "Go in peace to love and serve the Lord and one another."

Over the next weeks, the broken sign reminded me of the ways that God instructs His beloved to get moving: "Go into all the world and preach the gospel" (Mark 16:15, NKJV); "Go. First be reconciled to your brother" (Matthew 5:24, ESV); "Go and sin no more" (John 8:11, NKJV); "Go with them two miles" (Matthew 5:41, NIV); "Go ye therefore, and teach all nations" (Matthew 28:19, KJV).

So, today, instead of just thinking of and praying for ways to love and serve, I will go buy food for a funeral reception and go practice music for Sunday.

Father, I'm going! Bless me on my way.
—Gail Thorell Schilling

Digging Deeper: Luke 10:30–37

Live peaceably with all men. —Romans 12:18 (KJV)

I wore a skirt and a dressy jacket, and my husband wore a new suit. After all, it was a rare privilege to be given an interview with Dr. Martin Luther King Jr. and his wife, Coretta Scott King. Mrs. King met us at the door of their home in Montgomery, Alabama, and went to call her husband. Dr. King was recovering from a near-fatal stab wound.

Seeing John's suit, the civil rights leader apologized for appearing in a sweater. "I'm sorry I couldn't dress up a little better."

"Why don't you tell them," Mrs. King said, "why you can't wear your suit?"

"Now, Coretta," her husband said, "these people are here to talk about important things."

"What do you call important?" she asked him. And as the four of us sat down, she told us the story.

Dr. King owned two suits, and while he was in the hospital she'd taken them to the dry cleaner. When she went to pick them up, the store owner said, "I don't have anything here for a *Mrs. King*, but I have two suits ready for *Coretta*."

Every week since then she'd gone back to the same store. There was never anything for Mrs. King.

What do you call important? Justice, certainly. Equal rights under the law, of course. Fair housing, a living wage. But maybe the struggle for human rights begins closer to home, with each one of us right here, right now, simply respecting the dignity of every human being we meet.

Father, help me to honor each person You send my way today. —Elizabeth Sherrill
Digging Deeper: 1 Samuel 2:8

Tuesday, January 17

Therefore, as God's chosen people...clothe yourselves with compassion, kindness, humility, gentleness and patience. —Colossians 3:12 (NIV)

My mittened hands fumbled to open the latch of the barn door. I'd been outside only a few moments, but already my cheeks ached from the cold, which matched my heart—way below zero. I'd run into an acquaintance who had a reputation for being difficult. She snarled at me when I said hello. *Next time I see her, I'm going to totally ignore her!* I thought.

I swung open the barn doors. The light from my headlamp cast its beam as I loaded the sled with flakes of alfalfa for the horses. Two eyes glowed from the top of the stack. A skinny tortoiseshell cat sat huddled in a ball, trying to keep warm. As soon as the light danced across it, it scooted backward to hide. "Aw, kitty, did somebody dump you out here? I bet you're hungry." The gold slits of its eyes glared at me.

After feeding the horses, I went into the house and filled a bowl with cat food. My heart felt warm from the kindness I would offer. But as soon as I stretched on my toes to set the bowl on the hay, the cat swatted my hand and disappeared. I chuckled at its antics.

I heard a still small voice: *That's not how you responded to your acquaintance.* My spirit was grieving. I couldn't control how others acted, but I could control what I did.

A couple of days later I smiled when I greeted the woman. It didn't matter that she only nodded in return.

Lord, help me to walk in Your example of kindness. Amen. —Rebecca Ondov

Digging Deeper: 2 Corinthians 6:3–10, Galatians 5:22–23

Wednesday, January 18

So continue encouraging each other and building each other up, just like you are doing already. —1 Thessalonians 5:11 (CEB)

A man stepped onto the crowded subway train. "Would somebody please give me a seat?" he asked. It was the stop nearest the hospital, and he looked like he'd just come from an appointment. He had an unsteady step, thick dark glasses, a hearing device, and a loud but shaky voice.

Get up! I told myself. But I was in a corner seat, hard for the man to get to, and not closest to him. Besides, I was studying my Bible, as I often do on my morning commute. Before I could move, a woman two seats away gave the man hers.

You should have been the one! I chided myself. *Really now, wouldn't that have been the biblical thing to do?*

The man spoke to all of us and no one in particular, commenting on the subway, asking us if we were at 59th Street yet, exclaiming over the day's news, nervously wondering if he was at his stop.

When we did get there, people helped clear the way. Then the woman who had offered her seat sat back down in it. I was about to return to my reading when I stopped myself. I reached over and tapped the woman on the shoulder. "That was very nice of you," I said.

She nodded. "Thanks."

I can't always be the one. I'm not always in the right place. I don't have the right things to say or give. Sometimes I'm not quick enough. But when I notice someone else do something kind, I can thank and praise, and spread the good word.

**Lord, show me how I can best give of all
You have given me.** —Rick Hamlin

Digging Deeper: Galatians 6:2

Thursday, January 19

Eli perceived that the Lord was calling the boy. Therefore Eli said to Samuel, "Go, lie down; and if he calls you, you shall say, 'Speak, Lord, for your servant is listening. . . .'" —1 Samuel 3:8–9 (NRSV)

Cheep, cheep, cheep. Shutting my eyes against the sunlight, I consider the possibilities of this sound, finally concluding it's the smoke detector begging for a new battery. *Well, tough, it's not getting one today!*

I am depressed. The worst winter on record has dragged on. Everything is gray, white, brown, or some combination thereof. A good friend is sick; another is watching her child die. We've just learned that a structural problem in our building will cost hundreds of thousands of dollars to fix. I just can't cope anymore . . . with anything. *When will God show me what to do?*

Cheep, cheep, cheep.

I open my eyes. When I stop squinting, I see it's not the smoke detector. A male swallow perches on the side of the building outside my window and digs out moss and crumbling cement from a tiny crack between stones. A female swallow hovers nearby. This crazy bird thinks he can clear out enough space to build her a home. She flies away. I smile sourly. *Good luck, pal.*

Cheep, cheep, cheep.

An hour later, that swallow has dug out enough moss and cement to squeeze in between the rocks, and the female returns. I begin to think about how my daily routine, chipping away at things, little by little, always makes me feel better.

God has many voices. *Cheep, cheep, cheep.*

Father, when I feel I can do nothing, give me the humility to open myself to Your help. Amen.
—Marci Alborghetti

Digging Deeper: Exodus 3:13–15; Psalm 35:17, 22

Friday, January 20

On those living in the land of deep darkness a light has dawned. —Isaiah 9:2 (NIV)

We were attending a support group to learn how best to help our son who was suffering from depression. Truth be told, I was getting depressed myself because I was finding it harder to hold on to hope as time wore on. I posed the question "How do you help someone to see a glimmer of hope?"

One member said, "A while back I went on a tour of the prison on Alcatraz Island. They showed us the solitary confinement cell. The tour guide said that, if we wanted, we could go into the cell and he'd close the door for a moment, so we could get a feel for how dark it is in there. I went in with a few other tourists, and when he shut the door it was totally black. I've never experienced anything like it. Then when the guide started to open the door again, even just that tiny crack of light made all the difference in the world."

The next day I found myself trying to muster enough faith to pray for the progress I was beginning to doubt would ever happen. Then I remembered the solitary confinement door being opened and how even the tiniest sliver of light penetrates the darkness. The greater it was, the less light was needed to transform it.

It was okay that I didn't have a huge amount of faith to keep on praying. All I needed was enough to pray for a small glimmer of hope.

God, I think I have enough faith today to make a difference in this darkest of times. Thank You.
—Karen Barber

Digging Deeper: Psalm 112:4, John 1:1–5

Saturday, January 21

You save humans and animals alike, O Lord. How precious is your steadfast love, O God!...
—**Psalm 36:6–7** (NRSV)

My sister Sharon and her husband, Tom, moved to Oklahoma from Colorado. Until they build a house, they are living on our farm, in my mother-in-law's old house, which has been vacant since she died. It's a nice arrangement—handy for shared meals and shopping.

One problem, however, has been the matter of dogs. Their elderly Shiba Inu, Andy, is an indoor dog, feisty and territorial but frail. Sharon and Tom dote on him as they would on a toddling son.

Our two Labradors, Moe and Erica, and two beagles, Sawyer and Russell, roam the farm in the way of country dogs and consider my mother-in-law's house part of their domain. Since Sharon's at home more than the rest of us (and gives dog treats all the time), our four dogs have taken to hanging out on her porch. They tolerate Andy and sniff his nose when he bites at them through the pen Tom built for him out back. Sharon lives in terror, though, that Andy will escape, pick a fight with them, and be killed.

It may happen. That doesn't stop Sharon from giving our dogs treats though. Or putting out water for them. Or loving them. Or sitting on her porch, watching them chase cows, then calling to tell me about it.

When it comes to dogs, Sharon is like God: all-loving. If only we were the same about humans.

Oh, Father, let me love others as You do. —Patty Kirk

Digging Deeper: Matthew 10:29–30

Sunday, January 22

**I listen carefully to what God the Lord is saying, for he speaks peace to his faithful people....
—Psalm 85:8 (NLT)**

The invitation to preach at my family's gathering weighed heavily on my heart. It had been only a month since Uncle Adolfo had been diagnosed with stage four pancreatic cancer; he had a few months to live and was homebound. His daughter Elizabeth asked the family to come together for worship at her home, so he could attend.

What words will bring comfort? I wondered. *What can I say to my cousins and their children that might alleviate their distress?* I was at a loss. So I did what I always do when I'm asked to preach. I prayed, "Lord, guide and help me offer words of encouragement."

Finally, after what seemed like a long wait, I felt led to Psalm 100:5 (NLT): "For the Lord is good. His unfailing love continues forever, and his faithfulness continues to each generation." The text was perfect because my uncle also taught us how to be faithful; he never wavered from God.

Although I was to give the benediction, I asked Uncle Adolfo to do it. We stood in a circle, held hands, and he gave us a blessing. It would be the last time he stood before the whole family.

Lord, thank You for Your unfailing love and faithfulness that continues forever. —Pablo Diaz

Digging Deeper: 2 Corinthians 5:7, Colossians 1:10

Monday, January 23

Then Jesus told his disciples a parable to show them that they should always pray and not give up. —Luke 18:1 (NIV)

The oddest thing I prayed for this year was a hat.

My wife performed a concert in London, and the stylist borrowed a couture hat from a famous designer for her to wear onstage. I told Julee to call me from the car after she landed stateside, but when the phone rang, all she could say was, "They can't find the hat!"

Julee accidentally took it with her in the taxi to Heathrow Airport. She realized her blunder, doubled the fare on the meter, and begged the cabbie to return it to the hotel concierge to be retrieved by the stylist. She called London the minute her plane landed—no hat.

"That hat costs a thousand dollars!" Julee cried.

"Find that hat!" I said.

"Pray," urged Julee. "That's all we can do. Ask your colleagues to pray."

But sitting in Guideposts Prayer Fellowship, I couldn't bring myself to ask people to pray for a hat, not when people needed prayers for health issues and financial stress. So I said a quick silent prayer, slightly embarrassed and feeling hopeless.

Though not for long! It turns out the London cabbie tracked down the designer, based on the label in the hat, convinced some assistant that he indeed was in possession of the one-of-a-kind headwear, and returned it forthwith.

Father, there is no problem too small or too big to bring before You. Thank You for that honest taxi driver and for reminding me that there is nothing trivial when it is said in prayer.
—Edward Grinnan

Digging Deeper: Psalm 37:5–6, Romans 8:18

Tuesday, January 24

Trust in the Lord with all thine heart; and lean not unto thine own understanding. —Proverbs 3:5 (KJV)

I'd seen a pair of carved wooden angel wings and just had to have them to hang on the new vintage-inspired floral wall covering in my guest bedroom.

But when I pounded the nail in the wall, I was left with the distinct impression that those angel wings were not mine at all.

Instead, God brought a special friend to mind. This woman owns a beach house, and I knew they would be ideal for her room, which features a luxurious queen-size bed with a mosquito net canopy and overlooks the pool.

When I mailed the gift to my friend, I prayed that the guests who got to see the angel wings would be comforted by their presence. A week later, I received a thank-you note. She did not keep the wings but felt led to pass them on to a missionary in Romania who runs a home for abused and neglected girls. "She gives those girls their wings," my friend told me.

In the new owner's hands, the angel wings became a symbol that God really cares about what happens to those girls. And by releasing my gift, I began to care about what happened to them too. Thanks to that pair of traveling angel wings, I now pray for the girls regularly and eagerly await the news of what God is doing in their lives.

When I give a gift, dear Lord, help me to trust You with the outcome. —Roberta Messner

Digging Deeper: Proverbs 3:6, Romans 8:28

But through love serve one another.
—Galatians 5:13 (NAS)

When my husband, Gene, broke his hip, I loved waiting on him. He adored having me bring him breakfast on a tray while he watched the morning news. I'd bought a special nonstick pan and learned how to poach eggs perfectly. But by month eight, my enthusiasm waned.

Early one morning Gene called out to me, "Are you fixing my eggs?" He knew I wasn't. I was on the phone and pretended not to hear him. He found me, opened his mouth wide, and pointed to it with one finger. I got off the phone and stared at him.

"How about some eggs and bacon?" he asked, smiling hopefully.

"How about I show you how?" I said.

"No thanks."

"I bought the cereal you like so much."

"No thanks." He settled down in his chair and turned on the news.

I stomped to the kitchen and slung the nifty pan onto the stove. When I served his breakfast on a tray, he beamed. "Thanks, honey."

"How's your hip?"

"I'm getting there," he responded, not meeting my eyes.

As I crawled back into bed, I remembered how I'd hated to cook breakfast for my first husband, Jerry, who died in 1983. One day, in desperation, I'd confessed my ugly attitude and asked God for help. So thirty-plus years later, I prayed:

Thank You, Father, that I have someone to cook breakfast for. —Marion Bond West

Digging Deeper: John 12:2, 21:9

Thursday, January 26

Always be humble, gentle, and patient, accepting each other in love. —Ephesians 4:2 (NCV)

My stomach plummeted as I read our son's report card. Christian had two failing grades, and the other two weren't much to speak of either. My husband, Anthony, and I shot questions at our middle-schooler: "When were you going to tell us how poorly you were doing?" "Why didn't you tell us about these missed assignments?" "What's your plan for improving your grades?"

Christian mumbled a few short responses, and Anthony and I felt confident he was remorseful and determined to work harder. I e-mailed his teachers, promising to assist him in his efforts to complete the missed assignments and to study harder.

A few days later Christian approached us with the truth behind his failing grades: he had taken my parents' recent deaths very hard, and focusing on schoolwork had been nearly impossible. I thought of the many days after my parents died that I had put off my responsibilities. I'd had the opportunity to take time out and step away. My son hadn't been given the same freedom; he had returned to school just days after the funerals.

I needed to give Christian time to mourn his grandparents, to allow him to talk through his feelings, and to make sure he was getting the extra rest his mind and body needed.

Lord, help me to extend to my children the same grace that has been extended to me.
—Carla Hendricks

Digging Deeper: Colossians 3:12–13, 1 Peter 3:8

Friday, January 27

Though I am surrounded by troubles, you will bring me safely through them.... —Psalm 138:7 (TLB)

An insidious hacker invaded my computer and destroyed everything: my books, stories, letters, photos, e-mail addresses, and file folders. The guys at the computer fix-it store said the assault on my computer was one of the worst because it locked all of my data with army-level encryption. Once the process was complete, my computer was useless. The only solution was to erase everything and start over.

I cried a lot the first two days. Okay, I wailed. It felt like the death of my career, plus contacts with loved ones and all the photos of family events and travels. I could hardly breathe. I did have some of my documents on a zip drive, but that had not been updated for three years. Luckily, I had copies of three projects I was working on stored on my husband's computer. But everything else was gone.

"Lord," I began to pray, "help me accept this and go on." Finally, I rationalized that it was useless to be angry at myself or even the perpetrators who'd put a lock on my files.

Jack reminded me that I still had what was most important in life: family, friends, good health, and the ability to move forward. I reminded myself that all we have in life is the present and the future, and if I would just concentrate on that I would be fine.

So I worked hard to create a new future for myself. I did some new writing, took new photos, painstakingly reentered hundreds of e-mail addresses, and gradually understood that no computer tragedy was going to ruin my life.

Lord, when something of value is taken from me, keep me sane and keep my life in proper perspective with You at the helm. Thank You. —Patricia Lorenz

Digging Deeper: John 14:27, Hebrews 12:14–15

Saturday, January 28

"Those who pay regard to vain idols forsake their hope of steadfast love." —Jonah 2:8 (ESV)

I had been asked to share encouragement with a group of women. The ladies were compassionate and kind. But I was scared. The week before this event was an all-out battle. I was pummeled by negative thoughts. I saw myself tongue-tied, fainting and falling, breathing too fast and hyperventilating, my knees knocking together so hard the roof would fall. I recognized these as irrational, it'll-never-happen thoughts, but they hawked me just the same.

One morning I sat in my quiet-time chair and let the fear spill like water. It was a fast rush. Worry streamed from a deep well. The bottom line was that I was afraid I'd be shamed, embarrassed, humiliated by my own ineptness. And what I understood, what was spoken to my spirit after I let the waves of worry crash free, was this: *You are making an idol—an idol of yourself, for yourself.*

This truth was both tough and tender. But, suddenly, I had fresh vision and I could see the circumstance for what it was. My eyes weren't on the Lord. They were on me. Who would've thought I could build an idol this way?

I repented, and God's grace and compassion met me in a gentle, vulnerable place. So did His strength and provision, because when I talked with the women, His Spirit was there. I wasn't afraid. The words were slow and easy, and the message was strong.

Lord, keep my eyes and heart on You.
Amen. —Shawnelle Eliasen

Digging Deeper: 1 Corinthians 10:14, 1 John 5:21

Sunday, January 29

At midnight I will rise to give thanks to You....
—Psalm 119:62 (NKJV)

I can usually handle whatever life throws at me, as long as I can sleep at night. So when I developed a stubborn case of insomnia, I was frantic.

We went to see our daughter in Kansas City, and my son-in-law handed me a box. "I heard you weren't sleeping," he said. "Maybe this will help." It was a model airplane kit, the old-fashioned kind, like the ones I used to assemble when I was a boy, with delicate balsa wood and tissue-paper covering.

Back home, I set up a work area in my study, in case the insomnia persisted. It did. So at midnight, I cut out pieces of balsa wood and was soothed by the spicy fragrance. Using my hands was hypnotic. As I worked, my mind drifted back to my childhood, when I made many models, a time when I felt safe and happy, surrounded by a loving family. "Lord," I breathed, "thank You for my happy childhood. Give me back the peace of mind I had as a boy."

For several nights I trekked to my study, but then the excursions fell off as I began to sleep again. Having something fun to do loosened the grip of insomnia.

Handiwork and prayer. It's worth a try.

Waking or sleeping, Lord, Thy presence is my light.
—Daniel Schantz

Digging Deeper: Psalm 23, Proverbs 3:21–26

Monday, January 30

"As the Father loved Me, I also have loved you...."
—John 15:9 (NKJV)

Getting married for the first time at forty came with some interesting adjustments. The most notable was getting used to the fact that my fiancé, a divorced man with grown children, was already a grandfather. By marrying Randy, I would become an instant grandmother. I'd never once harbored any desire to be even a mother. It terrified me. Would the children like me? Would I like them? Worst of all, would I suddenly become old?

I hid my knocking knees when I met the grandkids for the first time. They didn't seem to have any such preconceived doubts. "Want to see my room?" Nolan asked. Natalie showed me flips she could do on the trampoline. Huntley wanted a ride on the four-wheeler. And Bridger just grinned, showing more dimples than teeth. Within minutes, I forgot all about being nervous and got down to serious playing.

At our first big family get-together, my niece and nephew were there. Since they called me Aunt Erika, the other children started to as well. The name stuck. Playing continued. I was just one of the kids, only taller.

It's turned into the best of both worlds. I don't have to be the parent. All I need to do is listen to them, play with them, and love them. That's easy to do. They don't make me feel old; they make me feel loved.

The only downside? Randy is wondering about when the grandkids get older, just how is he going to explain why their Papa is married to their aunt?

Lord, thank You for guiding us all through the transition from my family/his family to our family. Blessed be Your name. —Erika Bentsen

Digging Deeper: Isaiah 54

There's a season for everything and a time for every matter under the heavens. —Ecclesiastes 3:1 (CEB)

When we bought it in 1979, the tandem-axle grain truck was state of the art. I drove it until I took an off-farm job with a social service agency. Thirty-plus years later the brakes were shot, the crank windows were cranky, and the motor used lots of oil. The truck was worn out, and my husband was wearing out too. Each year it was harder for him to work twelve-hour shifts and wrestle the heavy tarp in the Kansas wind.

So last winter Don parked the truck on a dealer's lot. I thought I would be glad to see it go but, instead, I was sad. Our last tie to farming was gone. The truck was useless and would likely be sold for scrap iron. I felt pretty useless, too, retired now.

When we drove by the dealer a week later, the truck was gone. An Oklahoma farmer bought it to haul seed wheat.

The truck's new life helped me to remember that my activities in retirement are different but still beneficial. While I don't have the agility to paint the house roof again, I am helping Don put up drywall in the basement. My swollen thumb joints keep me from playing difficult organ preludes, but each Sunday I play hymns for our small congregation. I don't speak to large groups about justice issues, but I do visit an elderly friend in a care home.

Different ages, different stages, different tasks—they're all part of God's perfect design.

Everlasting God, thank You for using a worn-out truck to give me a new perspective on the seasons of life.
—Penney Schwab

Digging Deeper: Psalm 37:25, Isaiah 46:4, Luke 2:36–38

IN GOD'S HANDS

1 _____

2 _____

3 _____

4 _____

5 _____

6 _____

7 _____

8 _____

9 _____

10 _____

11 _____

12 _____

13 _____

14 _____

15 _____

16 _____

17 _____

18 _____

19 _____

20 _____

21 _____

22 _____

23 _____

24 _____

25 _____

26 _____

27 _____

28 _____

29 _____

30 _____

31 _____

FEBRUARY

*I keep my eyes always on the Lord. With him
at my right hand, I will not be shaken.*

—Psalm 16:8 (NIV)

BEAUTY FROM ASHES: A New Home
I will dwell in the house of the Lord forever.
—Psalm 23:6 (NAS)

I had no idea that, come New Year's Day, I'd be helping my daughter find an apartment. Katie's divorce was imminent. Driving through the familiar tree-lined neighborhood toward her house, I told myself to hold it together.

In the kitchen, we boxed up her things as praise music floated into each hollow room. That night, I stayed over and prayed she could sleep. Tomorrow, we would go apartment hunting.

Early the next morning, we sat in the den, drinking coffee—probably the last time Katie would be here. Without a sound, she handed me her Bible. I turned to Psalm 23. "The Lord is our Shepherd," I said, my voice barely above a whisper. "He makes us lie down in green pastures. He leads us beside quiet waters. He restores our souls."

Calm filled the room. Suddenly, it felt holy, as though we were sitting in a stained-glass chapel. Moved by God's tenderness, Katie's brown eyes filled with tears. So did mine. We clasped hands and asked God to help us find just the right apartment.

By lunchtime, we'd toured several complexes. With each one, she shook her head. "Are we ever going to find it, Mom?"

Please, Lord, I begged. Making a U-turn, I spotted the apartments I'd been thinking of. We escaped from the cold, gray day into the toasty office—a welcoming smile, a fire, and chocolates. The woman behind the desk said she'd recently gone through a divorce, and graciously, compassionately, she led us to Katie's new home.

Thank You, Lord. With You living in our hearts, we always have a home. —Julie Garmon

Digging Deeper: John 14:23, 15:4

Thursday, February 2

...A time to keep, and a time to cast away. —Ecclesiastes 3:6 (ESV)

As my graduation from law school got closer, my wife and I started gearing up to move. I reluctantly agreed to start going through our stuff early and get rid of what we didn't need.

Emily had a plan: we would go through everything, one by one, and ask if it gave us "a spark of joy." If it didn't, we would give it away. It sounded silly to me, but I agreed to try. I've learned by now that Emily usually knows better than I do!

The experience was remarkable. As we went through all of our possessions—from old sneakers to books we'd never read—I found that I wasn't asking whether I got a spark of joy. Instead I was asking, "Is this thing right for me? Does it serve a valuable purpose in my life, or does it tether me more to material things?"

I wasn't ready to renounce all of my possessions, but I couldn't believe how many things I'd kept solely out of some vague fear that I would regret giving up something that had cost money. I didn't want all those fancy books I'd read in college; the only purpose they served was to show off to guests. I didn't want those shirts that didn't fit; there was someone out there who could actually use them.

I'd never appreciated the value of an organized bare space. I felt calmer, less troubled by the things of this world. In the end, we gave away 70 percent of our possessions and gained so much more in the bargain.

Thank You, God, for giving us everything we need in You. —Sam Adriance

Digging Deeper: Matthew 4:4, 6:19

Friday, February 3

OVERCOMING LOSS
Learning to Make a Joyful Noise
He put a new song into my mouth, a hymn to our God.... —Psalm 40:4 (JPS)

Every week, my husband and I used to bless each other at the beginning of Shabbat by singing together. "I Am My Beloved's" became our prayer song, and I ended up having its last line ("As the years go passing through, more and more I find the meaning of my life in loving you") engraved on Keith's headstone.

I stood next to him as he was dying. The hospice people and our neighbors had left the house several minutes earlier so that just he and I were left. The nurse had thought his "numbers"—whatever that meant—were improving, but I noticed that his hands and feet were ice cold, no matter how much I tried to warm them.

When his breathing became sporadic, I wanted him to know I was there and to understand how much I loved him. So with a serenity I still can't comprehend, I sang our Shabbat song. It seemed entirely natural to send him on his way wrapped in my cherishing.

I couldn't sing again after that. I couldn't even hum. I had to turn off music so as not to break down in tears. When the cantor or the congregation sang during services, I left the sanctuary because I could not join in. I became afraid that singing to Keith had been the last time I would ever sing.

Then, about fifteen months after his death, I was sitting at a service, not thinking about anything in particular. Suddenly, I became aware that I was singing with the congregation as we all answered the call to prayer. While I couldn't sing for myself yet, I could sing for God.

Stick with me, Eternal God, if it takes me a long time for the noise I make to become joyful.
—Rhoda Blecker

Digging Deeper: Judges 5:3, 1 Chronicles 16:23

Saturday, February 4

"Trust in God, and trust also in me."
—John 14:1 (NLT)

Our plane landed at 5:00 p.m. in Atlanta in one of the worst ice storms ever to hit the area. I was thankful to be there safely, yet my thoughts were on getting to our son Kirk and his family, including newborn Madison, whom we were meeting for the first time. My husband and I still had to make what was usually a two-hour drive to their Tennessee home.

Snow was falling fast as we turned on to the highway entrance ramp. Cars were stopped ahead. Several were even backing down the shoulder. As we inched along, I called Kirk. "Traffic's stopped for miles," he said. "You need to turn off and take the back roads."

"We'll get lost," I objected.

"Trust me," Kirk replied. "I know the way."

For the next few hours he navigated for us by phone as we pressed on through the storm's arctic obstacle course of ice-encased streets, accidents, and spinning, sliding, and abandoned cars. Kirk's voice remained calm and steady, and at about midnight, he told us how to get back on the highway. "I'll meet you at the next exit," he said.

Unknown to us, Kirk had been driving for three hours to meet us and lead us to his home. We spotted his truck, followed him, and arrived at 2:00 a.m. As I lay snuggled and warm in bed, grateful to be safe in my son's home, my thoughts went to another Son. *Trust me,* He said. *I know the way.*

Jesus, be my guide through all of life's storms.
—Kim Henry

Digging Deeper: Psalm 143:8, John 10:27

Sunday, February 5

"This is the will of him who sent me, that I should lose nothing of all that he has given me, but raise it up on the last day." —John 6:39 (ESV)

My wife Kate's sister, Liz, died after a years-long struggle with breast cancer. They had been close. As a little girl, Kate had donated the bone marrow that enabled Liz to survive childhood leukemia. But the radiation Liz underwent for the leukemia caused breast cancer four decades later.

We stood in Kate and Liz's childhood church, listening as family and friends recalled Liz's fierce intelligence, gentle generosity, and talent for friendship. Liz's ashes would be interred at the church columbarium, downstairs from the sanctuary.

Time for the post-Communion hymn. I heard familiar chords. It was number 335 from the Episcopal hymnal, "I Am the Bread of Life." To be honest, I don't like hymns. They seem stodgy. But this one I love. Its words are straight from Scripture, an adaptation of Jesus's astonishing claim in John 6:35 (NRSV): "I am the bread of life. Whoever comes to me will never be hungry, and whoever believes in me will never be thirsty."

The chorus is even better: "I will raise them up on the last day" (John 6:40, NRSV). Whenever that hymn is sung at our church in New York City, people cry. I was crying now. But they were not despairing tears. Jesus's words in that chorus are not a promise. They are a certainty. Liz was with Jesus, where she belonged.

**Confident in Your saving power, God,
I will live abundantly today.** —Jim Hinch

Digging Deeper: John 6:60–69

Monday, February 6

"In your anger do not sin...."
—Ephesians 4:26 (NIV)

We put our apartment on the market ten days ago and had a full-price offer within twenty-four hours. I felt great! I'd devoted hundreds of hours to plastering and painting our place, and it had paid off.

The day afterward one of my kids, stressed and angry about our impending move, dragged an armchair across the hardwood floor, leaving a bright white scratch. I looked at the damage and blew, shouting harsh words about carelessness and thoughtlessness and being a bad steward. My throat hurt by the time I was done. My heart did too.

Was there righteous anger behind what I said and did? Yes. Was there personal grievance as well? Yes. I'm far from being Jesus. I have my own agenda, flaws, and resentments, and they get mixed up with what actually needs to be said and done. What I'm left with is that some part of my actions was good and true—and the rest was not. The first part doesn't justify the other.

So what does one do with that? God asks me to confess the not-good parts, to apologize to the child, to go on, and to remember not to despair. Perfection awaits in the next world.

Holy Spirit, give me the words to say what needs to be said and seal my lips for the rest. —Julia Attaway

Digging Deeper: Matthew 21:12, James 1:20

Tuesday, February 7

Fix these words of mine in your hearts and minds; tie them as symbols on your hands and bind them on your foreheads. —Deuteronomy 11:18 (NIV)

If your in-box is anything like mine, you get a slew of e-mails touting tips to live longer, eliminate debt, reduce stress, improve your love life...you name it. There's no escaping the diurnal onslaught. And who isn't tempted to click through? This morning I got suckered into an e-mail that promised to reveal sixteen surefire ways to eat more healthfully. *Sixteen? Really?*

It struck me that all of this information that swamps my in-box can be found in a single definitive source: the Bible. I thought it would be fun to test the theory.

Live longer: "If you walk in obedience to me and keep my decrees...I will give you a long life" (1 Kings 3:14, NIV).

Eliminate debt: "Let no debt remain outstanding, except the continuing debt to love one another" (Romans 13:8, NIV).

Reduce stress: "And the peace of God, which transcends all understanding, will guard your hearts and your minds in Christ Jesus" (Philippians 4:7, NIV).

Healthful eating: "So whether you eat or drink or whatever you do, do it all for the glory of God" (1 Corinthians 10:31, NIV).

Improve your love life: "Love is patient, love is kind. It does not envy, it does not boast, it is not proud" (1 Corinthians 13:4, NIV).

So take that, Internet! You're old news.

God, technology may have changed our daily lives in so many ways, but You change our hearts. Let me always remember to click through to Your Word, the source of all wisdom and truth.
—Edward Grinnan

Digging Deeper: Psalm 119:105

Wednesday, February 8

This is the message that you have heard from the beginning, that we should love one another.
—1 John 3:11 (ESV)

It is really annoying when your child corrects your behavior based on what she's learning in preschool. This happened to me three times in as many days.

On occasion one, I was guiding her out the door on the way to school. We were running late. "It isn't nice to push people," she said. *Oops! I guess I was sort of pushing her.*

The next time it happened when we were home together and I became frustrated while trying to unscrew a lightbulb. I muttered something angrily to myself. "You should be happy, Daddy, not angry," she said. *Maybe.*

And then, just today, we were rushing to school but decided to return library books on the way. There was nowhere to park near the library, so I illegally pulled up in front. We jumped out of the car and hustled to the return box. A woman and her little boy were on the sidewalk, too, headed toward the box. "Let's let them go first, Daddy," my daughter said, grabbing my arm, smiling at the mother and son.

"Thank you, young lady," the woman replied. She looked at me. "What a kind daughter you have."

"Thank you," I managed.

How easily I forget!

Make me an instrument of Your kindness and love today, Lord. —Jon Sweeney

Digging Deeper: 1 John 3:14, 16

Thursday, February 9

God saw all that he had made, and it was very good.... —**Genesis 1:31** (NIV)

I have learned that God's most natural voice is laughter and delight. When the ancient God of Genesis created the world, He bellowed across the universe, "This is good! This is very good!" God's eternal voice resounds with glee. The fruit of His labor is happiness.

Too often I have reduced God to a stern and grim voice. In my youth, I feared that God would lead me where I did not want to go. I feared that God would demand that I do what I most disliked. The God of my childhood avoided all parties and celebrations. God was warped into a demanding taskmaster.

I now know this is a distortion of sacred truth. God wants me to live in His image and share in the ongoing joy of His creativity. God longs to set me free to be my best self and to find meaningful work.

When laughter has disappeared from my life for too long and dread is the order of the day, I find that God corrects my course and leads me in another direction. True, I have my difficult moments. But God is most intent on sharing the joy of His creation with me—and beaming when He sees the reflection of His image in my eyes.

Lord, to my heart bring back laughter! Amen.
—Scott Walker

Digging Deeper: Genesis 21:6, Proverbs 11:20

He went away sorrowful: for he had great possessions.
—**Matthew 19:22** (KJV)

"You can't take a quarter of all this," the Realtor told
my husband and me as we prepared to move from
our house to an apartment. But "all this" meant
the treasures of a lifetime! How could we part with
John's great-grandmother's soup bowls? My mother's
end tables? I decided I could part with a table lamp
here, a framed photo there, and then changed my
mind. (That lamp was a wedding gift!)

John came to my rescue with three words:
"Remember Uncle Trevor."

Uncle Trevor had adopted my friend Margery
after her parents died. When a trip took us to
Durham, England, we promised Margery we'd call
on him. "Sorry for the clutter," he apologized as
we moved single file along a passageway lined with
boxes. "I'm just clearing things out."

Books and clothes covered every chair, every
table in the living room. "Afraid the closet's full
too." Indeed, the door couldn't close against coats,
hats, sweaters, boots stacked floor to ceiling.
Kitchen counters were piled high with pots, dishes,
utensils. Uncle Trevor cleared three chairs, and
we had a wonderful visit hearing about Margery's
school days.

"We didn't see the house as you remember it," I told my friend when we got home. "Right now it's crowded with things he's clearing out."

Margery burst out laughing. "But that's exactly how I remember it! He's been clearing out for decades, but he can never let anything go."

I laid out boxes. I could give that lamp away after all...and the soup bowls...and the tables...

Don't let me be possessed, Father, by my possessions.
—Elizabeth Sherrill

Digging Deeper: Proverbs 15:16

Saturday, February 11

Love is patient; love is kind; love is not envious or boastful or arrogant or rude. It does not insist on its own way; it is not irritable or resentful.
—1 Corinthians 13:4–5 (NRSV)

The Valentine's Day volleyball tournament was named Sting of the Heart, and that's how I felt! Valentine's Day is also my wedding anniversary.

I'd looked forward to a day of celebrating love. Instead, I sat shivering on a plastic bleacher in a church gymnasium. To make matters worse, our daughter was riding the bench. She'd missed practice, and the coach had a policy of limited play for absences.

"I can't tolerate watching Micah not participate," said my husband.

"No use both of us being here," I agreed.

So here I sat—alone, cold, and feeling sorry for myself. Conversely, the girls were having a blast. Between matches, they giggled and snacked.

Standings were later posted. We went into the loser's bracket. I checked the time: 3:30 p.m. *If we lose, I'll be home by five o'clock,* I thought.

But it was a rival club team. The girls dug down deep and won in three sets. After a one-hour rest, they'd go to the finals.

When it was finally over, a teammate's family invited Micah out to eat. Back home, my husband surprised me with a steak dinner and a beautiful bouquet. I was asleep by 9:00 p.m.

I'd been too rushed for my quiet time on our anniversary, so I read 1 Corinthians 13 the next day. Love was everywhere in that gym yesterday: parents who sacrificed a Saturday so their daughters could play; spectators who encouraged players; coaches who instructed; the friendships of teammates. It truly was a day of celebrating love!

Loving Father, help me to remember that true love—real love—is never all about me. —Stephanie Thompson

Digging Deeper: Romans 8:37–39, 12:9;
1 Corinthians 13:13

Sunday, February 12

Every good gift, every perfect gift, comes from above. —James 1:17 (CEB)

"Too bad nobody gave me any of those good winter pears for Christmas," Mom said wistfully. "I like them so much."

Too bad indeed! I muttered to myself. If only I had had that key piece of information before Christmas and not after it. I wrote a blog confessing my own sense of inadequacy about gift-giving.

"Keep a list of ideas all year long," a kind Guideposts.org reader suggested. "I find it helpful to jot down ideas as they come to me. Then I don't feel panicky at Christmastime."

I did as he suggested and I was tempted to share this brilliant idea with my siblings, but then I changed my mind. They would have to come up with their own ideas; this one was a sure winner.

Alas, it barely got me to February. Valentine's Day was approaching, and I had this brain wave: *Why not get some of those pears for Mom now?* I logged on to a Web site and ordered them with the message "Happy Valentine's Day, Mom!" And then a box for "From" popped up. I paused a second. Of course I'd put down my name, but what if I added the names of my siblings? Why keep such a good idea to myself?

"Hey, guys," I e-mailed my brother and sisters, "I just sent Mom a box of winter pears. She says she likes them. And I signed all of your names. xo, Rick."

A present for Mom and the best brother and sisters you could ask for. I was grateful to God for that good idea. Now I had ten months to think of some more.

Lord, teach me how to be generous at all times and in all ways. —Rick Hamlin

Digging Deeper: 1 Timothy 6:18–19

Monday, February 13

"As for me and my house, we will serve the Lord." **—Joshua 24:15 (NKJV)**

"Have you thought about your wedding someday?" Aunt Yvonne asked me when I was sixteen.

"Yeah. When I find the right guy, I'm gonna get married in jeans."

We'd laughed at the time, but I got so busy cattle ranching that I was nearly forty when I met the right man.

Optimistically, I opened a bridal magazine. My expectations plummeted the more I flipped through the pages: designer dresses, designer cakes, designer venues, designer honeymoons, hair, makeup, shoes, entertainment, party favors. "Expect to pay seventy thousand for a proper wedding," the article stated.

"You're kidding, right?" I asked the model on the page, who looked sullen in a sleeveless fifteen-thousand-dollar dress. Wasn't this supposed to be about the promise we would make before God? I didn't need to be a princess for a day; I simply wanted to be a wife for life.

"That's not me," I announced to my fiancé. "It's so commercial!"

"If you showed up like *that*," Randy gestured to the magazine, "I wouldn't believe it was you. I'm marrying you for you, not for what you wear."

"I'm holding you to that," I said.

"You'd better." He grinned.

So, dressed in jeans, I took Randy's hand in his living room, surrounded by family and more roses than I'd ever imagined (a surprise from Randy), and solemnly vowed with my whole heart, our lives forever joined with God's blessing.

Lord, it's getting harder to find You in this modern world. May You always come first in all that I do.
—Erika Bentsen

Digging Deeper: Exodus 23:22–25, 2 Chronicles 34:33, Psalm 100

When we take your gifts to those who need them they will break out into thanksgiving and praise to God for your help. —2 Corinthians 9:11 (TLB)

On Valentine's Day, when her husband, Wally, was hospitalized with serious flu symptoms, Shirley went home to discover a huge bouquet of flowers near her front door. The note read, "It has been a beautiful life, thanks to you. No matter what happens to me, I will always keep you in my heart. Love, Wally."

After a few tearful moments, Shirley began to wonder who'd really sent the flowers. Wally's late-stage Alzheimer's disease meant he couldn't drive or use a computer or a telephone. He couldn't remember anything longer than about ten seconds.

Shirley asked her neighbors, friends—anyone she could think of—but all were as baffled as she. The day she called me to see if I'd sent them, I was so impressed by her story that immediately after I got off the phone, I decided I could fill my husband's car tank with gas without telling him. I could send my children and grandchildren gifts or letters when it wasn't their birthday. I could write thank-you notes to caregivers. I could even send flowers to those who really needed a boost.

After sleuthing for days, Shirley finally found out that Jim, one of their dearest and oldest friends in Wisconsin, had sent the bouquet. Little did he know that he had inspired a number of people in Shirley's circle of friends to be more spontaneous, and sometimes even anonymous, in their own gift-giving.

Father, help me to be more aware of things I can do to help others who are going through tough times.
—Patricia Lorenz

Digging Deeper: Matthew 6:1–4,
2 Corinthians 9:5–9

Wednesday, February 15

LESSONS IN STONES
Written on the Heart
So he cut out two stone tablets like the former ones, and Moses rose up early in the morning and went up to Mount Sinai, as the Lord had commanded him.... —Exodus 34:4 (NAS)

Moses, leading the Israelites to the land God promised them, was not a young man when he climbed Mount Sinai in Egypt—nearly 7,500 feet. This was not his first climb. God declared, "I will write on the tablets the words that were on the *former* tablets which you shattered" (Deuteronomy 10:2, NAS).

Moses was roaring mad. He'd come down from Mount Sinai with this treasure from God, only to find the Israelites had tired of waiting and betrayed God with idol worship. Moses threw the tablets to the ground and "shattered them at the foot of the mountain" (Exodus 32:19, NAS).

This is what anger can do: shatter things—a relationship, a reputation, a promise, a hope. I came so close, in an angry moment caring for my elderly mother, to hurtling the terrible words: "You never helped *your* mother!" I knew the circumstances between them had been different: my mother worked full-time with two children in a one-bedroom apartment, and my dad was temporarily unemployed. They were barely making it.

Even so, I thought, frustrated.

After Mom died, I discovered a letter from her mother asking to come live with her. On the envelope my mother had written, "How I wish I could have done what she wanted, but it was impossible."

Moses experienced eruptions of anger. So do I. I am encouraged that God rewrote His words on the stones and arranged them for their preservation. He told Moses, "Arise, proceed on your journey" (Deuteronomy 10:11, NAS). I am not defined by my bursts of anger unless I do nothing about them.

God is always there to rewrite on the tablet of my heart.

> **As Saint Francis prayed, "Lord, make me an instrument of Your peace."** —Carol Knapp

Digging Deeper: Exodus 34:1–14, Luke 9:51–56, Galatians 5:19–25

Thursday, February 16

For everything that was written in the past was written to teach us, so that through the endurance taught in the Scriptures and the encouragement they provide we might have hope. —Romans 15:4 (NIV)

My mother-in-law, Sybil, died almost a month ago and tonight my husband is missing his mom. It makes no difference that she was ninety-four and he is over fifty. It doesn't matter that she suffered from dementia and failing health, that her quality of life was all but gone, or that we prayed for her to go to heaven.

Tony looks off into the darkness before sleep and asks if it will always hurt like this. I tell him, "No, you're just not used to it yet."

When my sister, Maria, died suddenly in her sleep, I held on to that sentiment, believing and repeating, "Not used to it yet," because those were her words. Maria told me a story years ago from when she was in the hospital visiting my brother, who was healing from a motorcycle accident. The man in the bed beside my brother had just learned he was paralyzed from the neck down. Maria said she felt terribly awkward being in the same room with only a curtain between them and overhearing such devastating news. And a day or so later, again behind the curtain, Maria heard the man crying. The nurse came in and asked if he was in pain. He answered, "I'm just not used to it yet."

Maria's eyes brimmed with tears when she told me the story. "So filled with hope, don't you think?" she said. "That we can go on. We can bear such difficult things and go on."

Dear Lord, guide us through the hard times and help us face the days ahead with hope. —Sabra Ciancanelli

Digging Deeper: Psalms 3:4, 50:15

Friday, February 17

Yet I will rejoice in the Lord, I will be joyful in God my Savior. —Habakkuk 3:18 (NIV)

I shoveled my driveway today for the first time in years. After two decades of living in California, I moved back to New York last year. Shoveling was novel, kind of fun, in fact. But weeks into winter I know the thrill will wear off and I will be as jaded as any New Yorker. I'll be tired of scraping my car in the morning and bundling up just to go get the groceries. I'll be weary of driving on slippery roads and worried about pipes freezing.

I'm reminding myself today to hang on to the fun parts of the season: the quiet of the first snowfall, the delicate patterns of ice crystals, the blanket of white that covers the backyard and dresses the trees, the cozy feeling of being safe inside.

It reminds me of my faith life. In the beginning, everything was wonderful. I felt a peace I'd never known and wanted to hold on to it for life. It was my new life. But those feelings wore off as day-to-day living wore me down. How to recapture that spark? How to find a way back to the wonder? How to enjoy shoveling?

I remind myself in gentle ways. I put up a sticky note on the bathroom mirror: "Pray today." I pause during my quiet time to soak in the devotion I am reading. I remember my good manners and use "please" and "thank you" all day long. These are simple things, little ways to rejoice in the faith-filled life I am living.

Dear Father, thank You for the change of season. Remind me of the good things about winter. Amen.
—Lisa Bogart

Digging Deeper: Psalm 37:4, 2 Corinthians 1:3–5, Philippians 4:4

"The spirit of God has made me, and the breath of the Almighty gives me life." —Job 33:4 (NRSV)

I was busy this year: conferences, trips, my sister coming to live here, work projects. Both of my daughters were home for longer than usual and had friends visiting. As a result, I struggled to maintain my twice-weekly Hot Yoga schedule and, eventually, ended up taking off most of the year.

After things settled down, I motivated myself to start going again, but I found I'd lost most of my skills. I could no longer do wheel or side plank—poses I'd invested a lot of time in mastering—and I struggled with ones that had never given me any trouble. Halfway through that first class back, I got so light-headed, it took everything in me to drop into child's pose, as my yoga instructor recommends in such instances.

I concentrated on my breathing. In. I consciously slowed my heart, narrowed my nose, filled my chest. Out. Even more slowly, I emptied myself entirely. In. Out. Soon I was in a rhythm, taking it in, letting it leave me.

As if she were part of the air itself, my yoga instructor chimed in. "Breathe in. Receive," she coached. "Breathe out. Let go. Receive. Let go."

Such a foundational teaching: breathing. The task of a newborn. The spiritual work of every child of God.

Father God, I receive You. Help me to let go.
—Patty Kirk

Digging Deeper: Genesis 2:7, John 20:19–23

Sunday, February 19

"On that day you will know that I am in my Father, and you in me, and I in you." —John 14:20 (NRSV)

"While I am on my commute back and forth from Philly to New York, I pray," my professor said. "I paraphrase John 14:20: 'I am in you and you are in me and we are in God.' I look at each individual in my train car and mentally recite that verse."

During my next commute, squeezed into an overstuffed subway car, I thought, *This is my chance to give it a shot!*

I looked at the first person. At a distance of about four feet, there were twelve people between us. I took a deep breath. "I am in you and you are in me and"—He looked up and caught my eye. I quickly looked away. I hadn't counted on making eye contact with other people. In hindsight it seemed obvious, but in New York City, where everyone is looking somewhere else, it hadn't occurred to me.

I gathered my nerves to try again. This time I chose the woman sitting in the seat in front of me; she had on sunglasses. I took another deep breath and recited the verse. The guy next to her? Done. The teenager over by the door? He looked up, and I said the verse quickly.

And so I continued for the rest of the ride, in fits and starts, with successes and failures. I'd love to say it got better and I got braver, but the truth is, it didn't. Regardless, I felt a connection to people I would never see again, whose lives I intersected for fifteen minutes one morning while we all waited in an underground tube.

Thank You, God, for reminding me of Your Presence in others and that every space is a sanctuary.
—Natalie Perkins

Digging Deeper: John 4:11–16

Monday, February 20

The government shall be upon his shoulder: and his name shall be called Wonderful.... —Isaiah 9:6 (KJV)

For a social studies project, a young neighbor friend had chosen Abraham Lincoln as the hero she wanted to know more about. I don't think she really grasped underlying social issues such as slavery and war, secession and union. I think she was fascinated with his top hat and beard. She spent weeks memorizing a short biography: "My name is Abraham Lincoln. I was born in 1809 in Kentucky...." Sporting a tall black hat, she proudly recited the paragraph at a school program.

To encourage her interest, I promised I'd drive her across the river from Virginia to Washington, DC. "We'll go see the Lincoln Memorial. It's got a very big statue. I think you'll say, 'Wow!'"

And so we went. We walked up the long marble stairway crowded with tourists. Inside the open-air building, dwarfed by the huge figure, we stood together, looking up. *Wow!*

I pointed out a plaque, reading it silently: "In this temple, as in the hearts of the people for whom he saved the Union, the memory of Abraham Lincoln is enshrined forever."

Always curious but not a keen reader, my friend asked, "What does it say?"

I summarized simply: "That we'll remember Abraham Lincoln forever."

"Like Jesus," she said.

I wasn't sure if it was a question or a statement, and I immediately saw that the comparison wasn't perfect. But I smiled. "Yes," I answered, "like Jesus" (a hero in a different realm).

On the way back to the car, she recited her Lincoln lines, but by the time we got home we were singing a favorite tune: "He's got the whole world in His hands."

Lord, as we honor and appreciate our historic leaders, we give our deepest praise and thanks to You.
—Evelyn Bence

Digging Deeper: Psalm 98

PARENTING ANEW: A Nesting Place
The birds of the sky nest by the waters....
—Psalm 104:12 (NIV)

The sound of twittering birds caught my attention as I jumped from my chair and ran to the window. Sure enough, finches were flying around the back porch, stopping to rest on the chain of the porch swing.

At our house, finches are a guarantee of spring's arrival. But so soon? Even in north Florida we still have bouts of cold weather through February. However, there was no doubt about the presence of red-breasted males and gray-brown females fluttering from porch to tree to fence.

"Chuck, the finches are back!" I exclaimed to my husband.

He and Logan joined me at the window. "They're looking for their nesting place. Are you going to put one out?" Chuck asked.

"Guess I'll have to, if I can find one in the store."

For the past five years, I had hung a fern from the porch eaves, taking it down when the cold weather froze it and replacing it with a new one each spring. Every fern I put out soon became home to a finch nest.

At the nursery, I smiled when buying the first fern of the season, knowing I was getting it for the birds. Back home, the finches lost no time in discovering the plant, disappearing into its fronds as they built their new home.

With a pat of self-satisfaction on my back, I was happy to know I'd provided them, and my grandson, a home—a home until it was time to leave the nest.

Lord, thank You for the opportunity to care for Your little creatures in need. —Marilyn Turk

Digging Deeper: Deuteronomy 32:10–12

Wednesday, February 22

For since the world began, no ear has heard and no eye has seen a God like you, who works for those who wait for him! —Isaiah 64:4 (NLT)

I phoned my mom to find out when my dad's appointment was for his biopsy results. "Two o'clock," she told me.

"Great, I will go with you," I said. It had been weeks of waiting. Sometimes I prayed in spite of my concerns; other times with great faith and hope. The time had come for answers.

In the waiting room, the nurse called my dad's name. "You go in with him," Mom said, to my surprise.

Dad and I sat and waited in the cold little room. I had plenty of time to observe my father. He was deep in thought, his hands folded together. *What if the news is not what we want to hear?* I worried. Once again, I prayed.

Finally, the doctor came in. "How are you doing, Mr. Diaz?" he asked.

"*Bueno*" (Fine), Dad said in Spanish.

The doctor sat at the computer, stared at the screen, and then turned to Dad. "The test results are good. You don't have cancer," he said.

Dad exhaled, releasing all of the tension he had been feeling. I did too. We walked out into the waiting room, and I gave Mom a thumbs-up.

I was happy that I had been able to be there with my parents, and even more so that God had been with us too.

Lord, thank You for working on our behalf during this waiting time. Help me to keep my eyes, at all times, on You. —Pablo Diaz

Digging Deeper: Psalm 37:4, Hebrews 4:16

Thursday, February 23

If anyone can control his tongue, it proves that he has perfect control over himself in every other way. —James 3:2 (TLB)

A friend and I were chatting when my phone sounded. I didn't think my anxiety showed, but she asked, "Bad news?"

"Just a meeting notice," I replied. "I haven't had an upsetting text in a month, but I still panic when I hear that tone."

"You may be associating the sound with trouble," she replied. "The problem is the tone itself. It's shrill, like someone is yelling at you. Change the tone, and I guarantee you'll change your reaction."

I took her advice, and the results were gratifying. My new tone sounds the way marigolds look: bold but friendly. My stress has nearly disappeared, and I'm able to calmly handle negative messages from family and friends.

As an unexpected bonus, my new alert reminds me to watch my tone of voice. When a store clerk snapped at me, I took a deep breath and kept my voice pleasant. He apologized, and we both smiled when the transaction was finished. The same thing happened when I had a disagreement with someone on our church mission committee. I choked down a snippy comment and lowered my tone before I gave my views.

It took a moment to permanently change my cell tone. Changing my voice is a work in progress, but I've made a sound beginning.

"Let the words of my mouth and the meditations of my heart be pleasing to you, Lord, my rock and my redeemer" (Psalm 19:14, CEB).
—Penney Schwab

Digging Deeper: Proverbs 15:1, 16:23–24; 1 Corinthians 13:1

Friday, February 24

"As water wears away stones and torrents wash away the soil, so you destroy a person's hope."
—Job 14:19 (NIV)

Things will never change and get better.

I put on the outward appearance of everything being okay, but inside I felt paralyzed by worry and fear. Nothing seemed to help.

Then, one day, I attended a talk by a counselor who explained something that psychologists call automatic negative thoughts (ANTs). He said that without realizing it, ANTs spontaneously come into our minds and we believe them because we've thought them for so long. He went on to say that people can be taught to question the truth of these thoughts in order to get their thinking unstuck.

At home, I sat down with my journal and wrote myself a question: "What is my biggest fear today?" Right away I wrote down, "That things will never get better with a problem at church and with our son Chris." Next I wrote, "See what words are crushing hope." I looked back at my statement and circled the word *never*.

I thought for a moment and wrote, "I challenge the word *never* by asking God to show me one way that each of these situations has actually improved." The next thing I knew, I had written down two small ways that each one seemed a little better. Then I wrote down an affirmation: "With Your help, O God, progress can be made and is being made."

Dear Holy Spirit, I challenge these ANTS by holding them up to You. Amen. —Karen Barber

Digging Deeper: Psalm 119:116, Romans 4:18–25

Saturday, February 25

**For the Lord is good and his love endures forever....
—Psalm 100:5 (NIV)**

"Is he a good baby? How is he sleeping?" As a new mom, I hear those questions everywhere I go. The checker at the supermarket, my coworkers, and strangers all want to know. Not how I am. Not how he is. But if he is good and how he is sleeping, as if the two are linked.

I struggle to find an answer. James is a good sleeper, but the truth is he isn't a *great* sleeper. And getting only ninety minutes of sleep at any single stretch was making me a not-so-great human being.

One night, unable to soothe this tiny human, I found myself crying out to God: "Why have You given me a child who won't sleep?" Then I looked down at James. He wasn't upset or angry. In fact, he was cooing.

It dawned on me that James was good. He might not sleep well, but he was good. He was James, just as God had made him.

I gazed down at my son and thanked God for the tiny person He had given me, the one I was still getting to know and already loved. If he never slept again, would he still be good in God's eyes and covered with God's grace? Yes, he would. Because God is good.

Lord, remind me that the "least of these" are those I'm called to love and serve. How lucky I am to get the chance to do so!
—Ashley Kappel

Digging Deeper: Genesis 2:2–3, Exodus 33:14

Sunday, February 26

And He shall not judge by the sight of His eyes....
—Isaiah 11:3 (NKJV)

My daughter and I were out walking, when a woman passed by. I made a wisecrack about her weight, but my daughter didn't laugh. "You know, Dad, you have a tendency to judge people by their looks before you know anything about them."

That was a little too close for comfort, so the next day I monitored myself. Sure enough, I found myself avoiding a certain store clerk because he looked austere. So I forced myself to speak to him, and it was like I had pushed the On button. He lit up with a huge smile, and we had a stimulating conversation. Turns out he is bashful, tenderhearted, and remarkably funny!

In the afternoon, I met "the medical receptionist from Hollywood." *She is too thin*, I said to myself, *too blonde, too glamorous, a real lightweight and one with a past, no doubt. Maybe a model, a dancer.* But then I discovered she is the mother of four boys, a down-to-earth farmer's daughter with two college degrees and working two jobs to put her sons through school. She is soft-spoken and very smart.

All week long I met people who were wearing "disguises," but when I got to know them, their appearances changed. The "austere" clerk now looks like a teddy bear, and I can see a twinkle in his eye. The blonde receptionist is a model all right—a model of dedication.

I am having fun, discovering all kinds of fascinating people hidden behind the odd hairdo, the big nose, the strange tattoos. I am learning to delay my judgments until I know more about the people I meet.

Help me, Lord, not to trust my eyes alone when I'm sizing up people. —Daniel Schantz

Digging Deeper: 1 Samuel 16:7, John 7:24

Monday, February 27

"I would not forget you! See, I have written your name on the palms of my hands...."
—Isaiah 49:15–16 (NLT)

I sighed as I fluffed the down comforter around me. My family had been with me a few days, but now they'd gone home and the house seemed hollow. I whispered to God, "I feel so alone." Rolling over, I fell asleep.

Two hours later, the icy wind howled. I sat straight up in bed and gasped. *Oh no, I forgot to put out the heated water dish for Kitty!* The temperatures had been below zero, and if she didn't have anything to drink, she might get frostbite or even freeze to death. Kitty was a feral tortoiseshell cat who preferred to be wild and fend for herself.

Quickly I bundled up, donned a wool cap with my headlamp, and pulled on mittens. I hustled out to the barn, carrying a dish filled with water to tide her over until morning.

I swung the wooden door open and heard Kitty scamper across the stack of hay. She shivered as she lapped and lapped. I pulled off my mittens and touched her. Her body felt cold to the bone. I curled up on the hay and, although the temperature was twenty below zero, I unzipped my jacket and gently guided her next to my body. She didn't mind as I tucked my jacket around her and cooed. "I'm sorry I forgot you."

As Kitty leaned against my body, I felt the warmth of God's love and heard, *But I haven't forgotten you. I've been with you all along.* In my mind's eye, I saw God's huge hands cupped around me.

Lord, thank You for showing me how much You love me. Amen. —Rebecca Ondov

Digging Deeper: Job 12:10, Mark 1:15

For the Lord seeth not as man seeth; for man looketh on the outward appearance, but the Lord looketh on the heart. —1 Samuel 16:7 (KJV)

While perusing the wares at the local thrift shop, I once again noticed a crewneck sweater. It had been passed over for days. Immediately, my thoughts turned to my junior-high sewing teacher, Mrs. Barrett. "If you want to know the quality of a garment, always peek inside," she told us. "That's how you discover the real story."

I went right to the label. Its very design somehow looked expensive and indicated the garment had been made in Italy. Further scrutiny revealed that the seams of this sweater were intricately hand bound to prevent fraying.

Made of the softest, lightweight merino wool, the sweater would be great for layering and could be dressed up or down. I adored the colors too: a palette of stripes in muted turquoise, sage green, mustard, copper, and brown. It appeared as if it had never been worn and its lines were timeless. I envisioned it elegantly paired with a scarf and sparkling jewelry or casual with a button-down shirt underneath.

For three dollars, the sweater was mine. Once at home, I researched the manufacturer on the Internet.

I learned that the garment hailed from an Italian luxury fashion house that sews custom-made suits that command six thousand dollars and sweaters costing nearly one grand.

As Mrs. Barrett advised, the interior of my garment steered me right. And so it is with me. It is my heart that is my essence. That's what God looks at when He assesses how I'm living my life.

When You examine my heart, Lord Jesus, may You be well pleased. —Roberta Messner

Digging Deeper: Psalm 51:10, Matthew 6:21, Romans 12:2

IN GOD'S HANDS

1 _____

2 _____

3 _____

4 _____

5 _____

6 _____

7 _____

8 _____

9 _____

10 _____

11 _____

12 _____

13 _____

14 _____

15 _____

16 _____

17 _____

18 _____

19 _____

20 _____

21 _____

22 _____

23 _____

24 _____

25 _____

26 _____

27 _____

28 _____

MARCH

May your unfailing love be my comfort. . . .

—Psalm 119:76 (NIV)

All are from the dust, and to dust all return.
—Ecclesiastes 3:20 (ESV)

This morning my husband and I drove through
our old town, past our old house that I'd loved and
nurtured for almost a decade. We inched forward
slowly, but not slowly enough, to catch up to all the
memories. Then we passed the local grocery store,
where I shopped every day for years.

I loved the man who worked there stocking
shelves. Brian always greeted me with a heartfelt
"Hello there!" as if he hadn't seen me in months.

I learned from a friend he'd had a car accident
in high school. He spent a long time in a coma
and was lucky to be alive. And though he'd made a
miraculous recovery, he never fully regained all of his
abilities.

Once I had an awful day at work. I was exhausted
and starving as I snaked through the aisles, picking
up something for dinner. When I reached for a jar of
spaghetti sauce, I lost my grip and it shattered on the
shiny linoleum floor. Looking at the mess, I broke
down and cried.

Brian ran over. "It's okay. Accidents happen." I
noticed his forehead had a smudge of something as
he got a mop.

"Rough day," I sighed.

"Ash Wednesday," he said. I had totally forgotten. Brian went on. "Beginning of Lent. Forty days to get ready. Jesus saved me, you know. He saves me every day." As he mopped up the broken jar, I took his words to heart.

Dear Lord, it's easy to get caught up in the day-to-day of my life and forget what a blessing it truly is. Help me to use this special time to recharge and renew and draw closer to You. —Sabra Ciancanelli

Digging Deeper: Ezekiel 9:4, John 14:6

Thursday, March 2

Let us not become weary in doing good, for at the proper time we will reap a harvest if we do not give up. —Galatians 6:9 (NIV)

My older daughter loves blueberries. I can't keep them in the house; she devours them faster than I can make it back to the market.

That's why I decided to plant my own blueberry bushes in the backyard. I did some research and learned the importance of planting different varieties for cross-pollination, spacing seedlings far enough apart, and waiting to plant until the danger of frost had passed. I was so excited! I could picture my daughter and me, in the warm months to come, picking those plump, delicious treats off the bushes each morning, seeing who could find the most new berries, bringing them inside to have with our cereal and yogurt.

But Alabama is notorious for its crazy weather and—wouldn't you know it?—the week after I planted my new seedlings, an unexpected storm moved through, starting with heavy rain and promising ice as temperatures dropped through the night.

Frustrated, I trudged out to the backyard. As the cold rain poured down, I held an umbrella in one hand, using the other hand to place buckets atop my new plantings. It was awkward work, this woman-against-nature business. By the time I finished, I was soaked and scowling. "What a lot of trouble!" I grumbled.

Then I thought back to my vision of those summer days, picking blueberries alongside my daughter. How spoiled I was to expect a harvest without toil. Didn't all good things require nurturing?

I stood inside and watched the rain, thanking God not only for the harvest to come but also for the opportunity to sow in expectation.

Forgive me, Lord, when I complain. Help me to remember that all good things come from You in Your time. —Ginger Rue

Digging Deeper: 1 Corinthians 3:6–9, James 5:7

Friday, March 3

But God shows his love for us in that while we were still sinners, Christ died for us. —Romans 5:8 (ESV)

"Shawnelle," Lonny called from the stairwell, "we have a problem! Come down quickly!"

When I got to the kitchen, Lonny's legs protruded from under the sink. The kitchen was a wild mess. Dishwasher racks were on the floor, dinner plates spattered with sauce. The counters were littered with glassware, and the dishwasher sounded sick.

Lonny poked a hose in my direction. "This thing is stopped up. Water isn't making it through. I need to drain it." That explained the bucket.

I held the hose while it surged and spat. The dishwasher door was stretched open, and Lonny reached inside. His hair stood straight up, and his face was blotched with red.

I am my beloved's and my beloved is mine. It was from Song of Solomon (6:3), though I didn't understand why I'd recalled it at that moment. There was nothing romantic about the situation we were in. It was grimy. Disagreeable. The sights and sounds and smells left a lot to be desired. But love sometimes shows up in messy places.

I began to think that it's quite like my relationship with God. I'm human. My thoughts can be grimy. My actions show stains. The attitude of my heart often needs repair. Yet God is faithful to love me because of Who He is, not because of who I am.

Lonny lifted the full bucket and headed for the door. For a second, he caught my gaze and held it. There was still a mess, but we loved each other just the same.

Lord, thank You for loving me with grace despite my grime and stains. Amen. —Shawnelle Eliasen

Digging Deeper: Isaiah 1:18, Romans 8:38–39, 1 John 1:9

Saturday, March 4

With God all things are possible.
—Matthew 19:26 (KJV)

How could this have happened? In an empty restaurant, I sipped black coffee as bitter as my freshly severed relationship. My dear friend had betrayed me and now shunned me. I struggled to figure out what I had done—or not done— to deserve this. As the events of that fateful day replayed in my mind, each cruel word cut again like razor wire.

I finished my cup and headed toward the parking lot under leaden skies. Suddenly, a splash of red and green bobbled in the bleakness. *Can't be...* Yet there near my vehicle, a magnificent macaw roosted on the steering wheel inside an RV, bobbing and sidling, as though trying to find a better view of its hardly tropical surroundings. If a giraffe had loped by, I couldn't have been more surprised. The comical and incongruous creature startled me into a giggle that rolled into hilarity. I laughed like a lunatic— or perhaps like a woman finally releasing days of pent-up stress.

The more I reflected on glimpsing a tropical bird inside a car in gloomy New Hampshire, the more I understood that God was the source of the comic relief. My "chance" encounter with the colorful creature certainly lightened my mood. Perhaps, more important, it reminded me that God can do anything, including heal broken relationships. So I've tacked a picture of a macaw on my bulletin board to remind me that reconciliation is possible. That day will come. It will.

Lord, in the depths of my despair
You surprise me with joy. Yes, all is possible!
—Gail Thorell Schilling

Digging Deeper: Psalm 30:5

Sunday, March 5

Pray all the time . . . and keep praying earnestly for all Christians everywhere. —Ephesians 6:18 (TLB)

Although I appreciate technology, I never considered my computer and cell phone to be prayer partners. Then my friend underwent radiation after surgery for cancer. For the entire seven-week course of therapy, her mom sent text reminders to pray prior to treatment and to give thanks when it was completed successfully.

"I'm so sorry Mom bothered you with that," my friend said when I told her.

"It wasn't a bother," I assured her. "They were quick, helpful calls to prayer and praise."

Text messages directed my prayers for a sick child in our church family. I forwarded them to others to make sure we all had the same accurate information. We also texted appeals for a young man struggling with addiction and a friend facing job difficulties.

Along with thousands of other people, I participated in Guideposts' 40-Day Prayer Challenge during Lent. The daily Scripture prompted me to pray for a variety of needs around the world. My faith is strengthened through uplifting Scriptures, photos, and personal stories that are posted several times a day.

Our community has a telephone prayer chain to relay information and requests for individuals. The chain is important because not everyone texts, tweets, or has a computer.

For me, though, texting and social-media sites are now the main ways I ask for and receive prayer requests.

Thank You, imaginative, creative God, for the wonderful gift of technology, my new prayer partner.
—Penney Schwab

Digging Deeper: Matthew 18:19–20, James 5:14–16

Monday, March 6

So you have not received a spirit that makes you fearful slaves. Instead, you received God's Spirit when he adopted you as his own children. Now we call him, "Abba, Father." —Romans 8:15 (NLT)

I have to admit: I haven't always seen God as Father. I knew all about the concept in my head, but it hadn't quite sunk into my heart.

Usually, for a truth to travel the short distance from the cavity between my ears to the cavity in my chest, I need to experience it. I know in my heart that God is Jehovah Jireh because I've experienced Him as Jehovah Jireh in my life. I know in my heart that God is a place of refuge, because I've experienced Him as a place of refuge in my life.

But Abba? A loving, lavish Father Who not only created me but delights in my happiness? One Who longs to give me all things perfect and good? One Who rejoices in giving me the desires of my heart?

With years of infertility and a stalled adoption under my belt, I hadn't experienced that. At least not for a long time. So I made it my prayer: *Lord, I want to know You as Abba.*

I never could have guessed—not in my wildest dreams—that He would answer that prayer by delivering our long-awaited daughter into her earthly daddy's arms. As I watched my husband hold Salima from the Democratic Republic of Congo on US soil for the first time, I broke down in the best possible way.

Salima was finally home. After years of hope deferred, God gave me the desire of my heart. He delivered her. As I wrapped my arms around her small body, I felt Him wrapping His arms around mine. *This is for you,* He seemed to whisper. *A gift for My beloved daughter.*

Thank You, Lord, for not only being Lord and Savior, but Abba too. Help me to know You in this capacity more and more each day. —Katie Ganshert

Digging Deeper: Romans 8:26, 31

Tuesday, March 7

Be still, and know that I am God; I will be exalted among the nations, I will be exalted in the earth! —Psalm 46:10 (NKJV)

The morning was punctuated only by the singing of birds. I walked down my long driveway, breathing the chilled air and marveling at the postcard panorama stretched before me. I'm blessed to live in a mountain home, surrounded by snowcapped peaks and pristine forests. This walk was a chance to quiet myself and pray.

Then I saw those blasted weeds! My prayers came to a crashing halt as I bent over to pull out one of them. The snap of the taproot brought immense satisfaction, and I flung the offender down a steep incline.

Then another weed beckoned and another after that. Soon I was sweating despite the cool air, and my hands overflowed with weeds. Even worse, other chores called out to me: *Time to refresh the mulch. There's a bush that needs pruning. A tree needs trimming.* Serenity gave way to a disheartening burden.

I remembered back to the days when I was too poor to own a home. Then, I gave no thought to mowing the lawn, pulling the weeds, tending the landscape. It was the landlord's job and there was freedom in that.

So now on those early morning walks, I've started pretending I'm a renter. As the sun peeks over the horizon, I join the birds and sing, "When morning gilds the skies, my heart awakening cries, may Jesus Christ be praised...." For those shimmering moments, I'm free to worship.

Precious Lord, still my frenetic spirit for at least a little while each day. Amen. —Bill Giovannetti

Digging Deeper: Psalm 29:2

Wednesday, March 8

There are different ways the Spirit works. But the same God is working in all these ways and in all people. —1 Corinthians 12:6 (NIRV)

We fought in the break room. Not physically, of course. But Sue and I were really yelling at each other after a tense meeting during which she proposed an idea to our management group that I was against. I said as much in the meeting, but then it spilled over into the break room. Thankfully, no one else was around, but I'll bet they heard us through the walls!

So I came home from work early, frustrated and tense. On the bus, I remember staring out the window, throwing a few prayers into the air like desperation free throws. None seemed to land in the bucket. Each one bounced off the rim or fell short.

Now this will sound strange, but upon arriving home, all I wanted to do was pull out my jigsaw puzzle. There is something about a puzzle that allows me to work through a problem for hours without knowing that that's what I'm doing. Otherwise, my heart just spins around and around unhelpfully. The puzzle holds my attention—presumably for working out which piece goes where but also toward more than just that.

Two hours later, I called Sue. She was just leaving the office.

"I saw you left early," she said.

"Yes. And I'm sorry. You were right. I was wrong—both about the idea and in the way you handled things. Forgive me, please."

"No problem. See you tomorrow."

Knowing Sue as I do, that "no problem" was her simple way of forgiving, which I certainly needed. Thank you, God. I'm sure that we'll be doing this again, soon.

God, I'm right over here. And if it looks like I'm doing something else, thanks for working on me in the midst of whatever it is. —Jon Sweeney

Digging Deeper: Psalm 27:13–14

Thursday, March 9

OVERCOMING LOSS: Companion in Grief
My thoughts dwell on him still....
—Jeremiah 31:20 (JPS)

After my husband died, I needed his things around me. We have double sinks in the bathroom, so I left Keith's slippers neatly tucked together in front of his sink, as if he were standing there, brushing his teeth or washing his face. I wanted his hat on the hall tree by the front door, too, and his rain jacket on the chair in the kitchen. It wouldn't feel like our home without them.

The first time I came into the bathroom and found the slippers out of place, I thought I must have stumbled against them during the night. I carefully restored them to their original spot, but I discovered they'd been moved again. *Okay, so I didn't stumble over them while I wasn't even here*, I thought. Nor did I think it was a message from beyond. I put the slippers back once more.

The next time I went into the bathroom, the cause became clear. L.E., our tortoiseshell cat, who had made Keith her preferred person and stayed away from me after he died, was snuggling next to the slippers, her shoulder pushed into the side of one and her head resting on top of it. She was purring as she had used to when she lay pressed against Keith on the couch.

I understood that even though L.E. now came to me for petting and slept beside me, she still remembered and missed Keith as much as I did. The slippers were not just my way of staying connected to Keith; they were hers as well.

I thought I was grieving alone, Lord, except for You. Now I know You've provided me with a companion.
—Rhoda Blecker

Digging Deeper: Nehemiah 3:21

Friday, March 10

"I will bless her, and indeed I will give you a son by her...." —Genesis 17:16 (NAS)

I caught the history bug in school. In *Remember the Alamo*, I looked up to Jim Bowie and Davy Crockett as real American heroes. Later it was *Remember the Maine*, the sinking of the ship that helped steer the United States into World War I. In the 1960s it was *Remember the Pueblo*, the American ship and crew that were held by the North Koreans. Billboards all across our nation sent out a cry, so we wouldn't forget the ship's crew that was held for nearly two years before being freed.

I have another one to add: the story of Sarah. When my daughter-in-law Laurie and my son Dale decided to start a family, they ran into fertility problems. Years passed; it was disappointment upon disappointment. Laurie went in for IVF (in vitro fertilization), and after four attempts she was mentally and physically exhausted. Dale didn't want her to go through another letdown, but she wanted to try one last time. All the while I was praying, reminding God of His promise. That's when He said, *Remember Sarah*.

Jaxon Paul Macomber was born March 10, 2010. This child was God's special gift to Laurie and to our family because Dale died a year later.

Lord, may I always remember that You are faithful.
—Debbie Macomber

Digging Deeper: Psalm 127:3

Saturday, March 11

The mountain of the Lord's house shall be established as the highest of the mountains, and shall be raised above the hills.... —Isaiah 2:2 (NRSV)

My friend and I were on Highway 395, one of the most beautiful stretches of road in the country. It's east of the Sierra Nevada, running north to south through forested mountains, high desert, and the shimmering Owens Valley. To the west, the fourteen-thousand-foot escarpment of the Sierras rises abruptly in peaks of snowy granite.

I barely noticed because I was worrying. I always worry. This time I brooded over our impending move to New York City, where my wife had taken a job leading a large parish and I'd be resuming work at *Guideposts*. There were big anxieties (kids adjusting to new schools, Kate and I juggling work, and life in the big city) and smaller stuff (packing, visits to our parents before we left).

"Things are looking better, y'all," Steve announced out of the blue. That's a phrase he uses whenever the landscape turns particularly lovely.

I looked around. Sure enough, we were descending toward Mono Lake, a thirteen-mile-long, high desert lake surrounded by mountain peaks and sage-covered hills. An immaculate blue sky arched above, blending to hazy white at the horizon.

"Everything that is comes from God," Steve mused.

Something in me reached toward his words. "What do you mean?" I asked.

Steve gestured at the landscape. "You look at all this and can't help hearing God say, 'I made this. I am this big—no, bigger.'"

I'd felt small and isolated, overmastered by worry. Now, the size of my worries didn't seem to matter much. God is big—no, bigger.

Because You are my strength, Lord, I am free of fear.
—Jim Hinch

Digging Deeper: Mark 5:35–43

Sunday, March 12

Then he said, "The Sabbath was created for humans; humans weren't created for the Sabbath." —Mark 2:27 (CEB)

"Where's Margaret?" I asked two friends as we were leaving church. Her name was on the prayer list. "At Weill-Cornell," they said, the hospital where she'd been a nurse for many years.

"What room?" I said. "I'll give her a call."

They gave me the information and hurried off. I stood for an unaccountably long time, debating what I would do. I rather liked not doing anything on a Sunday—"observing the Sabbath," I'd say.

Then I thought about another day some twenty years earlier. I woke up in my hospital bed, feeling far worse than I'd expected, groggy from anesthesia and disoriented. There at the foot of my bed was Margaret. No telling how long she had been there, waiting for me to come to. "Rick," she said, smiling, "I'm glad to see you."

Margaret had done so many kind things for our family, I couldn't begin to repay her. At the very least I could go see her.

Margaret was on the fifth floor, just as my friends had told me, sitting up in her bed. She looked surprised. "How did you know I'd be here?"

"You weren't in church this morning, and word got out."

"I'm so glad you came," she said.

I sat down, and we had a long visit, talking about old times. It wasn't exactly what I had expected to do with my Sunday, but it turned out to be just the right thing.

Let me not give up the chance to serve You, Lord, by serving others. —Rick Hamlin

Digging Deeper: Matthew 25:36, Luke 6:37

Monday, March 13

For we know not what we should pray for as we ought: but the Spirit itself maketh intercession for us with groanings which cannot be uttered.
—Romans 8:26 (KJV)

I was only a kid myself, but it's always bothered me that I wasn't more supportive of my younger twin sisters. There was a five-year difference in our ages. Our mother was quite ill, and our father was an alcoholic. "Rachael and Rebekkah bore the brunt of it all," I agonized to a friend. "Oh, how I wish they could see that I tried my best and wanted only wonderful things to come their way! I just don't know how to tell them."

God showed me that He had indeed heard my heart. It was Rachael who telephoned and left a message on my answering machine. "You don't need to call me back," she said in a shaky voice, "but I have to tell you something. This year marks the fiftieth anniversary of *The Sound of Music*. That means Rebekkah and I were six years old when you took us to see it. It also means you were just eleven years old when you spent your hard-earned money on those tickets. I want you to know how special that makes me feel."

My thoughts traveled back to how I earned that money. A woman three doors down paid me seventy-five cents a week for taking care of her kids and straightening her chaotic apartment. I worked three hours a day, five days a week after school, which means I netted five cents per hour.

Rachael's recollection showed me that sometimes when we are being most effective for God, we don't even realize it.

Thank You, Lord, for prayers gently answered across time. —Roberta Messner

Digging Deeper: Psalms 4:1, 6:9; Colossians 4:2

Tuesday, March 14

Let the wise listen and add to their learning.... —**Proverbs 1:5 (NIV)**

I don't want to get less brave as I grow older, so I welcome challenges that stretch me—like agreeing to teach an hour-long Webinar about storytelling. *What could be so hard about sitting at my dining room table with my computer, sharing what I know about one of my favorite topics?*

Here's what's hard: I'd never done a Webinar before and had no idea how to make that happen.

"I can help you," my son-in-law David volunteered, reminding me how thankful I am that my daughter married him.

So I organized the content and created a digital file with my daughter's help. I sent the attendees an outline and instructions to the organizers about when to show a video during the presentation. Then I practiced and prayed.

The day the Webinar arrived, David's fingers flew across my keyboard to set everything in motion and soon I got the cue to start. Unfortunately, things went downhill from there: our dog began barking incessantly; a trash truck came rumbling through our driveway, loudly screeching to a halt; the video didn't work on cue. By the time we finished, all I could say was *Whew!*

The next couple of days I spent thinking of ways I could have made the Webinar better, but then I remembered why I had agreed to do it: to bravely stretch toward a challenge.

Lord, help me be brave enough to try new ways to share what I know and to learn what I don't.
—Carol Kuykendall

Digging Deeper: Deuteronomy 31:6, 1 Peter 4:10

Wednesday, March 15

"Therefore I tell you, whatever you ask in prayer, believe that you have received it, and it will be yours."
—Mark 11:24 (ESV)

I ran breathlessly into the meeting room, quickly scanning for an empty chair. I was late...again. "Sorry, sorry," I said...again.

I don't try to be late for meetings. Really! I check my calendar first thing every morning, so I know what is on the day's agenda. I lay out folders and other necessary papers in advance, so they're easy to find. I even have a reminder that pops up on my computer and on my phone fifteen minutes before an appointment.

So what's the problem? I also have this little habit of trying to squeeze in one more e-mail response or one more phone call or a few more paragraphs of that report in those last fifteen minutes. But then "one more" becomes "two more" or what I'm doing takes more time than I thought it would, and I'm scrambling.

Thank goodness I have a colleague who's given me a way to finally beat my late-to-meeting habit. "Do exactly what you're doing now, but when that fifteen-minute alarm goes off, stop what you're doing and close your laptop."

"But what a waste of fifteen minutes," I said. "That's when I do an e-mail or three!"

"Waste of time?" he responded. "Unless you use those minutes instead to pray for the work you are about to do, the people doing it, and those it will affect."

What an idea! Now I not only get to meetings on time, I get there with less stress and better prepared both mentally and spiritually.

Grant me the wisdom, God, to steward Your gift of time in faithful and fruitful ways. —Jeff Japinga

Digging Deeper: 2 Chronicles 6:12–42, Psalm 28

Thursday, March 16

They will receive blessing from the Lord.... **—Psalm 24:5** (NIV)

It's easy to feel gloom and doom when you're dealing with a difficult life situation. These feelings were heightened when I was driving home alone from a meeting and dark thunderclouds were blocking the last light of sunset. Then, as I drove around a curve, there was an unexpected break in the clouds. In this little piece of freshly revealed horizon, the sun was setting in all its glory, in vibrant pinks, deep purples, and bright golds. *How beautiful!* I thought. *I needed that.*

Then I wondered, *Could God have sent it to me?* I shook my head. *Don't be silly. It's just a weather pattern. Nothing more.*

I remembered something my sister said the last time we got together. When Susan discovered a few yards of gold fringe at a bargain price in a thrift store, she exclaimed, "I receive that!"

It seemed like an unusual thing to say, so I asked her what she meant. "It's my way of connecting God with good things that come my way," she answered. "It's different from just thanking Him for them. I'm actively accepting it and believing that it's an unexpected gift God sent specially to me."

I blinked at the sunset between the black clouds and said three simple words: "I receive that." Precisely at the moment, I experienced a feeling of being favored by God, Who intimately loves me and sends me good things even during the darkest times.

Today, God, when I confront something ordinary that warms my heart, help me to declare, "I receive that!" knowing it is a token of Your care. Amen.
—Karen Barber

Digging Deeper: Daniel 4:3, 1 Timothy 4:4

LESSONS IN STONES: Ebenezers
Then Samuel took a stone and set it between Mizpah and Shen, and named it Ebenezer....
—1 Samuel 7:12 (NAS)

There's a fascinating Old Testament story about the naming of a rock. A warring people had invaded the land of Israel. The prophet Samuel told the wavering Israelites, "Direct your hearts to the Lord and serve

Him alone; and He will deliver you" (1 Samuel 7:3, NAS). As the battle began, God "thundered with a great thunder" (1 Samuel 7:10, NAS). The enemy was confused and fled. Samuel set a stone in that place and "named it Ebenezer, saying, 'Thus far the Lord has helped us'" (1 Samuel 7:12, NAS). *Ebenezer* means "stone of help."

I once named three large boulders positioned around a fire pit we had. The flat one was *Sky* for times of lying back and searching out God's wonders in the sky. There was *Story*, a perch for the telling of tales around the fire's embers. *Sparrow* got its name from a little fox sparrow that landed there, reminding me of Jesus's words about His Father's knowing even the sparrows (Matthew 10:29–30). Those rocks later became a circle of meeting where I cried out to God for help in a fierce battle of the soul.

Samuel's stone is not the main attraction in the biblical account. What it stands for—God's deliverance—is. My life's path, were I to set markers, is chock-full of Ebenezers. Rescues from fear, sorrow, failure, disillusionment, regret—the list as elastic as human frailty. But those "stones of help," how firm and strong they stand.

Lord, You called the stars by name (Isaiah 40:26), You inspired Samuel to name a stone, and You know my name and just how to deliver in my every need.
—Carol Knapp

Digging Deeper: Deuteronomy 4:7, Psalm 71:3–5

"The flowers are springing up and the time of the singing of birds has come. Yes, spring is here."
—Song of Solomon 2:12 (TLB)

One reason I love living in Florida is the wildlife. There's a nine-foot alligator that lives in the nature reserve just a few miles from my home. I've named her Gussie and I love to visit her. She's there every time I go, lying in the shallow water with her full length exposed to the sunshine. On hot days, most of her body is submerged in mud.

I also love our big Florida birds. Hardly a day goes by that I don't see a tall white egret or a great blue heron walking around our neighborhood. On the dock across the street, I often spot my favorite: pelicans, waiting for the fishermen to toss their smallest catches. Watching a pelican eat a whole fish is a riot.

The best sighting of all is the pink roseate spoonbill, a large wading bird. The only time I've ever seen one is when it flies across the pool during water aerobics class between nine and ten in the morning. Every few weeks someone will shout "Pink spoonbill!" so none of us misses the beautiful sight. Up to thirty-four inches long with an average fifty-inch wingspan and a large spoon-shaped bill, the roseate spoonbill is a sight to see.

I am happy to find these amazing creatures right here in my neighborhood and start thanking God for all sorts of things: my good-natured husband; my beloved children and grandchildren; my friends who all appreciate and love nature the way I do....

All the birds and gators around me help pump up my prayer life. Whenever I see any of God's wild creatures, I find myself praying with gratitude and gusto.

Lord, thank You for the many blessings You have placed in my life. Help me to be mindful of them every single day. —Patricia Lorenz

Digging Deeper: 1 Kings 4:22–23, 32–33; Revelation 7:10–12

Sunday, March 19

Then our mouth was filled with laughter, and our tongue with singing.... —Psalm 126:2 (NKJV)

Why did I ever volunteer for this job? I asked myself on the way to the church. *I despise this kind of work.* I had promised to help collate pages of a devotional book, so it could go to the bindery.

About a dozen volunteers showed up. I looked at the big boxes of pages and cringed. At first it was the same old chore I remembered from my teaching days, but then volunteers began to chat: "My husband thinks shopping for radial tires is a vacation. We shopped twelve different stores, then sat in a stinky garage forever while they installed them."

Others made jokes: "How many church members does it take to change a lightbulb?" Answer: "Ten. One to change it and nine to say how much better they liked the old bulb." Soon we were all laughing, and then someone started singing "Blessed Be the Name" and we all joined in.

All of a sudden the task was done. "That's it? We are finished? I can't believe it! I was enjoying this so much!"

On the way home, I thought about why the morning was so much fun. The answer was the social element, like the old quilting bees and barn raisings when people did their chores together. I could add the social element to my work, such as inviting the grandkids to help me weed the garden and doing some of my paperwork at the coffee shop.

I have stumbled on to something that will add much pleasure to my work—and to my life.

Lord, help me not to be so independent but to let others in. —Daniel Schantz

Digging Deeper: Proverbs 13:20, 27:17

Monday, March 20

When I was a child, I spoke like a child, I thought like a child, I reasoned like a child; when I became a man, I gave up childish ways. —1 Corinthians 13:11 (RSV)

I love commuting on my motor scooter (weather permitting). I get to use the HOV lane, save money, park close to my office, and have fun. Win, win, win, win.

"Weather permitting" turns out to be a crucial parenthetical remark. "Skittish" is the kindest description of Pittsburgh's climate—the other words aren't suitable for this publication. In fact, I use those same unprintable words in reference to our local meteorologists, who are as reliable as a coin flip. Which is why I found myself in a part of town that's often in the news and rarely for the right reasons, parked underneath an overhang, waiting out a sudden, unexpected downpour. I was wet and seething at faceless forecasters.

Through the rain, I saw a woman under an umbrella walking toward me. "I saw you from my porch," she said. "Here's a poncho for you."

As God is my witness, the rain suddenly eased. I was grateful my face was wet because she couldn't see me tearing up. I thanked her profusely but declined her kind offer because it was now safe to drive.

My rage continued as I drove home, this time directed at myself. In my senseless anger, I couldn't see the vision coming toward me, the angel bearing gifts; nor did I see the life-giving rain. All I saw was delay, plus unwarranted resentment at meteorologists whose job it is to predict the weather, not control it.

Lord, I'm probably not mature enough to ride a motorcycle. Or vote. Or marry. Or make assumptions about neighbors from an unfamiliar block. I am a petulant child. In the words of Saint Paul, it's time to put away my childish things, like reasonless rage, and enjoy the grace of a random act of kindness. —Mark Collins

Digging Deeper: Deuteronomy 32:2

Tuesday, March 21

And the Lord, he it is that doth go before thee; he will be with thee, he will not fail thee, neither forsake thee: fear not, neither be dismayed. —Deuteronomy 31:8 (KJV)

My daughter is ill. My daughter has a condition. My daughter medicates herself—all day and night, every day, all week, all month, all year. I am her dad, and I am horrified and worried and frightened. How can this possibly end well?

My subtle, brilliant, devout, wise, gentle, gracious wife says, "Trust in God."

I say I will surely try to do so, but here I am at dusk sobbing in the currant bushes where no one will see me losing my cool. *Fear not,* You said to Isaiah, *for I am with thee. Be not dismayed,* You said, *for I am with thee.* But Isaiah had no daughters, did he? He didn't lie awake at three in the morning desperate to hear the grumble of the car returning safely. He didn't try to speak reasonably and gently to his daughter and get a blast of sneer back in his face like pepper spray, did he?

How do I trust You? That is what I would like to talk about, Merciful One. Are You attending to her even as You attend to the birds of the air, who reap not? Because it sure seems to me like she is headed for a crash, an arrest, a crisis. Do I keep playing perimeter defense and hope You are standing behind me like a huge, terrific shot-blocker? Do I accept that I cannot protect or defend her anymore? But that's an awful thing for a father to know. *You* are a Father—You know what I mean.

Suddenly, I have a flash of the oddest emotion, a terrible empathy for You, Who must watch so many of Your children flail and crash. O save her, Blessed

One. Please? Be with her even on her darkest paths. Please?

> Dear Mercy, almost always I show up here, hat in hand, asking You to save me from myself. But today I just beg desperately for my daughter. Heal her, bring her back to her deep sweet genuine self.
> —Brian Doyle

Digging Deeper: 1 John 5:14

Wednesday, March 22

Pray without ceasing. —1 Thessalonians 5:17 (NKJV)

Sonya and I carried on a neighborly conversation over a wooden-rail fence we shared. Although we both try not to dip too deeply into the bucket of negative topics, soon we shared about some friends' sicknesses and misfortunes. After we said our good-byes, my heart ached, wishing there was something I could do to help.

I slumped at my desk while finishing off my day's work and was greeted with a chime announcing an incoming e-mail. It was from Sonya. "What a great idea! It gives hope that something good is going on in the world," she wrote. I opened it to discover a link to a video featuring a new invention called an "ambulance drone."

The video showed a flying robot that could be dispatched as a first response from a hospital for patients who were suffering from cardiac arrest. The built-in GPS system guided the flying miniature ambulance, which resembled a two-foot-wide flying saucer, to the patient's side. The response time was only minutes. Voice instructions told a bystander how to use the defibrillator, which was housed inside.

As I marveled at the technology, God whispered to my spirit, *That's what prayer is like. When you pray, heaven responds immediately and is on the scene. It's your first response for those people around you who are hurting.* Instantly I started praying.

Thank You, Lord, for being our lifesaving First Responder. Amen. —Rebecca Ondov

Digging Deeper: Luke 11:1–4, Colossians 1:9–11

Thursday, March 23

"For the Lord will not forsake His people."
—1 Samuel 12:22 (NKJV)

A snowstorm struck our ranch. From the house, I watched the barn swallows line up on the barbed-wire fences, looking miserably cold. Then I spotted movement in the grass. A swallow was trying to fly to its friends, but it couldn't get off the ground. The snow was building quickly. In another minute, it would be buried.

I pulled on some boots and rushed outside. Cradling the motionless bird in my gloves, I brought it indoors and set it on a towel in a cardboard box. The bird lay still. Maybe I was too late.

I had to go to another ranch for the afternoon so I put another towel over the box. *Lord, why do I continually let my heart break over every lost cause I find?* I thought.

The storm ended a few hours later and the sun returned. When I got home, I found the bird on a windowsill, managed to recapture it, and released it outdoors. It flew strongly.

My barn swallow, a "lost cause," needed only the tiniest bit of care. How often do I seem like a lost cause to God? Yet, He doesn't give up on me. He promised. And I believe Him.

Your love is steadfast, Lord, no matter how lost our cause may seem. Please comfort and guide us through the storms of life. —Erika Bentsen

Digging Deeper: Psalms 38:21–22, 99:5–9, 138:8

Friday, March 24

"Truly I tell you, whatever you did not do for one of the least of these, you did not do for me." —Matthew 25:45 (NIV)

My wife, Pat, and I had moved to Brazil. We were warned from the day we arrived not to give to beggars. After months in hotels, we finally moved into our house. All day long I looked forward to dinner, the first meal in our new home.

As soon as we sat down to eat, the doorbell rang. *What if it's a beggar?* I thought. I could still hear those voices telling us not to help them. I could picture the lines of people we were told would come.

The man waiting at our gate asked for bread. "No, I'm sorry," I said.

His dark eyes stared deep into mine. "You don't have bread for me?"

I shook my head.

As I walked back inside, Jesus's words from Matthew 25:45 seared into my soul. Filled with sorrow, I took a loaf of bread from the pantry and searched the neighborhood for the man who only moments before I had turned away.

Never again did I say no to those who came by for food. The lines of people at our door never formed—just a few beggars on some days. But my attitude toward helping and listening was changed forever.

Dear God, forgive me when I stumble and say no to serving You. Amen. —John Dilworth

Digging Deeper: Matthew 25:35–45, Romans 12:10–13, Ephesians 6:7

I will sing.... —1 Corinthians 14:15 (KJV)

"I'm over here," my mother calls as I walk into the hospital's big gathering room. She has been ill and is here for an evaluation.

After we exchange the usual news, her voice drops. "Oh, you just can't believe the poor woman who shares my room," she says. "Last night was awful. She kept crying on and on."

I look at my mother. Her still beautiful face is filled with compassion.

"I tried to talk to her, but she wouldn't listen. She cried like a baby. Finally, I had an idea. Maybe it would help if I sang to her."

My mother described the long night and the songs she sang. Soon the woman became quiet, peaceful, and drifted off to sleep. A while later, she woke my mother asking, "Please sing to me some more."

So, through the night, my mother sang—church songs, children's songs, songs from the past.

I had come to the hospital worried. What if my mother was different, in pain, complaining, begging me to take her out of this place? But my worries were unfounded. She was the same: focused on the needs of someone else, never complaining, never talking about getting old or lamenting her loss of mobility or the fact that most of her friends had left the earth. She had become a love song.

Father, let me grow in kindness, in mercy, in love, like my mother, singing Your comfort to others.
—Pam Kidd

Digging Deeper: Psalm 103:2–4, Ezekiel 33:32

Sunday, March 26

And if the ear would say, "Because I am not an eye, I do not belong to the body," that would not make it any less a part of the body.
—1 Corinthians 12:16 (NRSV)

I attended Calvin College's Festival of Faith and Writing featuring so many great writers in every manner of venue, several at the same time, it was hard to choose which workshop to attend. Or find time to eat. Or have a genuine conversation. Or be by myself.

So, though I liked being there, I felt fractured the whole time. Just looking at the program agitated me. So many mouths and words. So many "me's" in attendance. I felt redundant.

Thus I found myself—late in the festival, late in the day—in a session by one of the most frenzied speakers. All I wanted was to escape to my room, eat, gather myself, maybe read awhile before bed.

But the stranger sitting next to me had dragged me along to what ended up being my most profitable session, where, apropos of nothing the speaker was saying, she suddenly shouted, "You are chosen and loved!"

I must have needed to hear that. Every nerve in me vibrated with its truth: God chose me—and everyone else—and loved us.

For the first time that weekend I felt not pulled apart and splintered, but part of one wholesome body—the best way to be.

Lord of all, thank You for Your body of believers and that You've chosen each of us with Your very hand.
—Patty Kirk

Digging Deeper: Colossians 3:15

Monday, March 27

He said, "My presence will go with you, and I will give you rest." —Exodus 33:14 (NRSV)

A million things to do! That's how it is most every day: housekeeping, shopping, preparing meals, volunteering at Bible study, and carpooling Micah to school and sporting events. Then I wake up and do it again.

The hectic pace exhausted me, so I was thrilled when my daughter had a day off from school. It would be the first time in weeks that I didn't have to wake before dawn. I turned off the alarm clocks and switched the phones to silent. Guess what happened?

I opened my eyes and gazed at the clock. 6:15. I tried to go back to sleep but couldn't. I had the idea of lingering over my Bible study and watching the sun come up. I grabbed a blanket and my materials and slipped out onto the back porch.

Our two dogs danced around my feet, then took turns jumping in my lap. No way could I get out my study notebook, but maybe I could read my Bible. Gusty winds whipped down the plains, flapping the pages. Exasperated, all I could do was sit, watch, and do nothing as the dawn broke.

Thirty minutes later, I went indoors. *Sorry, God. I didn't do much out there. The wind, the dogs—all I could do was sit and watch the trees blow while listening to the wind.*

A quiet knowing washed over me. This was just what I had needed.

God, help me remember that being with You is always better than working for You.
—Stephanie Thompson

Digging Deeper: 1 Kings 19:11–13, Psalm 139:7, John 15:5

I fear no evil; for thou art with me....
—Psalm 23:4 (RSV)

I once read that anxiety is the human condition.
After living six decades, I know this is true. Though
I may appear confident, uncertainty and fear often
grip me. A close friend was critically injured, and I
feared for his life. My wife, Beth, and I attended her
forty-fifth high school reunion. It was a wonderful
time of greeting old classmates, but we were grateful
for name tags with large, legible print. Then
we learned our son Drew and Katie Alice were
expecting a daughter. We were ecstatic, but with
all that comes fear about Katie Alice's health, the
baby's health, and on and on.

Beth and I escaped to a favorite cottage on the
Florida coast. Near midnight, I took a long walk on
the beach. The moon was full and the stars brilliant.
I gazed into the vast darkness and found myself
thinking, *Is God real or just a myth? Is eternity a*
wonderful new dimension of unimagined experience or
is death merely extinction? I prayed that I would see
my unborn granddaughter reach her wedding day.
Amid the beauty, thoughts pounded me. I felt tense
and tentative.

As I walked, I heard the Psalmist's calm voice:
"The Lord is my shepherd, I shall not want.... Even

though I walk through the valley of the shadow of death, I fear no evil; for thou art with me.... Surely goodness and mercy shall follow me all the days of my life; and I shall dwell in the house of the Lord for ever" (Psalm 23:1, 4, 6, RSV).

Slowly the rhythm of the surf embraced me. I knew that the God of holy mystery was near. I was no longer afraid.

Father, help me to accept my anxious nature and to follow You. Amen. —Scott Walker

Digging Deeper: Psalm 8, John 10:11–14

Wednesday, March 29

"For you are a mist that appears for a little time and then vanishes." —James 4:14 (ESV)

I looked up from sweeping the porch and noticed some new birds on my feeder in the backyard. They were small, with a black cap, black bib, gray wings, and black and whitish underside. *I'd love to sit down and watch you, if I didn't have so much to do!* I thought.

I saw the same birds a few days later while I was planting flowers in the garden and the next week too. *I sure want to find some time to watch you little guys!*

The following weekend, I finished everything on my to-do list. *Now for some bird-watching!* I grabbed my binoculars, picked up my bird book, and headed to the backyard. I sat and waited…and waited. *I'll try again tomorrow.* But there was no sight of them.

I stopped at the feed store to pick up birdseed and described the birds to the man behind the counter. "Sounds like Carolina chickadees," he said.

"Really?" I exclaimed. "I can't wait to see them!"

"Not this year, you won't," he replied. "They're seasonal birds. Gone 'til next year."

"Oh," I said, disappointed.

He peered over his bifocals. "My years of bird-watching have taught me one big lesson: special moments are fleeting. So we've got to stop and enjoy 'em when they're here." He patted my hand. "The chickadees will be back next year. In the meantime, there've been some indigo bunting sightings." He handed me my bag of seed. "And if they show up in your yard, I reckon you'd best sit a spell and watch 'em."

All I have is the precious present, Lord. May I never overlook Your daily gifts. —Melody Bonnette Swang

Digging Deeper: Psalm 90:12, Matthew 6:11

Thursday, March 30

For I have always been mindful of your unfailing love and have lived in reliance on your faithfulness. —Psalm 26:3 (NIV)

"The incision is healing nicely, but I'm afraid the mass in her spleen tested positive for cancer. I'm so sorry," said my eight-year-old golden retriever's vet, Dr. Maddie.

Millie wagged. I tapped. I wanted to know exactly what kind of cancer. I wanted a name.

"Hemangiosarcoma."

"How long?"

"Three to six months."

"How will we know?"

"She'll tell you. Pick the three things she loves most. When she stops doing two of them, it's probably time."

I felt my fingernails dig into my palms. At that moment, I hated cancer more than I had hated anything in my life. I was light-headed from hate. I had to sit down and pull myself together.

Millie and I went for a hike. We climbed Squaw Peak Trail to a point called the Devil's Pulpit, which afforded a magnificent, sweeping view of the hills we loved. We'd spent so much time at each other's side since she was eight weeks old and I made her climb Monument Mountain.

Finally, I gave in to my tears. I held her close and told her it was okay. Whenever she was ready she could go. I would be fine. She didn't have to hold on for me. Dogs will do that, you know. They will suffer as long as they can if you don't let them go. Love should not have to mean suffering, not for a dog. And there was no room in these final months for hate, not even hate for the thing that would kill a being I loved so much.

Dear Father, You have given me many dogs to love and to be loved by, each one more than the last, and each one has returned to You. But it gets harder every time. Help me love Millie through that hurt and pain. Let me be there for her as she has been for me... as You have always been.
—Edward Grinnan

Digging Deeper: John 16:33

Friday, March 31

"New things I now declare...." —Isaiah 42:9 (RSV)

The petition was making the rounds of our town. Community leaders, Realtors, garden club members were protesting the erection of an "ugly," "monstrous," "outsize" wind turbine. "An eyesore that will lower property values." "Totally out of keeping with our colonial character."

"What do you think?" I asked my husband when he'd finished reading.

"I'm thinking," John said, "about the Eiffel Tower."

This instantly recognizable icon of Paris was nearly petitioned out of existence before the first shovelful of dirt was dug for the foundation.

Alexandre Eiffel's design had been selected by a committee planning the 1889 World's Fair. When its choice was made public, the city's elite exploded with outrage. "We, the writers, painters, sculptors, architects, and lovers of the beauty of Paris do protest with all our vigor and indignation against the useless and monstrous Eiffel Tower."

The committee pressed ahead anyway. When completed, the tower was the world's tallest building and the sensation of the exposition. It changed forever the way we see the world, as millions of people for the first time viewed the earth from seventy stories up.

When the tower's lease was up in 1909, opponents attacked again. "Now that its 'novelty value' has worn off, it is time to restore the city to its former dignity." The tower doubtless would have been torn down, except for another "novelty." An aerial recently mounted on top of it provided fans of a new fad—the radio—with a longer-distance signal than ever before possible.

"Maybe," John added, "a sleek wind turbine will someday be considered the most useful and beautiful thing in town."

Changeless God of this fast-changing world, help me to not always and automatically resist the new!
—Elizabeth Sherrill

Digging Deeper: Philemon 1:6

IN GOD'S HANDS

1 _____

2 _____

3 _____

4 _____

5 _____

6 _____

7 _____

8 _____

9 _____

10 _____

11 _____

12 _____

13 _____

14 _____

15 _____

16 _____

17 _____

18 _____

19 _____

20 _____

21 _____

22 _____

23 _____

24 _____

25 _____

26 _____

27 _____

28 _____

29 _____

30 _____

31 _____

APRIL

*He reached down from on high and took
hold of me; he drew me out of deep waters.*

—Psalm 18:16 (NIV)

Saturday, April 1

BEAUTY FROM ASHES
Facing What's Ahead

For His compassions never fail. They are new every
morning; great is Your faithfulness.
—Lamentations 3:22–23 (NAS)

"What happens next, Mom?" Katie asked as we stood
in the kitchen of her new apartment.

With a divorce pending, she'd opened a new
checking account, made a grocery list, packed, and
brought her two dogs. Wanting to get everything
done quickly, she'd left some necessities behind at
the old house: a shower curtain, a trash can, and
dishes.

"Let's tackle your shopping list," I suggested.

In somewhat of a daze, we headed to the store.
"This doesn't feel real, does it?" she said.

I kept walking, afraid to give in to my emotions.
"What's first on your list?"

She read it out loud and paused. "I'll never forget
how good it felt when we prayed and read the Bible
together, even though nothing else made sense." I
nodded, remembering the sun streaming through
the windows and how we had sensed God's presence.
"I'm going to start every day the same way," she said.
She headed toward the stationery department.

"What are you looking for?"

"A prayer journal." She settled on a satiny one, Easter-egg blue, turquoise, and yellow, like the promise of spring. "Now I need a coffee mug."

"Don't you want a set of dishes?"

"Nope, I only want one mug, and my prayer journal. That's all I need."

"You're absolutely right, Katie. You've found the two essentials for your new home."

Oh, Lord, when You're all we have, You're all we need.
—Julie Garmon

Digging Deeper: Psalm 46:1–2, 2 Peter 1:3

Sunday, April 2

I make all things new.... —Revelation 21:5 (KJV)

It will be Easter in two weeks, my first without my mother, Bebe.

I think of long-ago sunrise services, reenactments of the first Easter when the women made their way to the tomb. Then, in a flash, everything changed. The bright light of Resurrection banished darkness forever.

"Up from the grave He arose," we always sang at Easter service when I was a child. I loved wearing my shiny new black patent leather shoes, white gloves, and pastel dress. Even my socks were new, because that's what Easter proclaimed: all things new! Afterward, we'd make our way back home for pancakes and chocolate bunnies, my mother's favorite.

Now the sun is taking shape, gathering the gold back into itself. "Low in the grave He lay," I begin singing softly, "waiting the coming day."

I miss my mother, but this Easter will be especially poignant. Our family will gather for our annual Easter feast. We will begin the festivities with our red-egg contest, hitting our eggs together while proclaiming, "Christ is Risen!" until only one egg is left uncracked. My mother liked being the winner...last egg standing!

My memories lighten as I sing on: "He arose! He arose! Hallelujah! Christ arose!"

Suddenly, I smile. This will be the first Easter of my mother's resurrection, undefeated by life, triumphant over death. For her, everything is new.

Father, all is new because of You. —Pam Kidd

Digging Deeper: Psalm 65:8

Monday, April 3

Lord, in the morning you hear my voice. In the morning I lay it all out before you. Then I wait expectantly. —Psalm 5:3 (CEB)

The water was boiling. I poured the five-minute Irish oatmeal into the pot and stirred, lowering the heat. Now what?

Meow, Fred said at my feet. He gazed up toward the top of the refrigerator where we keep his brush.

"Fred," I said, "I'm trying to figure out how to cook this oatmeal."

Meeeeooooow. Oatmeal or not, he wanted to be brushed. I grabbed the Zoom Groom and knelt down beside him.

"You're going to have to cooperate, Fred. Paws down." He stretched out, turning into a gray-and-white puddle on the floor. I ran the brush through his thick fur. Clumps rose off his lush coat, floating like fog and then dropping to the ground or getting stuck on my sweats.

I got up and stirred the oatmeal and then returned to Fred. He began purring. *Might as well pray,* I thought.

"Thank You, God, for a demanding cat, a bubbling breakfast, the snow that's melting, the run I made on just-plowed streets." Fred swiped a lazy paw at me, his signal that he was done. It wasn't very gracious, but that's his way. He'd already purred—that was my thank-you.

The clock on the stove said five minutes had passed. The oatmeal was ready, not stuck to the pot at all. Fred wandered off, his needs met for the time being. I poured my breakfast into a bowl, added some maple syrup and milk, and sat down to eat. It was going to be a good day.

I'll wait with You and for You, Lord, whenever
I have cause to wait. —Rick Hamlin

Digging Deeper: Mark 1:35

Tuesday, April 4

We all live off his generous bounty, gift after gift
after gift. —John 1:16 (MSG)

Reading the cake recipe, I felt my heart sink. I'd
forgotten the very thing I went shopping for earlier
that morning—eggs. The recipe called for two, and
I knew from this morning's breakfast that there was
one lonely egg left in the carton.

I didn't have the energy to go back out. Besides, I
had to make dinner and then get the boys to bed so
I'd have time to make up the goody bags for Henry's
birthday party. *How much difference can an egg make
anyway?*

Chocolate cake with vanilla icing is Henry's
favorite, and with all the fudgy chocolate goodness
who would miss one little egg? I got out my mixer
from under the cabinet and started putting together
the ingredients, all the while reassuring myself it
would turn out fine.

I opened up the carton and cracked the egg
against the bowl. For a second, I couldn't believe my
eyes. Two yolks stared back at me. I hadn't seen a

double-yolker in years! Growing up, we had chickens and were often surprised by double yolks, but I couldn't remember ever cracking open a double-yolk egg from the supermarket.

Yes, it was Henry's birthday, but I'd been given the gift.

Dear Lord, thank You for Your glorious surprises that show us how much You love us. —Sabra Ciancanelli

Digging Deeper: Numbers 6:24–26, Psalm 115:12, Isaiah 1:19

Wednesday, April 5

The Lord is risen indeed. . . . —Luke 24:34 (KJV)

"I met a new cashier in the hospital cafeteria," I said to my office mate Julius. "When I asked if Easter was a special holiday for her, she looked at me, perplexed, and told me, 'No, honey, my children are all grown.'"

Julius shook his head sadly. "I love my America," he said, "but back in Nigeria, Easter was different. We didn't have much materially, so the focus wasn't on bunnies and chocolate." At four o'clock on Easter morning, a small group of people would gather at Julius's parsonage. As the group trekked to the next family's home, they sang favorite songs of the Resurrection: "He's Alive," "He Arose," and others. On and on it went until the entire congregation circled the town and returned to the church at 8:00 a.m. There, they praised the Lord, nonstop, until two or three in the afternoon.

"We were filled with such joy, we never tired," Julius said, beaming at the memory. "All of that worship energized us."

Now I was the one who felt sad. I thought of too many church services where folks checked the bulletin to see how many songs they had to slog through or texted friends throughout the sermon.

Julius never had an Easter basket or even tasted cake or ice cream until he came to the United States at the age of twenty-six. In Nigeria, he didn't know the luxury of three meals a day. Though my friend scrambled to survive, because of Jesus, he never wanted for anything.

Thank You, Lord, for teachers from distant places who point me to the blessings of this nation.
—Roberta Messner

Digging Deeper: Mark 16:9, John 11:25–26, Acts 2:29–32

Thursday, April 6

Then he told them, "The Sabbath was made for people, not people for the Sabbath."
—Mark 2:27 (ISV)

My husband, Kris, suffers from stress every tax season. Each year we add exercise into his schedule, but he never ends up doing it, which only adds to his stress.

Kris suggested last year's failed plan: we buy a bike rack and take our bicycles to new trails forty-five minutes away.

"Why can't you just run like I do?" I protested.

"Running makes me sick," he said.

Soon, Kris was fantasizing about bike racks, researching them on the Internet, reading reviews out loud at breakfast, and pointing them out in parking lots. We'd stop at bike shops, so he could examine their brands and ask questions. He learned every dealer's name.

By summer, we'd spent money in what I knew would be this year's failure, but it turned out to be the best investment of our marriage. The expense motivated us to use our bikes, and we took long rides—the first one over twenty miles.

Afterward we were hungry. "If it were Switzerland, there'd be an alpine café," I huffed as we pedaled the last hill. At the top, as if I'd conjured it, stood a little restaurant with an alpine theme. It became our Sunday destination. We'd leave from church, ride for two hours, eat a late lunch, and then drive home, tired and happy. Kris stayed relaxed all week.

It wasn't exercise that he—we—needed most. It was time doing nothing other than being together, enjoying God's creation, a genuine day of rest.

Holy Creator, thank You for instituting the Sabbath. Such a good idea! —Patty Kirk

Digging Deeper: Exodus 20:8–11, Leviticus 23:3

Friday, April 7

"Now I commit you to God and to the word of his grace, which can build you up and give you an inheritance among all those who are sanctified." —Acts 20:32 (NIV)

I was taking Millie for her late-night walk, urging her on so we both wouldn't get completely drenched in a steady rain, when along came a shabby figure in the gloom, his gait wobbly, arms extended to greet my dog. The man looked at me with a boozy grin and asked, "Which way to Bellevue?"

"Straight across. Just keep going east," I answered.

A few minutes later Millie and I ducked into a bodega. There was the man again, trying to get people to give him cash.

"I think Bellevue is a better option, my friend. You'll get three squares and a bed," I urged. Then I moved on. But not totally.

I can't help but see myself in a drunk on the street. I've been there. Even now I still have that paralyzing moment of shock and recognition when I encounter someone in the throes of addiction. *That was me*, I think. *That could still be me.*

I woke up the next morning, still thinking about the guy. The rain had gone and the sky was a hard blue. I checked my phone. There was an e-mail alert about the worldwide weekend of prayer for the addicted.

A day rarely goes by when I don't pray for some suffering addict, even if it's just me. Today I know who will be in my prayers.

Lord, addiction has plagued humankind ever since the dawn of time. Yet recovery is possible with You, a day at a time, a prayer at a time.
—Edward Grinnan

Digging Deeper: Luke 4:17–19

Saturday, April 8

Likewise the Spirit helps us in our weakness....
—Romans 8:26 (ESV)

My younger daughter had been asking a lot of questions about how the Holy Spirit works in our lives. I found it hard to explain. "Sometimes, when you feel moved to do something good, even though you don't want to do it, you know that's the Spirit working on you," I'd told her.

A few weeks later, I got a crash course.

I was practically skipping down the aisles of the grocery store. Every other Easter my daughters are with their father, so I was beyond excited that this was my year. I'd been shopping all week for goodies for their baskets and planning my table setting for Sunday lunch. My parents and brother would be joining us, and this would be my first time to do the family lunch while my mom simply enjoyed it all. I wanted everything to be perfect. Today I was buying an egg-dyeing kit and all the side dishes plus dessert.

The young man who bagged my groceries offered to take them to my car. "Do you have a big Easter planned with your family?" I asked to be polite.

"No, ma'am," he said. "I'm a college student, and my family lives a few hours away."

I knew immediately what I should do, but I didn't want to. *There are already eight of us. I ordered the smaller ham. He's a complete stranger. This could ruin my Easter with the girls. We won't have many more before they're grown.*

"Would you like to join our family for worship and lunch?" I asked.

As I drove home, I laughed at myself for how relieved I was when the young man had declined. Clearly, the Spirit still has a lot of work to do on me!

Father, help me not only to do the right things but to do them with a joyful heart. —Ginger Rue

Digging Deeper: Galatians 5:22, Ephesians 3:16

AN OUTWARD LENT
Give Away Something

To this you were called, because Christ suffered for you, leaving you an example, that you should follow in his steps. —1 Peter 2:21 (NIV)

A stack of turquoise envelopes sat on my friend Mollie's counter. "What are these?" I asked.

"Every day of Lent, I'm writing to someone who I think needs a word of encouragement. I always give *up* something as a way to remember Jesus's sacrifice, but this year I want to give *away* something as well. I want to feed the souls of those who so desperately need to be fed even as I am fed," she explained.

I let the impact of Mollie's words sink in. One letter was addressed to a distant uncle. Another was being sent to a friend who was in prison. Yet another was to our pastor who gives to our congregation each week.

Yes, Lent is about introspection, but it's also about caring for others, about loving joyfully, and about living Jesus's calling through every step we take.

What better way to show gratitude than to look outward even as we look inward? To serve the poor as we search the poverty of our own souls? To embrace the downtrodden even as we examine our own inequities? To love like Jesus did even as we receive His grace, so willingly poured out for us?

I'm ready to change from the inside out. Are you?

Lord, reveal to me ways that I can show Your love to others. Amen. —Erin MacPherson

Digging Deeper: Ephesians 4:22–24, Philippians 2:5

Monday of Holy Week, April 10

AN OUTWARD LENT: Welcome Others
Carry each other's burdens, and in this way you will fulfill the law of Christ. —Galatians 6:2 (NIV)

I stood in the corner of the cafeteria, watching the drama unfold. There was a big table in the center of the room with girls already laughing boisterously as one girl with long blonde hair began telling a story. They leaned in close, hardly noticing the tiny girl with big purple glasses walking toward an empty table.

I swallowed hard. Memories of my own days in the school lunchroom raced through my mind— of mean girls, of being excluded, of feeling alone and unwanted. I stood on my tiptoes, vowing to intervene. Sure, I was just a volunteer lunch monitor, but I wasn't going to stand by as this little one was snubbed by those who didn't understand friendship.

The girl's steps seemed to echo across the cafeteria, drowning out the hum of chatter as she plodded toward an open table, her eyes searching, her lips pursed. Then the girl with the long blonde hair looked up and noticed her. But instead of turning back to her friends, she stood. "Hey, Sarah, want to sit with us?"

The tiny girl with the big purple glasses paused and then turned toward the table of girls. "Sure."

Space was made on the bench as she squeezed her tray between lunch boxes, and the laughter and storytelling continued.

Lord, help me to welcome each of Your children to my table without hesitation and with a heaping dose of Your love. Amen. —Erin MacPherson

Digging Deeper: Proverbs 11:17, 1 John 3:18

Tuesday of Holy Week, April 11

AN OUTWARD LENT
Share a Love Language
Each of you should use whatever gift you have received to serve others, as faithful stewards of God's grace in its various forms. —1 Peter 4:10 (NIV)

Pulling weeds is my dad's love language. Suffice it to say, it's not mine—especially in Texas, where stalks grow six feet tall and bugs swarm every leaf even as I struggle to yank out the roots from the unforgiving clay. It's a chore I do only when absolutely necessary, which wasn't today.

I was taking a much-needed break while my mom graciously watched the kids. So I sat on her front porch, sipping a tall glass of iced tea, and took a deep breath of the spring air ripe with the smell of the just-blossomed chinaberry trees.

As my eyes scanned the bright coral trumpet vines that lined my parents' garden fence, I caught a glimpse of my father, crouched in his rose garden, painstakingly pulling the tangled vines that threatened his precious plants. My breath caught in my throat.

This man, the one who had so indulgently attended every one of my track meets when I was in high school, sprinting across the field so he could cheer me on at both ends of the track. This man who paced the hospital waiting room as each of my children was born, eager to meet yet another sprout on his growing family tree. This man who hoists my kids up onto his shoulders and lets them look out from the vantage point of a giant. This man who gave me life and so much more.

I stood up and grabbed some gloves. "Hey, Dad, may I help you?"

He flashed a big toothy smile. "Of course! This one here needs two pairs of hands to pull it out."

Heavenly Father, show me today how I can love like You—selflessly, fully, and mercifully. Amen.
—Erin MacPherson

Digging Deeper: John 13:12–14, Philippians 2:1–11

Wednesday of Holy Week, April 12

AN OUTWARD LENT: Give Bravely

"For I was hungry and you gave me something to eat, I was thirsty and you gave me something to drink. . . . " —Matthew 25:35 (NIV)

I tried to push those deep-black eyes out of my mind, dark pools that held a desperation I probably couldn't even fathom, eyes attached to a filthy body and hands holding a cardboard sign that read, "Please help."

But I was in no place to help—not with my mortgage due and three hungry kids who needed new shoes and clothes.

I drove past the man and quickly pulled into the drive-through to grab some food before heading to basketball practice. "Three cheeseburgers and a large order of fries!" I almost shouted at the attendant. I handed my ten-dollar bill to the clerk, grabbed the bag, and pulled into a parking spot so I could distribute the food.

Ten burgers? I glanced at the receipt and confirmed that I had paid only for three. "Our mistake," said the worker. "Eat them or throw them away."

Then I remembered the man with the pitch-black eyes. I returned to the intersection, praying that God would use even my hesitant generosity.

"They gave me seven extra burgers. Do you want them?" I asked.

"Yes, ma'am, I do. I have four little ones at home, and I imagine they would right appreciate these." He took the bag and smiled.

"God bless." I struggled to get the words out and prayed that next time I would be willing to respond to a need before God smacked me over the head with a bag of burgers.

Lord, give me the courage to give bravely. Amen.
—Erin MacPherson

Digging Deeper: Philippians 2:3–4, 1 John 3:17

Maundy Thursday, April 13

AN OUTWARD LENT
Call on the Great Helper
Religion that God our Father accepts as pure and faultless is this: to look after orphans and widows in their distress.... —James 1:27 (NIV)

"Oh, Lord, I can't do anything." The prayer stuck in my throat, causing a lump that wouldn't go away. But the truth was obvious: I was in no position to help. With three young kids of my own, I couldn't drop everything to go to my sister's home. And bringing my three children—to add to her four—simply wasn't an option.

"If only I had a million dollars to hire her a nanny and a housekeeper," I grumbled.

Not only did my sister have four kids, but three were still in diapers. *And*, on top of that, her three-week-old baby had just been diagnosed with a birth defect that made breathing difficult. *And* they were in the middle of selling their house. *And* now her husband had had another lupus attack and would likely be unable to walk or to move his hands to hold a baby for months.

The *ands*, piled one on top of the other, seemed too great. "Lord, I feel so helpless," I groaned.

But this time, He whispered back: *No, daughter, you are not.*

I may not be able to give vast sums of money or time, but I have the Great Helper as a friend. *And* He can do what I cannot: He can heal, He can advocate, He can provide, He can comfort, He can save.

Lord God, please comfort the widows, the orphans, the sick, and the desperate, and show me, in a tangible way, how I can help them right where I am. Amen.
—Erin MacPherson

Digging Deeper: Psalm 41:1–3, 1 Timothy 6:17–19

Good Friday, April 14

AN OUTWARD LENT: Offer a Tiny Promise

In him was life, and that life was the light of all mankind. The light shines in the darkness, and the darkness has not overcome it. —John 1:4–5 (NIV)

Bright yellow daisies scatter across hillsides, mixing with Indian paintbrush the color of a ripe tomato and delicate bluebells that we can almost hear jingling on the wind. And in the center of it all are fields of bluebonnets, our state flower and the undeniable heartbeat of a Texas spring. The sheer abundance of wildflowers is breathtaking, leaving little room for the dreary winter that is now just a memory floating away in the Texas blue sky.

Which is why I warned my daughter that it would be a meaningless gesture when she grabbed a pair of scissors and headed outside to pick a bouquet for her grandmother. Who needs a mere vase of flowers when God has given us a multitude outside?

Grandma did, it seemed. Because when a small grubby hand offered her a bunch of flowers with broken leaves and bent petals, a little voice said with a smile, "When you see these, remember you are loved."

It was a seemingly insignificant gesture that meant the world to a heart in need of uplifting. It was a tiny promise that pointed straight to the much bigger promise from the One Who gives us more beauty, more abundance, and more life than we can imagine.

Father God, help every little promise to display Your splendor in a big way today. Amen.
—Erin MacPherson

Digging Deeper: Genesis 1:31, Psalm 23

Please join us for Guideposts Good Friday Day of Prayer. Find out more at guideposts.org/ourprayer.

Holy Saturday, April 15

AN OUTWARD LENT: Spread Kindness
Let your gentleness be evident to all. The Lord is near. —Philippians 4:5 (NIV)

My son Joey worked hard for that frozen yogurt. His Sunday school teacher had promised the kids a five-dollar gift card if they were able to memorize and recite Colossians 3:12–14. After weeks of work, Joey had been able to earn his reward.

He grinned as he filled his bowl full of chocolate and peanut butter yogurt before sprinkling it with gummy bears and chocolate pieces. He walked up to the counter and proudly waited for the clerk to ring him up.

"Your bowl is actually paid for, young man."

My son looked confused. "But I haven't paid yet."

The clerk smiled. "As a random act of kindness, a woman paid for the next customer. So your yogurt is free."

I felt the wheels turn in Joey's head. He stood there for a few seconds, clearly contemplating what had just happened. He bit his lip, frowned, and then smiled. He handed the gift card to the clerk and said, "May I pay five dollars toward the next person's yogurt? You know, as a random act of kindness?"

"Of course you may!" The clerk took his card, swiped it, and smiled. "Enjoy your yogurt."

I hugged my son close. "That was so kind of you, Joey."

"Well, God did say to clothe ourselves with kindness, and what's more kind than a free bowl of frozen yogurt?"

Father God, help me to spread random acts of kindness, goodness, and joy whenever I have the opportunity. Amen. —Erin MacPherson

Digging Deeper: Ephesians 4:29, Colossians 3:12–14

AN OUTWARD LENT: Radiate Hope

In the hope of eternal life, which God, who does not lie, promised before the beginning of time. —Titus 1:2 (NIV)

The pastor asked for a thousand pairs of brand-new shoes to give to homeless people on Easter.

I looked around our small congregation and wondered where the shoes would come from. We weren't a congregation of means; we were teachers and office workers and stay-at-home moms and people with a trust that God could do what we couldn't.

Shoes started to pile up in the foyer of the middle school where our small church met—ten pairs one Sunday, twenty the next. Hope began to grow.

On Palm Sunday, the pastor announced that we had more than seven hundred pairs. We cheered, and then wondered where the next three hundred pairs would come from. But they arrived, in shipped packages, in paper bags left on our pastor's front porch—eight hundred pairs, nine hundred, then one thousand.

We carried those shoes that Easter, not to a lily-adorned chapel but to an empty park, white tablecloths blowing in the wind on picnic tables with vases of daffodils, the worship band warming up with favorite songs. We cut watermelon and grilled burgers and waited.

As new faces arrived, trickling in with their own stories to tell, we linked hands, we sang, we prayed, and we dared to hope that a thousand pairs of shoes would make a difference to a thousand pairs of worn-out feet, to a thousand desperate souls.

Lord, help me to radiate the hope that comes with Easter. Amen. —Erin MacPherson

Digging Deeper: Romans 5:2–15,
2 Corinthians 4:16–18

Monday, April 17

"Let there be light in the darkness."
—2 Corinthians 4:6 (NLT)

My day went from bad to worse. It started with a phone call that rearranged my schedule for the third time that week. Then my computer crashed. While I frantically researched computer fixes, my husband poked his head in to tell me he'd invited family over at the last minute for Easter dinner and asked if I could pick up what we needed.

I let my bad mood flourish during my hour-long drive to town. "I know Randy's busy, but can't he see I'm busy too?" I growled. I got out of my pickup and slammed the door. The cross around my neck bounced against my skin. I stopped. It didn't match the frown on my face.

This is the wrong attitude, I thought. *Easter is about overcoming darkness, a celebration of joy.*

I had eight stops to make, and an idea presented itself: I vowed to make someone laugh in each store, even though I didn't feel like it.

Wouldn't you know it? All my negativity dissipated after the first stop. Joking about my surprise Easter dinner guests was enough to do it. Checkout clerks saw that a lot. Many had great ideas for shaving time off dinner preparations and told their own unexpected-guest stories. My darkness was vanquished. I even sang on my way home, much to the chagrin of BlueDog, my faithful cattle dog in the backseat.

"How was town?" Randy asked a little tentatively when I got home.

I smiled. "Awesome!"

Thank You, Lord, for making Your light shine to brighten my way. —Erika Bentsen

Digging Deeper: Psalm 119:105, John 1:5, Acts 13:47

Tuesday, April 18

Whatsoever things are pure, whatsoever things are lovely, whatsoever things are of good report; if there be any virtue, and if there be any praise, think on these things. —Philippians 4:8 (KJV)

"Can you use some ham broth?" I asked, eager to hand off some of the quarts I'd stacked in my freezer after boiling a picnic ham at Easter.

"I wouldn't know what to do with it," Sandra answered.

"Soup starter. Lentils or beans. Or maybe baked beans."

"I don't know how." Though after the briefest pause she added, "But I do have some ham in my freezer."

"Yes, that would intensify the flavor."

"I don't cook much anymore. I don't even know what lentils look like."

I pulled a storage jar from a kitchen shelf. "Lentils." I reached for an old cookbook, looking for a particular loose page unglued from its binding. "Here's my recipe. A diced carrot and onion and rib of celery, a grated potato, thyme, ham bits. You don't need to be precise."

Sandra copied the ingredients and accepted the frozen broth but not the lentils. I seasoned my good-bye with low expectations, envisioning the thawing stock discarded and drizzling down her kitchen drain.

Days later, Sandra left a phone message: "Evelyn, I did it! Thank you! This soup is delicious. I didn't even know I had lentils in my cupboard. You inspired me. I can do this. I'll put some aside for you."

There was no magic in the broth or the recipe. Liberally bulked with ham, her soup tasted better than mine. Yet I savor the memory of this exchange, for its full complement of encouragement—mine to her and hers to me.

Lord, let my actions and words encourage my family, friends, and neighbors. —Evelyn Bence

Digging Deeper: 1 Thessalonians 5:10–11

Wednesday, April 19

Thou wilt shew me the path of life: in thy presence is fulness of joy.... —Psalm 16:11 (KJV)

I'm two days back from a seven-week vacation where I finally completed writing a book I'd been working on for three years. So I'm feeling a bit at loose ends, uncertain what should come next.

Yesterday, hoping for some clarity, I walked the sunny fields around our Colorado home with my two Australian shepherds. As they trotted in happy reunion alongside me, I prayed, "Lord, what do You want me to do now?" I didn't receive any immediate insight.

This morning I awoke to freshly white-powdered pine trees and snow-carpeted fields. Not exactly the springtime weather I'd ordered. As I settled into my study chair for my quiet time, a dense fog rolled in.

Fog is not the norm where I live. The view from my window revealed only thick gray mist, the usually distinct cottonwoods now a blur through the nearly opaque air.

Maybe this is God's answer for the time being, I thought. Surrounded by haze, I'm not able to see into the distance as I ordinarily can. It's cold, and snow obscures the ground. But I have no doubt the sun will appear again, the snow will melt swiftly, the fog will disappear, and the landscape will become clear.

At this moment, sitting in my study, my Bible in hand, all that's important is I'm seeking God's will.

Lord God, I don't know yet what You have in store for me. But that's okay. You're with me, and that's all I need to know for now. —Kim Henry

Digging Deeper: Psalm 119:35

Thursday, April 20

**I praise you, for I am fearfully and wonderfully made. Wonderful are your works....
—Psalm 139:14 (NRSV)**

Benjamin and I sat on the sofa. Atop our stack of bedtime reading was one of my favorites: *Days with Frog and Toad* by Arnold Lobel. I like the Frog and Toad books because I identify with the character Toad. He's a worrier and always feels flummoxed.

Luckily, his best friend Frog is levelheaded and has a can-do attitude. Together, they overcome all manner of mild domestic challenges.

"I'll read this one to you," said Benjamin. My eyebrows rose. He had begun reading this year, taking Kate and me by surprise.

"Maybe this one is for slightly older readers," I said gently. I remembered Frances getting frustrated and giving up when she encountered difficult passages.

Benjamin ignored my suggestion. "'The Kite,'" he read slowly, his slender finger tracing under the title of one of the stories. "'Frog and Toad went out to fly a kite. They went to a large...' What's that word?"

"Meadow."

"'Meadow, where the wind was strong.'"

My eyes widened as Benjamin made his way through the story about Toad's repeated failed efforts to fly his kite. Eventually, with Frog's encouragement, he succeeds.

"'Frog and Toad sat and watched their kite. It seemed to be flying way up at the top of the sky,'" he finished.

I hardly knew what to say. Benjamin's reading had progressed by leaps and bounds. For a moment, I almost had vertigo envisioning all the regions and depths of his mind taking shape, all the books he would read in his life, even long after I was gone.

"Great job, buddy!" I said, holding him close. I felt like *we* were flying way up at the top of the sky.

Watching my children grow up, I see You at work, Lord. I give thanks for Your unending love and care.
—Jim Hinch

Digging Deeper: Psalm 31:14–16

Friday, April 21

OVERCOMING LOSS: Asking for Help
When arrogance appears, disgrace follows....
—Proverbs 11:2 (JPS)

Everyone said it was going to be hard for me to take over doing the things my husband, Keith, had always been good at. I wanted to prove them wrong, show them I was perfectly able to cope after his death. Some were "guy" things like plumbing and computer repair; I could hire people to do those. But other things, like taking care of the plants, I was too embarrassed to admit I didn't know the first thing about.

Keith had a water-level reader, three different kinds of plant food, and a schedule that let him nurture the fern, the rubber plant, the pothos, the two succulents, the bromeliads, and the Christmas cactus. I had no idea what that schedule was, which plants got what food, whether I should water them all or just wait for each plant's leaves to droop.

I was determined not to ask for help because, in my mind, I should have been able to take care of everything now that I was on my own. I thought I was putting up a very convincing front.

Then Mother Cat came over from the monastery to spend a night after an appointment. She is good at nurturing the monastery plants and has a green thumb like Keith had. I welcomed her warmly into the house.

"How are you doing?" she asked.

"I'm doing okay," I said. "Getting things in hand."

She looked skeptical but said nothing until she walked into the kitchen and saw all the plants. Then she turned to me, surprise on her face, and said, "Wow, you haven't killed them yet!"

I took a deep breath and asked for her advice.

Help me swallow my pride and ask for help from others, Lord. —Rhoda Blecker

Digging Deeper: Micah 6:8

Saturday, April 22

He has showed you, O man, what is good.... —Micah 6:8 (RSV)

She was wearing an orange head scarf, a man's suit jacket, a short skirt, and pale pink bedroom slippers. I'd been watching her from my car in the parking lot. She was picking up things from the pavement and putting them in a big black handbag.

Would she be offended if I gave her money? It was so much easier to write a check to the local shelter than to proffer assistance one on one.

I had to try. I got out of the car with the walker I use these days and went up to her. "May I add something to what you're finding?"

She glared at me. "I don't need your dirty money!" She waved the handbag in my face. "This bag holds *thousands* of dollars!"

"I'm so sorry," I apologized as I fled into the store.

Driving home with my groceries, I got to thinking about that handbag filled with trash, yet in its owner's eyes containing great riches. What was there in my life that I put an exaggerated value on?

I thought of the way I'd responded to an invitation. I didn't simply click Accept. Instead, I sent a long e-mail describing the ear infection that's left me with vertigo: "Don't be alarmed at the walker."

What made me believe that anyone would think twice about a walker? Why was it so important to tell everyone it was an ear issue, not (horrors!) old age that made me unsteady? Was my self-image the trash that I mistook for treasure?

Father, show me the values worth living for.
—Elizabeth Sherrill
Digging Deeper: Matthew 13:44–46

"I give you a new commandment, that you love one another. Just as I have loved you, you also should love one another. By this everyone will know that you are my disciples...." —John 13:34–35 (NRSV)

My husband, Charlie, is the kind of guy who occasionally gives me flowers for no reason. Always he brings roses, no matter the season, cost, or color.

The first plant he brings home each spring is one of those miniature rosebushes you find at grocery stores. They always show a few perky flowers and one or two tight buds that look ready to burst. It kind of drives me nuts because the leaves start dropping like confetti. Then the blooms fade and cascade. And those bright red buds? They swiftly turn purple without ever opening.

The thing is, while I stew and grumble about stores ripping off spring-starved shoppers, Charlie is always delighted with his purchase. The plants from seventeen previous spring shopping sprees have left no negative impression on him. He is invariably pleased with his miniature rosebush, and while I count the hours until I'll have to toss the thorny little deceiver, he admires the perfectly formed buds and velvety petals.

I survey this year's offering as the first petal hits the floor. I look at Charlie, about to suggest we heave the thing. He is gazing at the plant, and before I can speak, he says, "I know! Isn't it great? It's like God's way of telling us to hold on. Spring's on the way. Should we plant it outside with the pansies this year?"

I open my mouth. Close it. I turn, so he cannot see the tears in my eyes. "We should," I say. "We absolutely should."

God, Who makes all things new, transform my thorny heart into an opening bud ready to receive and give love. Amen. —Marci Alborghetti

Digging Deeper: Psalm 30:11–12,
1 Thessalonians 4:9–12

Monday, April 24

LESSONS IN STONES
Precious Cornerstone
The stone which the builders rejected has become the chief corner stone. This is the Lord's doing; it is marvelous in our eyes. —Psalm 118:22–23 (NAS)

Peter was Jesus's passionate, impetuous disciple— the one who vowed he'd die for Him. Yet after Jesus's arrest, Peter swore at those who claimed he was His follower. When Jesus first chose His inner circle, Peter was called Simon. Jesus renamed him Cephas—or Peter—which, in Greek, translates as "rock" or "stone." I imagine rock symbolism took hold in Peter. Years later in his letters, he calls Jesus a "living stone which has been rejected by men, but is choice and precious in the sight of God" (1 Peter 2:4, NAS). He cites Isaiah 28:16, where Jesus is called a "precious cornerstone."

A cornerstone is the first stone in a masonry foundation, the one that determines where all the others will be positioned. When Jesus renamed Peter, He was fitting him into his place in God's kingdom.

Peter is the disciple I most identify with. He acted impulsively. He got scared. Sometimes he seemed anything but a rock. Jesus had to tell him, "I have prayed for you, that your faith may not fail" (Luke 22:32, NAS).

When I am tempted to give up on myself or others, I remember how Jesus didn't give up on Peter. I read again how Jesus said to him, "And you, when once you have turned again, strengthen your brothers" (Luke 22:32, NAS). Not *if* but *when.* Jesus knew that those who crumble—and then rally— often make the strongest rocks.

You are the Precious Cornerstone, Jesus.
Fit me where I belong in Your work, Your kingdom.
—Carol Knapp

Digging Deeper: John 1:41–42, Acts 4:11–12, Ephesians 2:19–22

Tuesday, April 25

And he will make my feet like hinds' feet, and he will make me to walk upon mine high places....
—Habakkuk 3:19 (KJV)

I was out on my morning prayer walk, telling God how my life felt so unstable because of concern over my son's depression. *I need some solid ground to stand on*, I thought.

Caw! Caw! A huge crow sitting precariously on the very flimsy top twig of a tree drew my attention. It seemed to brag to the wind, not a bit worried that the puny branch it was on looked like it would snap under its weight.

What a daredevil! I thought. *If I were up in that tree, I'd stay down lower on a sturdier limb.*

A snippet of a Bible verse came to mind: "Hinds' feet...upon high places" (Habakkuk 3:19). I remembered that a hind is a mountain deer, but since I was watching a crow I tweaked it to fit the current scene. So why was the crow perfectly comfortable in such a risky place? What if the twig snapped? The crow had a strength and ability to fly that didn't show with its wings tucked tightly around it.

I looked up the Bible verse when I got home and discovered that the first part says, "The Lord God is my strength." I had found the solid ground I could always stand on.

Dear Father, I thank You that You don't just give me strength, but You are my strength. Amen.
—Karen Barber

Digging Deeper: Exodus 15:2, 1 Chronicles 16:11

Wednesday, April 26

Honour thy father and thy mother: that thy days may be long upon the land which the Lord thy God giveth thee. —Exodus 20:12 (KJV)

My mom and dad are deep into their nineties, and we sit at the kitchen table and discuss burial and cremation, and plots and headstones, and the lieutenant's discharge papers from the army (which I need in order to reserve space at the military cemetery), and what species of tree they would like to be near if possible (pine first, "because it is piercing and redolent," says my mom, ever articulate). After lunch, when they amble off for their naps, I sit out under the oaks and contemplate the sure knowledge that soon they will not be in this world, not in these forms, the forms I have loved for more than fifty years. And I weep.

But, I realize, they will always abide in me; they are in me, their genes and murmurs and caresses, their lessons and tenderness, all these years of stories and kindness, all inside me, all adamant against time and loss, if subject to the tides of grief. They were, as they taught me young and ever after, themselves the children of the Coherent Mercy, as am I, notes from the song of "What Is," spoken into being not once but uncountable times every moment, far beyond my capacity to understand.

So while I can and will mourn and grieve the looming deaths of my beloved mother and father, I know that they are my bones and blood, the musicians of my house, and always shall be. This afternoon, under the gnarled live oaks, beneath the drifting swallow-tailed kites, I take refuge in that.

Dear Lord, I know the time is coming when You will take these two wry, gentle, wise, gracious, tender, brilliant, kindly, diligent servants back. I do not know how I can bear their leaving, but thank You for the gift of them to me. They sang You, Lord, they did. I heard it clearly. I will hear their song always....
—Brian Doyle

Digging Deeper: Deuteronomy 5:16, 22

Thursday, April 27

"Behold, I am doing a new thing; now it springs forth, do you not perceive it? I will make a way in the wilderness and rivers in the desert."
—Isaiah 43:19 (ESV)

Last summer I bought my mother a beautiful orchid. My mother loved flowers and kept a charming home adorned with them. In the evenings she'd sashay through the house, watering and spraying life into her precious plant-friends.

Two months after I'd given my mother the orchid, she had surgery. Her doctor placed a defibrillator near her heart, hoping to compensate for a weakened one. I flew from Arkansas to Maryland to be with her and to assist Dad. When I arrived in their home, I was delighted to see the orchid healthier and donning more blooms than it had during the summer—my last one with Mom.

At Christmastime, she was hospitalized again. I spent nearly two months watching her body become sicker and weaker. When I returned to her home in the evenings, I noticed the orchid also becoming sicker and weaker. It mirrored the life of its owner. Soon Mom succumbed to an infection and passed away in the new year. I had no hope that her sweet orchid would survive.

Two months after my mother passed, I returned to Maryland to help my sister pack up and prepare our parents' house for the market. I was amazed to see the orchid. It had sprung to life, gorgeous and lush with purple blooms.

Mom's orchid reminds me that life continues. Even in our darkest hour, life is always growing and blooming and surprising us with unexpected joy.

Thank You, Lord, for being the eternal life-giver.
—Carla Hendricks

Digging Deeper: Psalm 96:12, Isaiah 35:1–2

Friday, April 28

"Look at the birds of the air: they neither sow nor reap nor gather into barns, and yet your heavenly Father feeds them. Are you not of more value than they?" —Matthew 6:26 (ESV)

In the months leading up to law school graduation, it seemed like I was getting an update from my mom every day. "We can't find a hotel room, so we're going to start looking for houses to rent for a few days." "Grandmummy and Grandaddy want to come." "Ned is going to take the train up from Washington." "What were you thinking for dinner on the Saturday before graduation?"

All this talk and effort my family was putting into the weekend was making me uncomfortable. It wasn't that I didn't want attention, though I can't deny I've always been shy. But even more, it seemed like everyone was intent on celebrating this accomplishment in my life and I didn't feel like I'd done anything special. I'd shown up to classes and done the work I needed to. I didn't want my family fawning over me about something that seemed so small.

I got a package in the mail. It was a graduation gift, a beautiful new briefcase from my father-in-law, himself a lawyer. The card read, "This is a big deal!" I laughed when I read it.

I kept thinking about that card, all through the graduation weekend. My grandparents had made long trips to be there. My brother had persevered. Even after the train line between Washington, DC, and New Haven, Connecticut, was shut down, he took a bus. Everyone around me was happy.

It didn't matter that graduation wasn't all that important to me. It counted to my family. And that meant, in the end, it was a big deal.

Thank You, God, for family that shows me what matters most. —Sam Adriance

Digging Deeper: Galatians 6:2, Philippians 2:3

Saturday, April 29

The Lord has blessed my master abundantly, and he has become wealthy.... —Genesis 24:35 (NIV)

Up on the roof deck of Liz's building, the view was gorgeous. The outline of the Palisades undulated across the horizon; to the south, the New York City skyline glittered; and below us cars twinkled across the George Washington Bridge. A silver moon periodically disappeared behind a wispy cloud. How splendid!

Eventually, real life beckoned. "I have to go," I said, sighing. "I have to do laundry tonight or my kids won't have anything to wear."

"Hey, I just learned something earlier this week that is changing my life," Liz replied. "Change one word and you change your attitude. Replace *have* with *get*."

I looked puzzled, so she elaborated. "Instead of 'I *have* to do laundry,' say, 'I *get* to do laundry.' As in, I get to do it because I have clothes for myself and my family. Instead of saying, 'I *have* to pay bills,' try 'I *get* to pay bills' because I can afford electricity."

I could see how this one-word switch could be life-transforming:

I *get* to wash dishes because I have running water.

I *get* to call the bank because I have a phone.

I *get* to take the computer in for repair because I have one.

I *get* to tend to my sick son because I have a child.

I walked home thinking of all the things I *get* to do, purely by the grace of God. There's a lot to be thankful for, if I look at it the right way.

Lord of the universe, I *get* to praise You only because You thought to make me. May my life give You glory.
—Julia Attaway

Digging Deeper: Deuteronomy 8:10

Sunday, April 30

At dawn on the first day of the week, Mary Magdalene and the other Mary went to look at the tomb. —Matthew 28:1 (NIV)

As I entered our church on Easter morning, I noticed a gigantic video screen placed front and center above the choir. It was totally dark, but when the singing began, I could see a sunrise faintly illuminating the horizon. Throughout the service, the sun continued to rise and the darkness began to disappear. By the time we ended with the "Hallelujah Chorus," the brilliant sunrise had pushed away all the darkness.

That image lingers with me, because a sunrise reminds me of my own faith journey. I can't mark a single dramatic moment when I became a believer and Jesus changed my darkness into light. Just as in that video, there was no single moment when night became day. My faith has been a slow process of the light illuminating dark places over and over again.

When I was diagnosed with cancer years ago, I sensed darkness all around me. But rays of hope gradually began to push it away: a friend's note, others' prayers, the gift of a Believe sign, my daughter's pregnancy. I can't pinpoint the moment the darkness of despair lifted, but it did eventually, and the sunshine of God's perspective began to change mine.

That video makes me wonder if God gives us the promised gift of a sunrise each morning as a hopeful reminder that Jesus has risen to push away the darkness in our lives—every single day.

Jesus, You are the Son-rise that pushes away the darkness. Hallelujah! —Carol Kuykendall

Digging Deeper: Genesis 1:3–5, Psalm 5:3

IN GOD'S HANDS

1 _____

2 _____

3 _____

4 _____

5 _____

6 _____

7 _____

8 _____

9 _____

10 _____

11 _____

12 _____

13 _____

14 _____

15 _____

16 _____

17 _____

18 _____

19 _____

20 _____

21 _____

22 _____

23 _____

24 _____

25 _____

26 _____

27 _____

28 _____

29 _____

30 _____

MAY

Even there your hand will guide me,
your right hand will hold me fast.

—Psalm 139:10 (NIV)

On the day I called, you answered me; my strength of soul you increased. —Psalm 138:3 (ESV)

"Mama, can I climb up?" Isaiah asked. We were deep into the night, and the bedroom was dark as pitch. But I heard my little son and pushed back the covers to welcome him.

He had a fever. Heat radiated through his pajamas. It seeped from his skin. "Where do you hurt?" I whispered.

"My throat. My head. My legs," he said.

I knew I'd move from the bed in a moment. Isaiah needed a fever reducer and a drink. But I paused for just a pulse of time because my son had settled in. His body curled against mine, and we fit perfectly. It came to mind, as we lay in midnight hues, that when he formed and grew under my heart, together our curve was convex. Now, we were concave. As he nestled against me, he fit into my hollow places and we were so close we were like one again. He was in need and found his way to me.

It was the same way that I'd gone to God so many times recently. Helpless. Hurting. Needing love and care, mercy and grace. I curled into Him. Rested in His shelter. Listened for His heartbeat—the perfect cadence that brings peace to pain. In His arms I found restoration and healing. Time and time again.

Isaiah whimpered softly, and it was time for me to slide from bed. I'd meet his needs. I wanted to love and comfort and care for my precious child with all that I am. And my God does the same for me.

Thank You, Lord, for caring for me when I'm hurting. Amen. —Shawnelle Eliasen

Digging Deeper: Psalms 46:1, 147:3; 2 Corinthians 4:16

Tuesday, May 2

Keep me safe, my God, for in you I take refuge. —Psalm 16:1 (NIV)

Every day I pray the same prayer: "Lord, keep my son safe." I'm not worried about gangs or thieves, but the police. Recent images of cities in flame— cities in which we've lived and worshipped—of black people, especially black men, lying in pools of blood do not help to alleviate my fears.

My family and I live between cultures, and I know many of my white friends would not understand. They don't associate these images with my family. They don't know how many times Chase has been stopped by police, who approach him with weapons drawn, who often apologize after they talk to him and see operatic music scores in the back of his car. My friends don't know my peace-loving son was first frisked and thrown against a car, without cause, when he was fourteen.

Because I live between cultures, I see that the police, who smile and serve in my middle-class neighborhood, don't behave the same way in the "hood." Instead, they resemble an occupying force. Their language and expressions say that they see enemies, not community. They frighten me.

Safe in my living room, I realize these police officers, with their high-powered weapons, are afraid too. Each one is some mother's beloved child. So as I pray for my own son, I also pray for them.

Lord, who taught us to fear each other?
Help us to see with our hearts. Help us to love.
—Sharon Foster

Digging Deeper: Psalms 18:3, 38:19, 138:7

Wednesday, May 3

Yet you do not know what your life will be like tomorrow. You are just a vapor that appears for a little while and then vanishes away. Instead, you ought to say, "If the Lord wills, we will live and also do this or that." —James 4:14–15 (NAS)

Errands. If any word undoes my son, that is it.

I watched as he came outside his school building, ran down the sidewalk, and climbed inside our van. "Mom, can we go play at the park?"

"Sure, buddy. But first we have some errands we have to run."

His entire demeanor did a 180-degree-turn. Gone was my happy little man. A big grump had taken his place. He told me he didn't want to run errands. He hated errands. Then he ended his little spiel with this gem: "You're wasting my time!"

I love how God teaches me lessons through parenting. Teachable moments for my son become teachable moments for me.

Earlier that day, I'd been struggling with this very thing. I had a schedule and a plan, things on my list I had to get done. Yet it seemed at every turn there were interruptions: a friend who asked me to watch her kid, a young woman I mentor in need of a listening ear, a couple of girls from junior high ministry sending text messages. Each time I responded like my son—with a whiny heart.

How easy it is to forget that my time is not my own. God gave it to me. I can start each day with my own agenda and look at every interruption as an inconvenience. Or I can start each day acknowledging that the hours belong to God. How would He like me to use them?

Lord, thank You for every second You give us here.
Each one is evidence of Your grace. Help me to be
a good and faithful steward of my time.

—Katie Ganshert

Digging Deeper: Romans 14:8

Thursday, May 4

"O Lord, God of my master Abraham, please grant
me success today and show steadfast love to my
master Abraham." —Genesis 24:12 (ESV)

The above passage in Genesis has to do with
Abraham's servant, the very one Abraham sent to the
country of his own relatives to find a wife for his son
Isaac. Before he approached Abraham's relatives, the
servant stopped to pray and to ask God's guidance in
choosing a wife for Abraham's son by Sarah.

Over the years I've struggled to build a solid
prayer life. I've tried silent prayer. I've written down
prayers in a journal. I've kept a log of prayer requests
and prayed down the list each morning. Sometimes
it feels as if my prayers float off into empty space. Yet
I know God answers; I've seen evidence of that more
times than I can count. Still, I have trouble focusing
on prayer. Prayers come at the end of my devotions,
and I find myself looking at the clock and rushing to
keep on schedule.

As I returned to that Scripture passage, the same one I've read a hundred times, something changed in the translation after Abraham's servant prayed for a wife for Isaac. He was no longer called "the servant"; he was called "the man."

In that moment I heard God telling me that He did hear my prayers and that my prayers changed me, elevated me. While I am a servant of the Lord, I am also His daughter. Prayer changes me, and it changes me for the better.

Father God, I am humbled by the fact that You hear my prayers. —Debbie Macomber

Digging Deeper: Psalms 4:3, 5:3

Friday, May 5

LESSONS IN STONES
The Everlasting Rock
He who did not spare His own Son, but delivered Him over for us all, how will He not also with Him freely give us all things? —Romans 8:32 (NAS)

I was thinking over recent events in my life. Everywhere I looked I saw the generosity of God. How He led my husband, Terry, and me to our "little castle" with its eye-popping view of sky and river and forested mountains. How He provided every ounce of strength I needed to travel Mom's dying journey with her. How He made it okay for us to leave our family with three grandchildren in Minnesota when we moved to Idaho—and now our Alaska family of eight is moving to our area. How He made a way for my husband, suffering damage in his legs and feet from a compressed nerve in his back, to get surgery two months before they had room for him in the schedule.

This is just a paragraph among pages of God's generosity! Jesus spoke of His Father's open hand in Matthew 7:7–11. He quizzed His listeners, "What man is there among you who, when his son asks for a loaf, will give him a stone?"(Matthew 7:9, NAS). He went on to say that if imperfect people know how to give good gifts to their children, "How much more will your Father who is in heaven give what is good to those who ask Him?" (Matthew 7:11, NAS).

I have learned not to be fooled nor to be discouraged when life seems to trip me up. My mother's dying or Terry's needing leg braces and a cane to walk could have appeared as hard, unforgiving obstacles. But God's gifting is in the loaves—in sustenance through difficult times—in abundant displays of meeting the heart's desire for those who "delight in the Lord" (Psalm 37:4).

"Everlasting Rock" (Isaiah 26:4), filled with
strength and power yet
overflowing in love and compassion, from Your heart
I seek Your good gifts. —Carol Knapp

Digging Deeper: Psalm 21:1–4; James 1:17, 5:11

Saturday, May 6

I long to see you so that I may impart to you some spiritual gift to make you strong—that is, that you and I may be mutually encouraged by each other's faith. —Romans 1:11–12 (NIV)

Our friends were celebrating their fiftieth wedding anniversary. I stood quietly, while conversations swelled, and admired photographs. There was a picture in an oval frame—young sweethearts, smiles shining joy. There was another of a fresh-faced mother with a child on her hip. And another of a couple gently brushed by middle age, arms entwined in a familiar, easy way.

"I'm glad you're here" came a voice from behind.

I turned to find my celebrated friend. "I wouldn't have missed it, Hilde," I said, hugging her. "Tell me your secret. What can you share to help Lonny and me make it to fifty too?"

"You need to be stubborn," she said.

I was surprised. I'd thought maybe forgiving, patient, kind. But not stubborn. "Stubborn?" I asked.

Hilde's arm curled around my shoulders. She leaned close. "Yes, stubborn," she said. "Stubborn to hold God's Word. Stubborn to let the small things go. Stubborn to put your focus on positive things."

I let the words sink in. Stubborn for loving, righteous, positive, peacekeeping things? Yes, I could apply that to my own marriage—and to every other relationship in my life.

Just then Hilde's son-in-law came near and took a picture of the two of us. Maybe the image would be pressed into a scrapbook, captured and preserved, held as a memory of this special day—just as I'd hold Hilde's words.

Thank You, Lord, for the wisdom of others who love You. Amen. —Shawnelle Eliasen

Digging Deeper: Proverbs 13:20, Hebrews 13:16

Sunday, May 7

For, lo, the winter is past, the rain is over and gone; the flowers appear on the earth.... —**Song of Solomon 2:11–12** (KJV)

Winter dragged on forever on the East Coast in 2015. Boston snowfall toppled all previous records. My hometown, Concord, New Hampshire, endured endless snow that reached halfway up to my daughter's kitchen window. Bone-cracking cold made even the hardiest Granite State natives consider moving to Florida. Toward the end of April, ponds were still frozen and dirty snow covered dead grass. Drifts of sand, detritus from road deicing, smothered any incipient life, anything green. What had happened to "April showers bring May flowers"?

Then, while walking downtown in the thin sunshine, despairing of the bleak landscape, I glimpsed a purple fragment. *A tattered trash bag?* I looked closer. Tiny clumps of violets sprouted along the edge of the sidewalk, wedged against a brick apartment building and growing out of matted dead leaves and sand. Apparently, the cement and brick retained just enough warmth from the southern exposure to coax these dainty flowers to bloom despite the blustery weather. I found myself smiling. These delicate bits of life had broken the gloom.

Hope is a funny thing: just a smidgen can refresh a mood and restore faith. A resilient spirit needs the tiniest of jump starts. As I continued my walk, I noticed tiny green threads of grass in the matted dun turf. If I looked closely, I could see half-inch spears of lilies and tulips poking through. I found the crocuses blooming by the library—late, yes, but wonderfully alive. Spring had been here all along. As soon as I expected to find it, I did.

Lord of All, may we always be mindful of
the tiny ways You lead us to great truths.
—Gail Thorell Schilling

Digging Deeper: Matthew 7:7

Monday, May 8

**Praise be to the God and Father of our Lord Jesus
Christ! In his great mercy he has given us new birth
into a living hope through the resurrection of Jesus
Christ from the dead. —1 Peter 1:3 (NIV)**

Early this morning I awoke slowly, immersed
in a delightful dimension between dream and
wakefulness. In my dream, I was eighteen years
old again—a tall, thin, athletic kid who could run
painlessly and, seemingly, forever. Standing on the
Furman University soccer field, I glimpsed each
of my teammates. They were youthful, handsome,
toned, and I knew each of their names and
nicknames. For a fleeting moment, youth was real.

My wife rustled in bed beside me, rising for her
first cup of coffee. Becoming more awake, I lay
there murmuring my teammate's names: Gary, Tony,
Leon, Jerry, Nipper, Ashby, George.... To revisit
young men I have not seen in forty-five years was a
precious gift, the past merging with the present in
dawn's faint light.

As I rose and dressed, I could not shake the aura of my dream. I remembered that the day before I had visited a friend struggling with the last stages of dementia. I watched a sound mind now in disarray, a strong body now frail, and sensed death was near. And I reflected on that eternal dimension we call *heaven.*

Is heaven a reality unknown on this earth? Entry into a fourth dimension? A dimension our eyes cannot perceive? Will it be like waking from a lovely dream of grand reunion only to realize that we are not dreaming?

I cannot know from this side of eternity. But Jesus promised that separation is leading to reunification. And His Resurrection was more than a dream. It is a glimpse—our hope—into the future.

Father, give me faith to believe that death is but birth into deeper life and marvelous reunion. Amen.
—Scott Walker

Digging Deeper: Luke 23:43, John 14:2–4, Revelation 22:5–9

Tuesday, May 9

May the Lord give strength to his people!...
—Psalm 29:11 (RSV)

We've needed a new kitchen counter since, oh, May 9, 1991, around 12:31 p.m., when our oldest child was born. Before kids, the counter would suffer the occasional spill; now it resembled a short stretch of bad road that smelled vaguely of old juice.

A new counter was impossible because we're low on cash—the aforementioned kid and her two siblings grew up and then entered college during a six-year span. So it was on to Craigslist.

A nearby woodworker was selling sections of an abandoned bowling alley. I had a crazy vision: use a bowling alley for a countertop! Not even our kids could damage that.

I ran the idea past Sandee, whom I fully expected to be the voice of reason (one of us has to be). Instead, my wife said, "Sure. Why not?"

I was off to the woodworker. As he was loading each eight-by-four-foot section on to my ancient truck, using a forklift, I thought, *Huh. I don't own a forklift.*

Once home, my fears came alive: how to wrestle several hundred pounds and thirty-two square feet of rock maple through a narrow kitchen door and into place. It would take a miracle.

Actually, no, it didn't. It took my strong friend Gary, my strong-as-rock-maple daughter Hope, and me (five feet eight inches of untenured professor), plus a surprising wife and good luck. When visitors admire the counter-cum-bowling alley, I tell them about Gary and my daughter and crazy ideas,

because sometimes vision takes good friends and
Hope to make them real.

**Lord, sometimes my vision outpaces my ability.
Thank You for providing family and friends to bail me
out of all-too-human plans. —Mark Collins**

Digging Deeper: Isaiah 12:2

Wednesday, May 10

**"In this way we remember the Lord Jesus' words:
'It is more blessed to give than to receive.'"
—Acts 20:35 (CEB)**

Franklin sits on an empty milk crate on Fulton
Street, a block down from my subway exit near the
World Trade Center. I don't know his whole story,
but I've garnered bits and pieces: he is estranged
from his son who struggles with some sort of
addiction. His wife died a couple of years ago. He
likes worshipping at a nearby church and drops in at
another one to get a shower and a free meal.

He has a cardboard sign that says "God bless you"
and a cup for donations, but he doesn't do much to
solicit funds. Most of the time he's too absorbed in a
small, well-thumbed copy of the New Testament and
Psalms. I like talking to him about that because he
reads carefully and loves God, which I find hard to
imagine considering the life he leads.

"Rick," he asked me one morning, thumbing through his Bible, "where does it say 'It is more blessed to give than to receive'? I think it's in the book of Acts."

"I'm not sure, Franklin," I said. "Let me check my concordance at the office."

Franklin was right. "It's Acts," I told him the next time I saw him.

I give him cash from time to time and things to read. Once I gave him a backpack with food, gloves, a parka, and a warm blanket, most of which were gone the next day. "What did you do with the stuff in that backpack I gave you?" I asked him.

"Gave it to a friend," he replied.

I was surprised but only for a moment. After all, wasn't it Franklin who reminded me where to find Jesus's words about giving?

Lord, let me be the cheerful giver You know I can be.
—Rick Hamlin

Digging Deeper: 2 Corinthians 9:7

Thursday, May 11

"For I know the plans I have for you," declares the Lord, "plans to prosper you and not to harm you, plans to give you hope and a future."
—Jeremiah 29:11 (NIV)

I was swimming outdoors, surrounded by the towering snowy mountains of the French Alps. The quiet rippling of the water and the majesty of my surroundings felt like a dream. I was taking a trip for the first time without my boys. It had been ten years since my last visit to France, and everything about this trip was magical. I was reunited with friends, celebrated a fairy-tale wedding in a beautiful chateau, and topped it off with skiing.

Is this really my life right now? I thought happily. I was enjoying a moment that seemed impossible not so long ago.

After years of heartache, struggle, and minimal rest, I'd assumed my life of adventure and excitement was a thing of the past. Being a mother had conditioned me to sacrifice my own needs and wants. Yet this week in France was just for me, and in every breathtaking moment I felt God whispering, *You're important too, Karen.*

How much I have needed to know that I matter, that I'm cared for, and that there's so much more to look forward to in this life!

**Thank You, Father, that I am Your child.
You know me, care for me, and have wonderful
plans for my life.** —Karen Valentin

Digging Deeper: Psalm 20:4, Proverbs 16:9

As thou knowest not what is the way of the spirit, nor how the bones do grow in the womb of her that is with child: even so thou knowest not the works of God who maketh all. —Ecclesiastes 11:5 (KJV)

Every time I see a heron, I see something of my brother Kevin. I do not know how this can be, but it is.

He loved herons, and everywhere we went we gawked at herons. Two herons flew slowly past his gravesite on the day he was buried under an oak tree in Illinois. He was tall and stern like a heron, although he was not much for eating frogs and mice. I think that what we call God was in him and me and you and in herons also.

I think mostly when I talk about God I don't have the slightest idea what I am talking about. I think I am better off using stories and examples to tiptoe toward God. I think God is a verb and that the noun God is a mistake because I begin to think I know something when I use a word as a handle for that which cannot be grasped. Maybe I should lean on metaphorical ideas like Light and Mercy and Imagination and Unimaginable Coherence. Maybe I am closer to sensing and celebrating God when I don't use words at all; so that river-ripple and thunder-rumble and the thrill of thrushes in thickets are prayers.

I think my brother Kevin is not ash in a stone box under a tree in Illinois. I think he is music and laughter and whatever it is that drives the tree toward light. I think that what drives the tree and you and me is what we mean when we say God. I think my brother is in Him and with Him and will always be so, in ways that I cannot understand but can do my heartfelt utmost to witness and salute and sing. So I do, so I do.

Dear Lord, may I see my brother Kevin again please? Anywhere, anyhow, anyway You grant us?
—Brian Doyle

Digging Deeper: Job 38:4–7

Saturday, May 13

He climbed its steps.... —Ezekiel 40:6 (NIV)

I'd become worn out praying for my son who faced depression after going through a divorce. It seemed impossible to ever cover everything he needed in prayer! On a retreat at Amicalola Falls in Georgia, I was hoping to find a way to overcome my prayer fatigue.

During afternoon free time, I visited the top of the falls, where a stairway leads down the mountainside to the bottom. A sign said there were

425 steps. I could see that it would be a strenuous climb. A strange urge came: *Go down. And as you climb back up, say a different prayer for Chris on each step.*

My knees creaked as I made it to the bottom of the stairs. Then I started back up. Step one: please heal Chris. Step two: restore his self-confidence. Step three: draw him closer to You. After twenty steps, it became more challenging to think of things that needed fixing. By step thirty, I was totally out of specific problems. So I started to pray blessings for Chris. On step one hundred, I started thanking God for good qualities my son had. By step three hundred, I resorted to praying the Boy Scout laws on each step: thrifty, kind, brave, reverent, clean....

At last I hit step 425, fresh out of anything more to pray. I savored the glorious view from up top; my perspective had changed dramatically.

God, thank You that even with gigantic life problems, there are only a few major things that need fixing. Help me to daily refresh my prayers by climbing a little higher up the heavenly stairway, past everything that's wrong, to the positive virtues and blessings You are eager to give. Amen. —Karen Barber

Digging Deeper: Psalms 3:8, 119:59

Sunday, May 14

Wisdom is more valuable than precious jewels; nothing you want compares with her.
—Proverbs 3:15 (CEV)

I love Mother's Day, having enjoyed thirty-plus years of sweet moments with my three kids. But there's one particular Mother's Day that will always stand out. The cost of the gift my daughter Jamie gave me was free, but the emotional value exceeded anything she could have bought.

Jamie handed me a piece of construction paper; her blue-green eyes filled with tears. What I recognized shining back at me was the beginning of an answer to a years-long prayer.

Up until Jamie left for college, she and I were close. But she went her own way, leaving me and her childhood roots behind. After her sophomore year, she dropped out of school.

Now, I gazed at the sheet of construction paper. She'd drawn a picture with crayons—a field of tulips, green grass, and a glowing sun. Neatly, she wrote in purple, "Happy Mother's Day, Mom. I'm turning this around. I promise. I love you."

A few weeks later, I took my gift to the best frame shop in town. Without asking any questions, the owner helped me choose a gold, chiseled frame. When Jamie was twenty-five, she graduated from college and moved into a new apartment. I presented her with her first housewarming gift, returning the picture with all my heart, just as she'd given it to me.

Father, being a mom requires wisdom, a gift that comes only from You. —Julie Garmon

Digging Deeper: Isaiah 54:13, 2 Timothy 3:14–15

Monday, May 15

"Fill the earth and subdue it, and have dominion over the fish of the sea and over the birds of the heavens and over every living thing that moves on the earth." —Genesis 1:28 (ESV)

My wife, Emily, and I began going on weekend hikes and found that just a short drive outside of New Haven, Connecticut, where we live, were all kinds of lush, green paths to explore.

One Saturday, we took a hike up West Rock Ridge State Park. We couldn't find the main entrance, so we found a back route, eventually making our way onto a marked path. It was lovely to be together in nature's beauty and calm.

When we came to the end of the trail, which turned out to be the beginning for most people, the woods opened up to a clearing. In the middle, we saw several enormous, rounded rocks lying on top of each other, forming an almost tentlike structure. The sign told us this was Judges Cave.

I later found out it was named after two seventeenth-century judges who had rebelled against the Crown in England. They fled there, and hid out here, being fed by sympathetic Puritans. It became symbolic of the American revolutionary spirit.

Thinking of how these rebels were able to use nature to serve their ends, I was reminded of the constant interplay between the world God made and our role in it. It is worthwhile to admire Earth's beauty as a thing separate from us, but I need to remember that God made it for us, to care for it, and to use it.

Thank You, Lord, for the gorgeous and fruitful Earth You have given to us. —Sam Adriance

Digging Deeper: Psalms 61:3, 115:16

Tuesday, May 16

A friend loves at all times.... —Proverbs 17:17 (NAS)

Six years ago, my husband, Gene, befriended a pair of Canada geese at the pond. He spoke gently and fed them cracked corn. Over time, they flew in and out of our lives.

Early one morning, I looked out the window and there they stood at our front step, like guests, waiting. I ran to wake Gene, but when he refused to get up, I poured cracked corn into a pitcher. Cautiously, I poured two small piles as I'd seen him do. They ate hungrily, seemingly unafraid of me.

The next morning they showed up with twelve friends, all staring at our front door! I ventured outside with a lot of cracked corn and poured fourteen small piles. They waddled around eating eagerly. I was beginning to feel like *Rebecca of Sunnybrook Farm* when I noticed that one limped badly. The others were ostracizing it. The wounded goose evidently knew it mustn't attempt to be part of the group. It knew not to eat, even though I placed food near it. It stood like the Leaning Tower of Pisa. I prayed God would heal its leg. As the others gobbled their food, it looked away. Daily, it flew in with the other thirteen but stood stock still, leaning, not eating.

Then the most amazing thing happened. Another goose stood with it, also refusing to eat. In a few days, Leaning Pisa stood straight with barely a limp and joined its friends for breakfast!

Father, help me remember: "Pity weeps and runs away; compassion comes to help and stay" (Janet Curtis O'Leary). —Marion Bond West

Digging Deeper: Proverbs 18:24, John 15:12–15

Wednesday, May 17

The Lord is like a father to his children, tender and compassionate to those who fear him. For he knows how weak we are; he remembers we are only dust. —Psalm 103:13–14 (NLT)

Nothing galvanizes swift action on my part like the guttural noise my dog makes when she's about to bring up her lunch. My action is especially speedy when Lacy chooses our nicest rug for this endeavor. One afternoon, I was too late to prevent the deed. This happened twice in the space of a half hour.

As I cleaned up after my precious friend, I grew impatient. I muttered and fretted and fumed. *Why this rug? Why not the tile floor? What's she gotten into to upset her stomach?*

With each spray of the carpet-cleaner bottle, I ratcheted up my complaint. I told my dog to go lie down and to quit making a mess—words I'm certain she completely understood.

That evening, I happened to read Scripture, in Psalm 103. The Spirit immediately convicted me with the knowledge that my Father in heaven just rolls up His sleeves and cleans up after me. He doesn't gripe. He doesn't complain. While there may be dog-shaming in me, there is no Bill-shaming in God. My Father knows how weak I am. He understands my limitations. He fathoms my upset stomach. His patience knows no bounds.

I set aside my Bible and called Lacy. I invited her onto my lap, gave her extra affection, and imagined my Father lavishing extra love on me.

Gracious Father, no matter how many times I mess up, You never sigh, never frown, never chide. You make all things new, over and over again. Thank You. —Bill Giovannetti

Digging Deeper: Revelation 21:5–7

Thursday, May 18

Ah Lord God! It is you who made the heavens and the earth by your great power and by your outstretched arm! Nothing is too hard for you. —Jeremiah 32:17 (NRSV)

Workshops are held in the seminar room of the college where I teach: a long narrow space with a large window on one end and a table just big enough for twelve, plus me at the head. We were about midway through a fiction workshop one day when the sun-filled window changed to a wall of rain.

"Oh no!" my students wailed, even as my heart filled with gratefulness. I saw in my mind my little spring garden beds—the lettuces, spinach, and cress that had looked so yellow and puny this morning all drenched in the downpour, green and happy.

"How can you hate rain?" I asked my students—all women this semester. They listed their answers: their plans, no umbrella, no coat, their hair!

We are, of course, just different. We have different lives—different desires and needs, different sufferings, different gratitudes.

I remember worrying, as a newcomer to faith, about other believers' prayers and my competing ones. *What if I pray for miraculous healing of a friend's terminal disease and someone else prays for her peaceful death? How can God answer both prayers?* My first faith struggle.

After a lifetime of miracles, though, I've come to worship a bigger God: the Doer of impossible feats. I rejoice as blithely as a child in my own momentary abundance—rain, health, the resolution of some current worry—and I leave the divvying up to God.

I believe in Your impossible power to please all Your children, Father. Thank You, thank You, thank You!
—Patty Kirk

Digging Deeper: Matthew 19:16–26

OVERCOMING LOSS
Doing the Right Thing
Now take my advice, so that you may save your life.... —1 Kings 1:12 (JPS)

My mother died of breast cancer so I don't do well with mammograms. In the thirty-six years we were together, my husband always came with me. My first mammogram without Keith was a fiasco, not because they found anything, but because it reduced me to near-hysteria. I needed him to be there.

When time rolled around to have another mammogram, I flirted with the idea of just skipping it, despite my history. My friend Gayle said, "I haven't gone for three years and I should. Let's make appointments for the same time."

We met at the clinic, and after the tests we went for coffee and talked about waiting for the results. The technician had told us, "If you don't hear anything by the end of Monday, you're probably fine."

Four days. I tried to keep busy and, of course, I prayed all the time. *If only Keith were still with me,* I thought, *then it would be worth going through this every year.*

All day Monday, I carried the phone in my pocket, praying it would not ring. By the end of the day, I took a deep breath and put the phone down. No call. The next Friday, the "all normal" letter arrived and I wondered why I had put myself through such worry. What difference had it made?

On Saturday morning, Gayle said, "If it hadn't been for you, I would have just ignored the mammogram again. Thank you for being my bosom buddy."

I am very grateful, Source of Strength, when You show me the reasons I need to do the right thing.
—Rhoda Blecker

Digging Deeper: Deuteronomy 30:19

Saturday, May 20

"He who offers a sacrifice of thanksgiving honors Me...." —Psalm 50:23 (NAS)

I gathered with retired and active clergy at the service conducted by the Military Chaplains Association to honor members who had died. Rabbi Paul came forward and read Psalm 121 and then, in unison, we read verse 8 (RSV): "The Lord will keep your going out and your coming in from this time forth and for evermore." The chaplains sang "My Country, 'Tis of Thee" a cappella; their devotion to God and country was strong.

I was deeply moved by each part of the service, experiencing feelings of sadness and nostalgia, reflecting on the lives and the sacrifices made by our military men and women. In the bulletin, I read the list of names of those who were being remembered. *In what war had they served? How many people had they helped? What had become of them after their years of service?* I wondered.

Retired Army Chaplain Ed announced the names followed by the ringing of a bell: George, United States Navy. Hugh, United States Army. Clason, United States Air Force. William, Department of Veterans Affairs. As the names were read, the chaplains, now many in their seventies and eighties, stood at attention, tears streaming down their cheeks.

Chaplain Lyman ended the service with the words "Grant perfect peace unto the souls of our comrades who have gone to eternity. Lord of mercy, bring them under the cover of Your wings, and let their souls be bound up in the bond of eternal life. Be their inheritance, and may their repose be in peace. Amen."

Lord, it is good that we remember. —Pablo Diaz

Digging Deeper: Ephesians 2:10, Colossians 4:17

Sunday, May 21

I have learned, in whatever state I am, to be content. —Philippians 4:11 (RSV)

"You can't do so much traveling," my doctor said. "At eighty-eight, you don't have the stamina you once did."

Sure, I had heart issues, balance problems, macular degeneration. But I rebelled at advice to slow down.

It was a wood carving in our church that changed my attitude. It depicts a soaring eagle, outstretched wings supporting the large service Bible. The eagle is such a common motif for church lecterns that I'd never done more than glance at it.

I walked up for a closer look. What on earth was the eagle clutching? There was no mistaking it: a diamondback turtle, head poking warily from the carapace.

Is there a Bible passage somewhere, I wondered, *about an eagle and a turtle?* "Ask the church historian," someone suggested. "Robert will know."

Robert did know. "The carving wasn't designed as a lectern. It was made five hundred years ago as a table leg." And the story was from *Aesop's Fables!* The tale goes that a turtle yearned to fly like the eagle. The eagle pointed out that the turtle had no wings. But the turtle insisted, so the eagle took it high in the sky and let go—with the predictable result.

"Wasn't an ancient Greek fable out of place in a church?" I asked.

"Not at all," said Robert. "The church has always taken ancient wisdom and found the Christian meaning in it. Here, the humility to accept our limits."

I looked again at that self-deluded turtle. I'd experiment with a little grounded living for a while.

Help me to accept each phase of life, Father, with gratitude and grace. —Elizabeth Sherrill

Digging Deeper: Proverbs 19:20, Ecclesiastes 5:18–20

Monday, May 22

Whoever dwells in the shelter of the Most High will rest in the shadow of the Almighty. —Psalm 91:1 (NIV)

The sun's morning rays danced through the pine trees that lined both sides of the dusty trail. My horse SkySong dawdled while I rocked side to side in the saddle, enjoying the birds' "good-morning chorus." After a mile of being fascinated with God's creation, my mind whirled back to my never-ending to-do list. Some of my weeks were so busy that I didn't know if I was in the lead or if I'd fallen so far behind I would never see daylight.

God, how am I going to get it all done? I felt guilty for taking a break for something as frivolous as horseback riding. The beauty faded away as I planned how to extract the most out of the day. Gathering the reins, I sat up in the saddle and squeezed my legs. SkySong groaned lightly as he picked up his pace.

The trail curved gently around the hill. Suddenly, SkySong swung his head to the left. His nostrils flared and he stared uphill. My eyes scanned the ponderosa pine-studded hillside. Nothing. Curious, I squinted at each clump of brush. A flick of movement caught my attention. A deer stood under one of the tall pines, hiding under the tree's shadow. At that moment God's still, soft voice whispered, *You need to do the same. Rest in My shadow right now.*

I slumped in the saddle. My list wasn't important to God, but my uninterrupted time with Him was. I sighed. *Okay, God, it's just You and me for the rest of the ride.* By the time SkySong and I arrived at the trailhead, I felt refreshed and rejuvenated, as if I'd been on a long vacation.

Lord, thank You for giving us rest when we rest in Your shadow. Amen. —Rebecca Ondov

Digging Deeper: Psalms 36:7, 63:7

Tuesday, May 23

Don't be deceived, my dear brothers and sisters. Every good and perfect gift is from above, coming down from the Father of the heavenly lights, who does not change with shifting shadows. —James 1:16–17 (NIV)

Moving from California to New York was a big leap. We took on the adventure when my husband got a new job. Seven months into our relocation, I still felt isolated. Every detail of our lives had changed and seemed foreign.

I started giving a friend a list of my complaints: "I can't find good hiking." "I want a new book group." "I can't even find my favorite pickle relish!"

She laughed. "It'll come."

"I know it takes time, maybe even years, but this storm is lasting so long." I sighed.

"Can I make an observation?" she asked.

Here comes the count your blessings speech, I thought.

"You have your health." *See, I knew it.* "You are free from financial worries. You have a strong marriage. And you have your faith. Those all make a great foundation. With such solid things in place, you can weather this storm. Yes, it's hard and sad. But imagine how difficult it might be if you were missing any one of those building blocks?"

Huh, maybe my perspective was a little off. I thanked my friend for her wise words. Slowly, I began to change my point of view. Counting my blessings hadn't helped, but thinking of those blessings as a foundation was a new idea. I saw them as my anchor in the storm. Maybe, rather than crying out at the waves, I could begin navigating them.

Thank You, Father, for being my firm foundation and for giving me the blessings that help me daily. Amen.
—Lisa Bogart

Digging Deeper: Colossians 2:5,
Hebrews 6:18–20

Wednesday, May 24

Shall vain words have an end?... —Job 16:3 (KJV)

Some people call it "putting your foot in your mouth." My father expressed it a bit differently: "Engage brain before putting mouth in gear."

No matter the description, I'm just one of those people with a talent for saying the wrong thing at the wrong time. "God must have really loved my daddy," I told a friend, "because He took him to heaven so quickly." My friend's face clouded and she said, "My father was in excruciating pain for over a year before he died. Do you think God didn't love him as much?"

One evening I sat at the modest table of a family who lived in a small house overlooking Zimbabwe's Lake Kariba. I thought I might make them feel rich as I explained that such a beautiful site would be high-end real estate in the United States. "I'll bet your children love playing in the lake. Do you have a boat?" I gushed.

The room fell completely silent, every eye fixed on me. "We would never put our children in such danger," the mother replied icily.

My heart fell to my toes. Of course, hippos and crocodiles would make a meal out of a child in two seconds flat!

I'd like to say that I've finally taken my daddy's advice to heart but, honestly, I am a work in progress.

Father, thank You for never giving up on me.
—Pam Kidd

Digging Deeper: Proverbs 10:19, Ecclesiastes 5:2

Thursday, May 25

Do not fear, for I am with you, do not be afraid, for I am your God; I will strengthen you, I will help you, I will uphold you with my victorious right hand. —Isaiah 41:10 (NRSV)

I'm afraid of umbrellas. As a child, I'd always get my fingers pinched trying to close them, and they never worked in the wind anyway. Even now, especially in a sudden shower, the button sometimes sticks or the umbrella only opens partway or one of the metal spokes breaks.

My chronic "umbrellalessness" has earned me strange looks over the years, not to mention comments. Most are along the lines of "Hey, don't you know enough to come in out of the rain?" Occasionally, people try to give me umbrellas. During a recent downpour, a woman, whom I vaguely recognized from church, darted out of her house with one. I was about to refuse, but she opened it herself and stuck it in my hand, saying, "Now, dear, all of God's children deserve to stay dry!"

What an interesting thing to say, I thought. I'd been thinking a lot lately about what I deserve when it comes to God. I've never been able to fully believe that I deserve His mercy, healing, love, even grace. But I'm beginning to understand that because I don't feel worthy, I can forget that God's grace is the gift that comes because I really *can't* be worthy.

I may still be scared of umbrellas, but I'm learning not to be so fearful of being receptive to God's grace.

Gracious God, thank You for showering Your grace and gifts upon me wherever I am, however I am. Amen. —Marci Alborghetti

Digging Deeper: Romans 1:1–7

Friday, May 26

Devote yourselves to prayer, being watchful and thankful. —Colossians 4:2 (NIV)

This week we received thrilling news: Mary has been accepted into the conservatory program at a ballet company! The one drawback: my daughter will be leaving home this fall.

Mary knows how to cook and do laundry; she gets her schoolwork done; she balances ballet and babysitting and spending time with friends. She's responsible and does what needs to be done with competence, common sense, and faith. Still...she's only sixteen.

I consider inquiring, "God, why do You ask this of me?" but it's not a serious question. Mary is determined to dance and, heaven help me, I am surely the last person to stand in her way. Still...she's only sixteen.

Over the years I've learned that when my mind veers off into what-could-go-wrong territory, I need to steer it back to the ways God has been good. I focus on being thankful for the gifts God has given my daughter, for the gift of being her mom, and for the opportunity Mary has been given to do what she loves.

Yet because Mary is sixteen, sometimes I get a bit weepy. In a way this makes me smile and thank God too. For I am absolutely certain that one reason He made the day twenty-four hours long is so that mothers have 2:00 a.m. in which to cry, alone.

Jesus, take my tears and water the souls of those
I love so that they may grow in wisdom and faith.
—Julia Attaway

Digging Deeper: Ecclesiastes 3:4

Saturday, May 27

"I'll share my heart with you." —Proverbs 1:23 (NLT)

"I got a box, Granmom!" My four-year-old grandson
Wyatt held it up for me to see over Facetime. The
box was about one and a half feet long and had a
top. It contained one small rock. I tried not to look
puzzled. "It has my name on it too!" Wyatt pointed
to the lettering.

"Tell me more about your box," I said.

"Daddy gave it to me. He said to put things in it
that I want to show him when he gets home. We can
talk about what I find or want to share."

"Oh, how wonderful!" Now I understood. His
dad, my son, was deploying overseas again and
would be away for several months. He didn't want to
miss any of Wyatt's discovered treasures and wanted
his son to save things for them to talk about when he
returned.

That gave me an idea. The next morning in my
quiet time, I envisioned pulling out a sharing box

of my own, opening its lid, and lifting out items, one by one, to show my heavenly Father. "This is a sunrise I watched from our back deck this week. It was magnificent. Thank You." "This is a book I started reading yesterday. I have a few questions and want to know what You think." "Here's something that's been worrying me. I need Your guidance."

I felt God smiling.

Heavenly Father, thank You for the reminder that You are interested in everything I want to share with You.
—Kim Henry

Digging Deeper: Psalms 5:3, 21:6, 71:6

Sunday, May 28

"Men of Galilee," they said, "why do you stand here looking into the sky? This same Jesus, who has been taken from you into heaven, will come back in the same way you have seen him go into heaven."
—Acts 1:11 (NIV)

I am often on the road for business; the longest trips are usually book tours. It took almost one month for the twenty-city tour I did for a book called *Twenty Wishes*. My husband, Wayne, said, "If you'd titled the book *Three Wishes*, you would have been home a long time ago."

Life on the road is often a challenge. There've been days when I've schlepped my way through four different airports in a single twenty-four-hour period. By the time I arrive back home, I'm exhausted and eager to spend alone-time with Wayne and my family.

I have a ritual I perform when I've been away for several weeks. I move from room to room, touching the things that are most precious to me: the photograph of my parents on the piano, the stack of books on my nightstand, the projects in my yarn room.

As we celebrate the Ascension of Jesus, I wonder if He, too, experienced that deep sense of welcome—the welcome of heaven, the joy of being surrounded by all that was familiar after such a long absence. I wonder if we, too, will share that same experience with Him when we cross over that bridge from life to death to new life, that sense of homecoming, that welcome, that at-home feeling of all that's right and familiar.

**Lord, remind me that my true home is with You.
I already know that the welcome
is going to be amazing!**
—Debbie Macomber

Digging Deeper: 2 Peter 1:10–12

"And the heavens proclaim his righteousness, for he is a God of justice." —Psalm 50:6 (NIV)

My sister and brother sent me a fascinating item from our family history. It was a letter to Mrs. Sarah A. Daily, my father's aunt, dated November 19, 1919, from a US Army chaplain, expressing condolences for the death of her son. "I am so sorry we could do nothing to heal his poor, maimed body, but it was otherwise decreed." He went on to say that Leonard was a beautiful boy who "won the hearts of all of us with his bravery." He congratulated Mrs. Daily on having such a fine son "who did his full duty." He concluded the three-page, typed letter by assuring Mrs. Daily that he prayed with Leonard until the moment of his death and describes the gentle French hillside where her son was laid to rest.

My hands were shaking when I finished reading. How many such letters were written by chaplains to families through the years, through the centuries? The events happened decades before I came into the world, yet I could not help feeling both heartbroken and proud, a tiny echo of what Leonard's mother must have felt.

A soldier once said, "War is not hell. It is the gates of hell." Memorial Day is when we remember those who have fallen at those gates. We call it a holiday, but it really feels more like a day of collective mourning, a day when we grieve those beautiful boys and young women who made a sacrifice that can never really be repaid.

Father, bring into Your kingdom all who have fallen in the defense of a just cause, all for whom it was otherwise decreed. —Edward Grinnan

Digging Deeper: Psalm 116:3–6, 15–16

Tuesday, May 30

We know also that the Son of God has come and has given us understanding, so that we may know him who is true.... —1 John 5:20 (NIV)

I never would have known about Sarah, a girl the same age as my daughter who had grown very sick very quickly because of an undetected tumor, if I didn't browse Facebook. I watched Sarah's story turn darker and darker, thinking of my sweet Olivia tucked in safely upstairs. I found myself pausing during the day to pray for this little girl and her parents, strangers weighing on my heart.

As I prayed, I often called out to God, "Please, no! Don't let this toddler lose her life." And over and over, I heard back from God, *Please, know that I am working.*

Parenting a toddler means I'm used to rejection. "Put your shoes on!" *No, Mama.* "Want to go to the park?" *No, Mama.* "Who's up for ice cream?" *No, Mama.* So I can only imagine God's rueful glance as I stomp and beg and pray my "Please, no!" about rain on a family vacation, losing a smartphone, or burning dinner again. But what about when I'm praying my heart out on behalf of family, friends, or even strangers who are in desperate need of God's attention?

God gently reminded me that silence isn't the same as absence. He is there in the trials and in the triumphs, and He is listening. "Please, no!" I cry. And "Please, know," He answers.

Calling out to You makes me feel so much better, Lord. Knowing that You are listening sets my heart at ease, even in a world of uncertainty and pain.
—Ashley Kappel

Digging Deeper: Matthew 12:15, 2 Corinthians 1:8–11

Wednesday, May 31

I will give thanks.... —Psalm 9:1 (NIV)

"Brock, we need to leave soon!" my wife called from the kitchen.

Two down, one to go, I thought as I tied my tie. Finally, the last graduation ceremony of the season. I longed to stay home and write. I was rotating off a board after nine years and would be offering my farewell message that very week. Working with the poor through Nashville, Tennessee's oldest nonprofit organization had been gratifying and I wanted my parting words to be profound.

Corinne and I found seats in the bleachers. We looked to the podium, expecting a wave of weighty advice. Instead, we were pleasantly surprised. "As a Southern lady, my mother always spoke of the importance of writing thank-you notes," a fresh-faced girl began with a hint of exasperation. The crowd chuckled. "But as much as I hate to admit it, my mom was right. So this morning, I have written a thank-you note to all of you." Her words were poignant and expressed her appreciation for everything she had gained from her teachers, friends, and school.

"Best graduation talk ever," Corinne said on our drive home. I agreed, my mind churning.

Two nights later, I stood before the board and pulled out a simple thank-you note.

Dear God, thank You. —Brock Kidd

Digging Deeper: Romans 1:8,
1 Thessalonians 5:18

IN GOD'S HANDS

1 _____

2 _____

3 _____

4 _____

5 _____

6 _____

7 _____

8 _____

9 _____

10 _____

11 _____

12 _____

13 _____

14 _____

15 _____

16 _____

17 _____

18 _____

19 _____

20 _____

21 _____

22 _____

23 _____

24 _____

25 _____

26 _____

27 _____

28 _____

29 _____

30 _____

31 _____

JUNE

*In peace I will lie down and sleep, for you alone,
Lord, make me dwell in safety.*

—Psalm 4:8 (NIV)

Thursday, June 1

Many are the plans in a person's heart, but it is the Lord's purpose that prevails. —Proverbs 19:21 (NIV)

I am walking the dog, and though the days are getting longer, it's near dark now. From the yard, the Christmas tree lights pinned to the front porch of our house shine. They're hooked up still, and when you turn on the outside light, they go on.

I look at them and groan. Time has gotten away from us. We have packets of seeds that need to be planted, fertilizer to be spread, the annual swap of winter clothes to summer ones, giving outgrown boots and even swim shoes from last summer to charity, putting away the shovels, and now the lights too.

I go to bed preoccupied with prioritizing. The next morning I get up and remember that I forgot to get the mail yesterday. When I go outside, I see my neighbor getting the newspaper. She's nearing ninety and waves at me.

"I have to tell you," she says, "I love seeing those lights at night!"

I'm about to roll my eyes and explain how we've been meaning to take them down, but then I remember the lights were hers. I got them a few years ago. She was having a huge yard sale because "you can't take it with you." When I tried to pay for the lights, she refused to take any money, saying that she was happy I wanted them.

On my way back inside, I scratch off one thing on our to-do list.

Dear God, I am in awe of Your mysterious ways— how even the small stuff is part of Your big plan.
—Sabra Ciancanelli

Digging Deeper: Proverbs 3:5–6, 16:9

Friday, June 2

This is the day the Lord has made; we will rejoice and be glad in it. —Psalm 118:24 (NKJV)

I tried not to look at the corral as we drove past. The neighbors were branding today. For twenty years I had been a cattle rancher, until I hurt my back so badly I had to quit. My husband had a day of fishing planned for us. Until now I'd been excited. *I should be helping them, not fishing.*

A strong work ethic was in my DNA. As a rancher, I used to go months without a day off. Sitting still didn't sit well with me.

We launched the boat onto a high mountain lake. Dark-green pines surrounded the sky-blue water. Snowcapped mountains towered above us in breathtaking splendor. The sun lifted, reflecting across the water in what looked like millions of sparkling diamonds. I felt its warmth relax the chilly bite of morning. I watched the hypnotic dance of the pole as we trolled. Cormorants, coots, and ducks bobbed noisily around us. Eagles soared overhead, calling to one another.

I felt guilty. Even though my back wasn't anywhere near strong enough to safely be around cattle, the feeling of needing to be there remained.

Randy seemed to read my thoughts. "Sometimes it's okay to enjoy yourself."

I laughed. He was right. This was the day the Lord had made, this day for healing.

Dear Lord, help me remember to take time to celebrate this life You have given me in this beautiful world You have created. —Erika Bentsen

Digging Deeper: Ecclesiastes 3, Romans 14:17–18

Saturday, June 3

For whosoever exalteth himself shall be abased; and he that humbleth himself shall be exalted. —Luke 14:11 (KJV)

I found myself living for a week in Australia in a rambling old stone house with a dozen priests and brothers. I met one man who had spent forty years in

the jungles of New Guinea and another who had lived
for thirty years on Bougainville Island, where he once
managed to delay a battle by inserting himself between
the opposing forces and engaging them in spirited and
hilarious debate all day. His devious plotting failed in
the end and the battle commenced, but his attitude
was that he had cut a day off the fight, which perhaps
saved some lives.

Another elderly man taught me a great lesson.
He had endured thirty years in the Australian
outback, and every time we sat over tea to swap
stories he would begin with a long silence. "I want to
remember to be humble before I speak," he said. "I
want to remember that I am one of the uncountable
miracles granted life by the Lord, and that *my* first
work is to witness and revere *His* work, and that I
can do that best while abashed with my head bowed.
So I try to begin every conversation with a few
moments of silence, to get my priorities straight.
I find it helps me to not be a prattling idiot and
to keep my temper. I learned it from a Waluwarra
man whom I much respected. We learned a great
deal about our own spirituality from each other. In
the end, all substantive religious pursuit is about
witness and attentiveness and humility and service to
miracle."

I have tried, ever since those bright parrot-filled
eucalyptus-spiced tea-steaming days, to remember

his wise counsel. Perhaps you will remember it now too.

Dear Lord, do, if You are not especially busy, remind me occasionally that humility is the final frontier. Be gentle. A hint is enough for me, after much abashment.
—Brian Doyle

Digging Deeper: 1 Peter 5:5

Sunday, June 4

"But I say to you, love your enemies, bless those who curse you, do good to those who hate you, and pray for those who spitefully use you and persecute you." —Matthew 5:44 (NKJV)

Do I really have to do this, Lord?

An invisible hand reached up inside me and choked off my prayer. I'd been nursing grudges for years now: people who hurt me; folks who betrayed me; those in ministry who, in my opinion, shouldn't have been.

My wounds ran deep. Many times I caught myself wishing them ill. I even prayed against them. But the Holy Spirit had been convicting me the whole time. I knew God wanted me to pray *for* them, not *against* them. I just didn't want to.

Things came to a head last weekend. I was preparing to preach a particularly difficult passage of

Scripture. The message had been tough to compose. It was time for our service, and I had no confidence. As I readied myself for worship, God's Spirit whispered, *Pray for them.*

I sighed and I prayed. There was no great relief, no lightning bolt, no deep emotion—just a still, small voice and a free-will choice.

I prayed for those who cursed me. I prayed for their success. I prayed blessing on their ministries. I prayed for their families. And then I went to preach and found unusual power.

It's been two weeks now since that day. I've prayed a few more times for those people. It gets easier every time.

I don't know what God is doing in their lives, but I do know what He's doing in mine: God is setting me free.

Compassionate Father, release me from the prison of my own bitterness. Create in me a forgiving heart, and let Christ's gentle grace flow through me.
—Bill Giovannetti

Digging Deeper: Psalm 51:10

Monday, June 5

"I have set you an example that you should do as I have done for you." —John 13:15 (NIV)

"Stephen, do you want to help Jeremy sell lemonade this afternoon?" I call to my eleven-year-old.

I get an eager "Yes!" By the time I text Melissa asking when she wants Stephen to arrive, my son is busy making origami paper cups and gathering pitchers. If there's an activity involving Jeremy, Stephen's there in a heartbeat.

Jeremy is five, and Stephen thinks he's the greatest kid on earth. They started playing together a year and a half ago, after Melissa had another baby. Melissa pays Stephen a nominal amount as a mother's helper; the real profit has been to my son's character. Whenever he comes back from Jeremy's, he stands taller, feels more mature. He's patient with the younger boy, playing games, finding new ways to approach Jeremy's special interest in math, and even sometimes remembering to clean up when they're done.

I used to wonder how I'd teach my youngest child the kind of generosity of self that's forced upon an older sibling. As it turns out, I didn't have to do the teaching. Jeremy's presence in his life achieved that. It's funny how God sometimes steps in, providing us with the right person to help us grow in ways we hadn't considered.

Jesus, thank You for those who have helped me grow into more of the person You want me to be.
—Julia Attaway

Digging Deeper: Titus 2:7

Tuesday, June 6

Always be prepared to give an answer to everyone who asks you to give the reason for the hope that you have.... —1 Peter 3:15 (NIV)

"John, how do you always stay so calm, even in the tough situations?" a colleague asked.

I was sitting across the desk from the division president of my company for one last meeting. We were chatting, wrapping things up, before I formally retired. Not expecting the question, I rambled, mentioning my faith and that I hadn't always been calm. I talked about reading Dr. Norman Vincent Peale's books in my younger days and how they had helped me.

Later, I felt disappointed that my answer hadn't come close to capturing God's work within me to overcome the biggest struggle of my life: crippling fears and anxiety. I asked God to help me overcome all of my turmoil and inner conflict. I learned ways to live my faith. I began to pray and read the Bible daily. I used many of the action steps that Dr. Peale outlined to deal with daily life and to practice peacefulness. From that beginning, God guided me on an incredible journey, step by step, to a life of deep tranquility and quiet confidence.

I wasn't prepared to give an answer when the question was asked. I missed an opportunity to tell firsthand what God had done for me. However, the conversation may have been another step that God intended for my journey. It caused me to look back and see more clearly than ever His presence and faithfulness throughout my life—and that He is "the reason for the hope" I have.

Dear Lord, help me be ready to boldly share stories of Your faithfulness whenever an opportunity comes. Amen. —John Dilworth

Digging Deeper: 1 Chronicles 16:9; Psalms 13:5–6, 71:23

Wednesday, June 7

"Do not worry about your life...."
—Matthew 6:25 (NIV)

"Hi, Carol," the e-mail began. "As you know, I'm graduating soon and looking for places near my high school for a party—which brings me to my point. Would you allow me to host it outside at your house? If not, I totally understand. Love, Tianna."

I knew we'd say yes to this request from my brother's oldest grandchild because that's the right thing to do. So Tianna stopped by a few days later to talk about her vision for the party: how many (about one hundred); what time (noon); which activities (volleyball and other games); and food (lots). She assured me her parents and grandparents would do everything, even provide a tent and an outside toilet. I wouldn't have to worry about anything.

She left, and I started worrying about the number of guests, parking, bad weather, and everyone crowding into our house.

Sure enough, party day dawned gray and drizzly. The parking area was a muddy mess, and guests piled into the small tent as the drizzle turned into a downpour and then hail. As I headed into the house, I invited the wet and cold guests to follow, and many did.

Hours later, I sat with my brother and his wife, reminiscing about the party. "Everything I worried about actually happened," I confessed, "and it was still a great party."

Lord, I'm thankful Your grace is greater than my worries. —Carol Kuykendall

Digging Deeper: Psalm 55:22, Philippians 4:6–7

Thursday, June 8

**The wise woman builds her house, but the foolish tears it down with her own hands.
—Proverbs 14:1 (NAS)**

It was a powerful moment alone inside my mother's car, taking a break from the hospital vigil.

Mom's hope was fixed on heaven. I'd watched her lips form "It is well with my soul." At nearly ninety-two, she was our family matriarch—faithful to listen and help and remember and teach. We cherished her "pray without ceasing" (1 Thessalonians 5:17) prayers for us. How we would miss her.

I know just where I was on the highway when the moment happened. God seemed to reach into my mind with the story of the prophet Elijah throwing his mantle on his successor Elisha, while Elisha was out plowing in the field (1 Kings 19:19–20). I clearly understood that another mantle—the matriarch mantle—was passing to me. I would be the oldest woman now on my side of the family: mother to four, grandmother to eighteen. I would be the one to listen and help and remember and teach. My prayers would be offered to God for the needs and dreams of the family. I recognized the great privilege—the responsibility—that I was inheriting from my mother. I answered God with tears of acceptance, already feeling Mom's absence and crying, "Yes, I will!"

It's been nearly a year since that mantle came to me. We are about to have grandchild nineteen. A son-in-law is seeking the right place to start a practice with his new veterinary medicine degree. Our daughter has needed help after suffering a concussion in a car accident. The family matriarch position keeps me seeking and serving God more than ever before. I am learning just how good it is for my soul.

It is a great honor, Lord, to be the matriarch in a family. Bless those who carry this mantle in Your name, giving Your love and nurturing care.
—Carol Knapp

Digging Deeper: Psalm 100:5; Philippians 1:3–6; Hebrews 10:23–24, 36

Friday, June 9

He has made everything beautiful in its time. He has also set eternity in the human heart; yet no one can fathom what God has done from beginning to end. —Ecclesiastes 3:11 (NIV)

Ten pairs of shoes lined the bright red Do Not Cross line just outside of airport security, leaning forward, getting as close as they could without going over it. Even the stern-faced guard cracked a smile as tiny legs arched on tiptoes and wide eyes craned for that first glimpse of their cousin from Ethiopia.

And then a familiar face appeared in the crowd of travelers pressing toward home. My brother Troy walked toward us, holding a bundle in a yellow sweatshirt: Isaac. The long-awaited one. The one our hearts had cried for, prayed for, yearned for.

A mussy-haired head slowly lifted off his daddy's shoulder, and black eyes turned to the crowd that waited expectantly just across that line. Isaac blinked once, twice, a third time, and then a slow smile spread over his lips.

"He smiled!" my daughter Kate screamed, and the other cousins began to cheer and laugh as Troy walked over that line. The guard stood stock-still in the chaos, watching closely, reminding us there was no going back now, no turning around, no do-overs.

Isaac had crossed that line and was finally home. And I remembered that we, too, are slowly walking toward that line, pressing in, holding tight, until the day when we cross over and are finally home.

Father God, thank You for guiding me slowly but surely toward You. Amen. —Erin MacPherson

Digging Deeper: John 14:2, Hebrews 11:16

Saturday, June 10

But I trust in you, Lord; I say, "You are my God." —Psalm 31:14 (NIV)

"Nice job, Logan!" my friend Steve shouted. "You're doing great!"

I looked down from the faux-stone wall I was clinging to. Steve was teaching me how to rock climb. He tightened the rope clipped to his waist. It connected to a pulley on the ceiling and down to my harness.

I was shaky from being so high up, but I also felt exhilarated. I swung my torso as I grasped for the next handhold, and I missed it. Suddenly, I was hanging from the rock face by one hand. I looked down at the gym floor, and my stomach clenched.

"It's okay, Logan!" Steve yelled. "That's why I'm here! You can let go now! I've got you!"

I was afraid. Instead of trusting Steve, I clawed and scrabbled to find a grip. *What if the rope isn't tight enough? What if it snaps? What if I weigh more than Steve and plummet to the floor while he rockets to the ceiling?*

"Logan, you have to trust me," Steve said, calm and steady.

I understood that I needed to release my grasp. But I struggle with surrender. I'm the firstborn of five, and I've got the personality that goes with it. Relying on myself feels safe and certain.

Now it was time to do the opposite: to relinquish and release control instead of claw for it. I uncurled my fingers. I dropped, but the slack in the rope tightened. Then I hung, suspended peacefully in the air. Steve had expertly braced himself. He began to lower me to safety, and I breathed easy.

It's a good thing to be in capable hands.

Lord, thank You for sending friends who teach me more about surrender and trust. —Logan Eliasen

Digging Deeper: Psalm 56:3, Proverbs 3:5–6

Sunday, June 11

He went…apart to pray…. —Matthew 14:23 (KJV)

"Two solid hours of just praying, every single day?"

"Yes," said David.

David Wilkerson was a tremendously busy man. His work with teen gang members and drug-addicted kids kept him on the streets of New York City from six in the morning till six at night, listening, counseling, preaching.

"You're so busy!" I said. "How can you take off two hours?"

They didn't come off the workday, he explained. He would set his alarm clock for 4:00 a.m. and spend the next two hours literally on his knees. "It's precisely because I'm so busy that I have to pray so long."

My husband, John, and I kept in touch with David after he left New York. His once-solo ministry became a huge organization, Teen Challenge, with chapters all over the world. And every time, before the conversation ended, we'd ask, "Are you still praying two hours a day?" The answer was always yes.

Later David moved back to New York to a church in Times Square, then a neighborhood of crime, prostitution, and sleaze. We asked our perpetual question. "No," he said, "I can't do two hours here."

I caught John's eye and knew what we were both thinking. Too often we'd watched ministries fall apart when the leader got so involved with building, fund-raising, chasing donors, that he let his own spiritual life drift.

"Here the job's so big" said David, "I couldn't possibly get along with only two hours of prayer."

Help me remember, Father, that when I'm busiest is when I need the most time with You.
—Elizabeth Sherrill

Digging Deeper: Psalm 119:93, Colossians 4:2, Hebrews 12:28

Monday, June 12

Look… that you may see! —Isaiah 42:18 (RSV)

My husband, David, and I and our eleven-year-old granddaughter Abby were up with the sun, on our way to Atlanta to spend the day with Bernard Lafayette Jr., an icon of the civil rights movement. A professor at Emory University and chairman of the Southern Christian Leadership Conference, Dr. Lafayette has spent his life teaching nonviolence. We hoped Abby would learn valuable life lessons.

"I read about your nonviolent reaction to the assassin who tried to take your life in 1963," said Abby. "The way you got back on your feet over and over again as the man struck you with his gun. Does such a reaction apply to the kids in my school who are victims of bullying?"

Dr. Lafayette smiled, pleased with her observation. "In any confrontation, from a disagreement to an attack," he said, "the first thing you must do is to find a way to look your adversary in the eye. Something unexpected happens when we look directly into the eyes of another. As we force them to acknowledge our humanity, they sense that we, at the same time, are acknowledging theirs."

As our visit ended, I felt that Abby had learned a lot. But it wasn't until a few days later that I understood how much I had learned too. A disagreement with David stoked my anger, and I was in attack mode. Suddenly, I stopped and looked directly into his eyes. As Dr. Lafayette predicted, something unexpected happened. Being right no longer mattered. I remembered love.

Father, let me look and see. —Pam Kidd

Digging Deeper: Psalm 145:15, 2 Peter 1:9

Tuesday, June 13

Look! I'm doing a new thing.... —Isaiah 43:19 (CEB)

"Have you seen God at work in your life lately?"
At the pregnancy resource center where I volunteer,
the teacher instructed me to pose this question for
discussion.

Glancing around the room, I remembered one
young couple was staying in a rent-by-the-night
motel, a father needed a job, a single mother awaited
test results on her infant son. *Lord, they have so much
heartache. This question will make them feel even more
hopeless.* I swallowed hard. "Does anyone want to
share how God's working in your life?"

A man to my left smiled. "Praise God, I do.
After my divorce, I wanted to commit suicide.
Feeling desperate, I prayed, 'Lord, help me make it
just one more day.' I prayed that for months. Then
I met my beautiful bride." He hugged the woman
beside him. "We just found out we're having twins.
God is so good."

A woman piped up: "A year ago, I was involved
in a drive-by shooting. I shouldn't have made it. And
I was pregnant at the time. Now I have a baby girl,
and she's doing fine."

Another woman said, "Eleven years ago, I wasn't
expected to live. Ovarian cancer. Doctors said if I

survived, I'd never have children." Her husband sat beside her, bouncing their baby boy on his knee. "See how good God is? He works miracles. How 'bout you, Julie?" she said.

Melted by their transparency, gratitude bubbled inside me. "When I started volunteering here, I'd gone through a rough time with clinical depression. I doubted I had anything left to give. But God had a plan, didn't He?"

The woman kissed her miracle son. "God always does."

Lord, You're doing new things in all of us! Thank You.
—Julie Garmon

Digging Deeper: Psalm 136:1, 2 Corinthians 13:14

Wednesday, June 14

"From the lips of children and infants you, Lord, have called forth your praise." —Matthew 21:16 (NIV)

I detest washing dishes! I'll take a mountain of stinky laundry, a dingy tub, or sticky floors over a sink full of dirty dishes! I dislike the smell of old food, the slimy bits of leftovers on my fingers, and the monotony of sponging forks, plates, and pans.

I admit that I let them sit for a while until I can't ignore them anymore, which only makes the job worse. I dream of owning a dishwasher, but I can only dream because it's not allowed in my apartment building.

One day after dinner, my boys wanted to try washing dishes. I pulled up two chairs by the sink, handed them wet, soapy sponges, and showed them what to do. They couldn't have been happier, bathing each dish and themselves in water and bubbles. "This is so much fun!" they exclaimed. "Why do you hate washing dishes, Mom?"

Watching my little ones find such joy in a chore that I dread was amusing. But it also helped me look at dishwashing and every undesirable task I do in a new way. If my boys can find the happiness in it, then surely I can too.

Thank You, Lord, for helping me to change my attitude toward things I need to do. Help me to find a bit of gladness in all things. —Karen Valentin

Digging Deeper: Colossians 3:10

Thursday, June 15

Then the Lord God formed man from the dust of the ground, and breathed into his nostrils the breath of life; and the man became a living being. —Genesis 2:7 (NRSV)

"Well, how'd the test go?" I asked my dad.

He had always been a light sleeper and, as a result, was known to nod off during the day. He had finally agreed to go in for a sleep test. "They woke me up in the middle of the night and told me that I had stopped breathing," he said. "It was really scary—a terrifying experience."

I had never heard my dad describe anything as "scary." *Dad forgets to breathe?* And then I was scared. *My goodness, Dad could have died all those times he woke himself up!*

While I was frightened by the news, I also felt a sense of relief that Dad finally knew why he'd always been such a light sleeper and that he now had some help to manage the problem. And I was relieved that I too had language for what occasionally happened to me at night—what I'd been afraid to acknowledge—when I sometimes awoke gasping for air.

The story of God breathing life into mud is one that is important to me. This is where I feel the presence of God most sincerely—the communion of the Divine in me and in the world is my breath. We take somewhere around twenty-one thousand breaths a day without even thinking about it. It's one thing not to notice them, but it's quite another not to take them. So I cherish my breath—the *ruach*, the wind of God—as I breathe deeply into my abdomen, knowing the next breath is not promised.

God, I am grateful for every breath You give me and the experience in it of communing with You, whether I am aware of it or not. —Natalie Perkins

Digging Deeper: Job 33:4, John 20:22

Friday, June 16

When she speaks, her words are wise, and kindness is the rule for everything she says. —Proverbs 31:26 (TLB)

Today marks my fifth wedding anniversary to Jack, my favorite husband by far. Sometimes I tease him and say he's my favorite husband *so far*. In reality, Jack is a good man and I know we will be together until death do us part.

I suppose many couples wonder if they're doing enough to make their marriage happy. I think about it often, perhaps because I still feel like a newlywed and want this marriage not only to work but to be downright joyful.

Sometimes I'm quick to judge or am critical when Jack does something differently from the way I would. I worry that he may feel neglected when I get busy. After reading a book about marriage, I decided I needed to do two things to help make our marriage sizzle. The first was to use kind words, to say something positive every single day: "You're a great help in the kitchen, and I appreciate it." "I am so proud of what a good job you do as president of our building association, and I know everyone else is happy that you're taking care of things."

The second thing was to simply touch him. In church or at the movies, I reach for his hand. At home, I often give him a love tap. It wasn't long before he started reaching for my hand whenever we were out walking. I also noticed more neck and back rubs. It's amazing how powerful human touch is.

I may not have it all figured out, but I can do little things like this to bring us closer together.

Heavenly Father, when I'm tempted to say something critical, zip my lips and help me speak with kindness instead. —Patricia Lorenz

Digging Deeper: Proverbs 31:25–31, Ephesians 4:31

Saturday, June 17

But if anyone does not provide for his relatives, and especially for members of his household, he has denied the faith and is worse than an unbeliever. —1 Timothy 5:8 (ESV)

I never know what to get my dad as a present for Father's Day. He's a complex, thoughtful man, but he has simple tastes. He loves running his own business, helping companies work through their internal communication issues. He feels like he makes a real contribution to those people.

When he's not doing that, he spends time with my mom and rounds out his days with some television and Solitaire. I've bought him tools to encourage his handyman streak and books and movies that have meaning for me. He's always grateful, but I'm usually left dissatisfied with my gift.

This year I racked my brain to think of something more interesting, more creative. I knew what my dad valued was simply my love and thoughtfulness, but I was a little old for a homemade gift.

Then my wife, Emily, showed me an article about GiveWell, an organization that rates charities based on how effectively they help people. I read about the Against Malaria Foundation, one of its top-rated charities, which provides insecticidal mosquito nets to Africans vulnerable to malaria. I'd never made a donation in someone else's name, but my dad didn't need a shiny new toy; he wanted to help other people.

I gave him his Father's Day card and told him thirty nets had been donated in his name. He was delighted! We hugged, and I knew I'd finally found the right present.

Thank You, Lord, for continuing to lead me toward the righteous path. —Sam Adriance

Digging Deeper: 1 Timothy 4:14–16, Hebrews 13:16

Sunday, June 18

**Be thankful in all circumstances, for this is
God's will for you who belong to Christ Jesus.
—1 Thessalonians 5:18 (NLT)**

"Guess how old I am?" At least once a day my dad
would ask some new friend this question while we
visited my mother in the hospital. Every time he'd
light up when the person asked the inevitable, "I
don't know. How old?"

I'd flown to Maryland from Arkansas as soon as
my dad called. My mother had taken ill, and her
doctors had rushed her to the ICU. While I would
have loved the opportunity to visit during a happier
occasion, I was grateful to sit by my father's side
while we supported Mom during the fight for her
life. It also afforded me many precious moments:
daily conversations; fixing my dad eggs and toast for
breakfast; hearing him brag about his age.

Dad wasn't just proud that he looked at least a
decade younger than his actual age; his true pride came
from reaching the age of "fourscore" that the Bible
speaks of. He often quoted Psalm 90:10 (KJV): "The
days of our years are threescore years and ten; and if
by reason of strength they be fourscore years...."

Even when he lay in a hospital bed a few weeks
later, having succumbed to his own illness, Dad was
still thankful: "Well, God gave me eighty years." Two

weeks later, he passed away, three weeks to the day before my mother lost her own battle.

Today, I remember Dad's gratefulness for life. It encourages me to be thankful for the years God has given me—years full of life, love, joy, and a wonderful relationship with my sweet dad.

Lord, may I always marvel over the precious years You've blessed me with. —Carla Hendricks

Digging Deeper: Psalm 34:1, Ephesians 5:20

Monday, June 19

By faith Abraham... went out, not knowing where he was going. —Hebrews 11:8 (NKJV)

I never anticipated how quiet retirement could be, so I decided to join a nearby gardening club.

"It sounds interesting," I said to my wife, Sharon, "but what if I hate it?"

"Then don't join. But you do need to check it out. You might love it."

When I opened the meeting-room door, I found fourteen elegant elderly women seated in a semicircle. I took the one empty seat, right in the middle, and felt like a rutabaga in a rose garden. The meeting started with a lengthy presentation about trees, which one woman had written in the form of a poem—an incredible feat! Her lecture was followed by such a spirited business meeting that, at one point, I felt my life might be in danger.

At break time, these women were as sweet as the tea and cookies they served. They truly made me feel welcome: "We would love to have a male in our group. Are you married?" I could see that the group was not a glove-fit.

"It wasn't a mistake," Sharon assured me. "The only way to know some things is to show up and have a look-see. Now, check out the next group on your list."

She's right, I thought. Whether I am looking for employment, a better apartment, or a different church, sooner or later I need to get out of the house and put some shoes on the ground.

Thank You, Father, for the freedom to make mistakes while I am learning. —Daniel Schantz

Digging Deeper: 2 Timothy 1:7

Tuesday, June 20

We do not know what we ought to pray for, but the Spirit himself intercedes for us through wordless groans. —Romans 8:26 (NIV)

The vagueness of prayer e-mails for a friend in the final stages of cancer made me unsure whether to visit her. I worried about being in the way, but beneath my worry was a deeper concern: I didn't know what to say. Finally, I made myself go.

I sat on the edge of the hospice bed in the living room and held my friend's hand while her husband talked about the past weeks—hospital stays, visitors, how nice the hospice people were. I said little more than the occasional listening noise: "Oh." "I see." "Uh-huh."

My friend closed her eyes while her husband talked. "Listening," she explained during a pause, "not asleep."

Gradually the visit lapsed into a rhythm of okayness. *She probably already knows whatever I could say anyway*, I thought. In fact, it occurred to me, maybe she wasn't listening to her husband but to God.

"Is God talking to you?" I asked during another pause.

Her eyelids flew open, and she nodded.

"What's He saying?"

Her forehead crumpled with the effort of getting the words out. "Not how it should be," she said. And then, "Nearby."

She repeated both messages several times to make sure I understood, her face bright with hope. Those profound messages and her confidence in them have comforted me many times since. The suffering of this world is not God's plan for us, not our future. Meanwhile, He's nearby.

Digging Deeper: Psalm 139

Wednesday, June 21

...Fixing our eyes on Jesus, the pioneer and
perfecter of faith.... —Hebrews 12:2 (NIV)

For most of my life, I've been waiting for some
fulfillment. On a grand scale: school graduation,
career gratification, relational satisfaction. In a daily
context: a friend's invitation, a client's confirmation,
a boss's affirmation.

Lately I thought I'd hidden the inclination, but
then I walked through my upstairs, assessing the
pictures hanging on the walls. Could I make room
for a new art print I'd received as a gift? In one room
and then another, I identified an underlying theme
in the illustrated covers of vintage sheet music I'd
framed: one featuring a moonstruck title "When I
Was a Dreamer," another expecting "A Signal from
Mars," a third anticipating a "Farewell."

*Oh my, all these pieces are wistful, wishing for some
desired but not present "other" something or someone,
somewhere over the rainbow.*

Seeing the displayed art in this light, my heart
gravitated toward the bold brick-red tones of the

new print. Called "Sanguine Head of Christ," its bearded visage, the pleading eyes, summoned: *Come to Me. Fix your eyes on Me. I am with you. I will give you rest. Here and now.*

Could I find room for the new print? That was no longer the question. I *wanted* a switch-out. The longing sentiments seemed outdated, no longer edgy, just plain old. Envisioning a new frame of reference, I've replaced "When I Was a Dreamer" with the loving face of Christ.

Lord, help me to look to You, here and now, as the fulfillment of my heart's need. —Evelyn Bence

Digging Deeper: Matthew 11:25–30

Thursday, June 22

OVERCOMING LOSS: Contentment
I forgot what happiness was.
—Lamentations 3:17 (JPS)

My friend Caryn, who already had a concussion, got rear-ended and sustained a second concussion as she was riding to the doctor's office. The compound injury to her brain kept her from reading, listening to music, watching TV, or using the computer, which meant she could not return to work until she was fully healed.

One year later, she was still on disability and falling into a seemingly endless depression. She asked a group of us for help. "Tell me what makes you glad to be alive."

One person answered that she found the world a fascinating place. Another spoke about experiencing moments of being in harmony with the world. A third said she was curious about everything. I thought those were good answers, but after my husband's recent death I was still missing him so much that none of them applied to me. I kept it to myself because I felt that people would think I was lingering too long over my loss.

Caryn wanted answers she could believe in and I wanted to help her, but I wasn't feeling glad to be alive and didn't want to lie. I thought carefully about the fact that we were both in basic survival mode. She was asking us to help her survive, and if I wanted to be honest, I had to look at how I was managing to do it without gladness. "I'm content to be alive," I said. "I know you're impatient to get back to normal, but you can't rush God's time."

"Ah," she said, "I can understand better now."

Over the next few days, I, too, figured out that while I wanted to get back to feeling glad, I couldn't rush God's time either.

Even in my times of desolation, God, I know You are there. —Rhoda Blecker

Digging Deeper: Isaiah 16:10

Surely your goodness and love will follow me all the days of my life, and I will dwell in the house of the Lord forever. —Psalm 23:6 (NIV)

I was awakened by a golden retriever's snout plopping down next to my pillow. Millie. *Oh no,* I thought, *do you have to go out? It's pouring rain.* As if on cue, the rain did a windswept paradiddle on the bedroom window.

Millie was a good dog. She only woke me up in the middle of the night when she had an emergency.

"Just a sec, Mil," I mumbled, grabbing my robe.

Millie preceded me down the stairs but stopped abruptly just two steps from the bottom and stared up at me, then looked down again at the landing by the back door.

"See?" her eyes seemed to say. "It's raining inside."

I did see. The roof had sprung a leak. The entire landing was soaked. How did Millie know this was something important enough to wake me up for?

"Good girl," I said. Her eyes followed me as I snatched one of her dog towels off a hook and sopped up the water. I found a bucket and positioned it under the leak to catch the drips till morning when I could call a roofer.

Millie seemed satisfied with my work, and we headed upstairs. I climbed back under the covers, and Millie lay down on the floor with a contented sigh. Before falling back to sleep, I said a quick prayer.

Thank You for making my dog so vigilant, Lord. Please keep her that way. —Edward Grinnan

Digging Deeper: Psalm 119:62

Saturday, June 24

Our heart is glad in him, because we trust in his holy name. Let your steadfast love, O Lord, be upon us, even as we hope in you. —Psalm 33:21–22 (NRSV)

I'm becoming aware lately of how often I ignore the joy God has strewn in my path. For example, when I reach out to a stranger or someone I don't know well, it tends to be because that person looks downhearted or distressed. A happy or seemingly content person is unlikely to get my attention, and someone who is positively giddy will often cause me to do an inner eye roll and keep walking.

My husband, on the other hand, is drawn to happy people. Charlie will often joke with strangers or make unsolicited comments that seem a bit forward or even silly to me. Occasionally I mention this to him, but he shrugs off my restraint with typical affability. Yet I can't help but notice that no one he greets or jokes with seems at all disconcerted by his approach. Indeed, I can't remember one person who has brushed him off or been offended. Quite the opposite: most people laugh or joke right back with him.

Yesterday, on our walk, we passed a popular outdoor clam and ice cream shack, and a woman was returning to her car, clutching two handfuls of small sundaes and cones. Children, excited and clamoring, were waiting in the car. I don't know what came over me, but I made as if to grab the bounty from her, saying, "Oh, for me? Thank you!" She laughed, the kids shrieked, and Charlie grinned and said, "Good one, Hon."

Come to think of it, I do know what came over me. Sometimes God's gifts are just too good to ignore.

Creator of joy, help me to more clearly and more often recognize all of the opportunities You give me to participate in joy. Amen. —Marci Alborghetti

Digging Deeper: Isaiah 35:10, Luke 4:18–21

Sunday, June 25

Jesus answered, "Everyone who drinks this water will be thirsty again, but whoever drinks from the water that I will give will never be thirsty again. The water that I give will become in those who drink it a spring of water that bubbles up into eternal life." —John 4:13–14 (CEB)

One night, my husband noticed a sharp decrease in water flow when he showered. When I turned on the kitchen faucet the next morning, I got a trickle. Don chalked it up to watering the grass, but turning off the hoses hardly increased the pressure at all.

The repair people immediately spotted the problem: the water table in our well had dropped. The motor was submersed, but part of the pump was out of the water and couldn't generate much flow. The fix was easy: they lowered the pump and motor forty feet so that both sat deeper in the well.

The next morning I read the *Daily Guideposts* devotion, as always, and shut the book without looking up the Digging Deeper Scripture verses. But then I thought about the abundance of water that resulted from fully immersing the pump and wondered, *Am I missing out on the fullness of each day's message?*

The Scripture for that day was Philippians 1:3 (CEB), so I turned to it: "I thank my God every time I mention you in my prayers." It reminded me to give thanks for the faithful prayer warriors in my church. Another day's reading was 1 Peter 5:7 (CEB): "Throw all your anxiety onto him, because he cares about you." They were the perfect words for an upcoming conference that might be divisive.

Not all of the readings speak directly to my specific situations, but digging deeper into the Word each day renews my soul in the same way that my body is refreshed by the abundant flow of water from our well.

Thank You, loving Lord, for refreshing my body and soul through Water and Word. —Penney Schwab

Digging Deeper: Isaiah 43:20–21,
2 Timothy 3:16–17

Monday, June 26

But land that produces thorns and thistles is worthless and is in danger of being cursed....
—Hebrews 6:8 (NIV)

A truckload of horse manure once taught me a valuable lesson in humility.

I had just moved from Boston to Lander, Wyoming, and couldn't wait to start my first vegetable garden. Yet here where cows and horses outnumber humans, I found stores selling twenty-pound bags of manure. I asked my neighbor, "Why pay money for something free for the asking?" He assured me store-bought treated fertilizer was better. I ignored his advice.

So when a friend who raised horses offered me all the manure I wanted, I loaded up a borrowed truck, hauled my freebie home, and spread it on my garden—all twenty-five-by-forty feet of it—smug that I had saved a few dollars. As the weather warmed, my vegetable seeds sprouted in tidy rows, but thistles, prickly thorny weeds, grew in crazy profusion, often smothering my seedlings.

I complained to my rancher-friend about the infestation of stinging weeds. He nodded. "Yup, that can happen when stock grazes in the wrong pasture. Digestive juices don't harm the seeds a bit. I'm afraid you've got yourself some thistles."

For the next seventeen years, I wrestled thistles from my garden. Along the way, I learned that this weed with stinging spines could sprout vertical as well as lateral roots. If I yanked them straight up and out, the remaining root grew sideways. If I chopped them with a hoe, I just made more pieces, which grew into more plants. Interestingly, the locals who purchased the treated fertilizer didn't have my problem.

I now know that the composting process generates enough heat to kill unwanted seeds and bacteria. Well-composted or commercially bagged fertilizer costs little and saves years of frustration. I now also know I need to listen to people wiser than I am.

Creator God, only You could use manure to make me a better person! —Gail Thorell Schilling

Digging Deeper: Proverbs 12:15, 24:30–31

Behold, he that keepeth Israel shall neither slumber nor sleep. —Psalm 121:4 (KJV)

"You were a no-show for your surgery today," a woman informed me via a message on my cell phone. "We do hope everything is okay."

It couldn't be! I was to be scheduled for an operation to remove a facial tumor at a medical center several hundred miles away. But no one had ever telephoned or sent written notification of my appointment date. Now I'd missed it. As a nurse, I knew it was a mistake that had inconvenienced a lot of staff and would cost the institution a significant amount of money.

The next morning, I told my office mate about the mix-up. Julius is a nurse from Nigeria and has an unshakeable faith in God. "Oh, that was no mistake to God," he assured me. Julius turned to the verse he'd read earlier for his devotional time, Psalm 121:4, and inserted my name in place of *Israel*: "'Behold, he that keepeth *Roberta* shall neither slumber nor sleep.'

"You sleep, Roberta, but God never does. He looks after you more than you look after you. There was some reason God didn't want you to have that tumor removed yesterday. I'm sure of it."

I rescheduled my surgery with confidence that when people mess up big time, God is ever on the job.

Dear Lord, I am safe and free from care in any place when You are there. —Roberta Messner

Digging Deeper: Joshua 1:9, Hebrews 13:5

Wednesday, June 28

"I set My bow in the cloud, and it shall be for a sign of a covenant between Me and the earth." —Genesis 9:13 (NAS)

I rode my bicycle eastward on Highway 98 as it hugs the tropical coast of the Florida panhandle. A brilliant sunset was cast across the sky behind me. I grew frustrated because I could not watch the sun descend and continue to pedal. Finally, I stopped and turned. With sudden splendor, the sun exploded as it dipped beneath the sea and cast a dazzling spectrum of color across the expanse. I glimpsed that moment of sun touching earth and sea and sky, and I was delighted.

But as I mounted my bike and resumed my path, my mouth fell open in amazement. Illuminated by the dying rays of the setting sun was a radiant and complete rainbow arcing across the highway. I shouted with glee! I remembered God's ancient promise that life shall be preserved and all will be well. I had seen the beauty of what was behind me and what was before me, all within a magnificent moment.

As I traverse life's journey, I must reflect on the past and approach the future simultaneously. But God is beyond time, not captured by past or present or future. God is ever present, and the words of Jesus are true: "And lo, I am with you always, even to the end of the age" (Matthew 28:20, NAS).

Father, may You fill my days with sunsets and rainbows and the memory of the covenant You have made with us. Amen. —Scott Walker

Digging Deeper: Revelation 1:8

Thursday, June 29

"For the Lord does not see as mortals see; they look on the outward appearance, but the Lord looks on the heart." —1 Samuel 16:7 (NRSV)

Are you a leader? I hope you didn't look at your paycheck or your job description or your bank account or whether your name has ever been in your local newspaper to answer that question. Though it wouldn't be surprising if you did. In our culture, people like me, with "executive" in our job title, are judged to be leaders far more quickly than an assistant or a stay-at-home mom or a retired factory worker.

But decades ago, around a humble table in a restricted black township in South Africa at the height of apartheid, I learned a different definition of leadership. Women and men, with virtually nothing to their names and against all odds, were feeding their children and those of their neighbors, operating schools, building churches. They had no education, no titles, no authority given to them. What they did have was character, determination, humility, relationships—habits of the heart. Not only would they make a difference in their neighborhoods, but they also truly changed the world from the inside out.

We live in a world desperately in need of leaders who, like my long-ago mentors in South Africa, are willing to exercise their God-given gifts to bring good news to the people around them, not for their own profit but for their community.

And so I ask you again: Are you a leader?

I know I am gifted from You and called by You, God. Show me from Your own heart how I might serve You.
—Jeff Japinga

Digging Deeper: Psalm 133, Acts 6:1–7

Friday, June 30

His way is in whirlwind and storm, and the clouds are the dust of his feet. —Nahum 1:3 (NRSV)

"I'm sure it won't rain."

Kate and I gazed above the peaks: a little cloudy but nothing unusual for early evening in the Sierra

Nevada. We were backpacking with the kids, camped at a high-altitude lake, to experience God in the wilderness.

The clouds thickened. A few raindrops speckled the granite around our campsite. "Frances, Benjamin, come closer to the tents!" Kate called. The kids jogged back from the lake, where they'd been playing.

The rain grew steadier. "Okay, everyone inside," I said. Frances and Kate ducked into one tent. Benjamin and I crawled into the other.

Suddenly our voices were drowned out. Thunder boomed and rolled. Rain poured onto the tent. The rainfly sagged. A few drips plopped onto our sleeping bags.

"Daddy!" cried Benjamin. I drew him close. The rain turned to hail. Wind shook the tent. I didn't voice my fear: that the hail might puncture the fabric; that the tent might collapse. The Sierras in summer are usually placid—until they're not. It can snow heavily at high altitude in August. Gale-force winds can snap tent poles like matchsticks.

The hail crescendoed to a roar. "Let's pray!" I shouted. In as calm a voice as I could muster, I prayed for the storm to end, for God to keep us safe.

At last, the hail slackened and turned to rain. The rain slowed to a drizzle and stopped. I let go of Benjamin, and we unzipped the tent and peered out at the clearing sky. Kate and Frances were peering out too. We grinned at one another, relieved but also awed by the storm's sudden fury.

God in the wilderness. We'd experienced Him, all right: His power, His mercy, the power of His mercy.

Your power will be sufficient for me today, Lord.
—Jim Hinch

Digging Deeper: Exodus 15:1–18

IN GOD'S HANDS

1 _____

2 _____

3 _____

4 _____

5 _____

6 _____

7 _____

8 _____

9 _____

10 _____

11 _____

12 _____

13 _____

14 _____

15 _____

16 _____

17 _____

18 _____

19 _____

20 _____

21 _____

22 _____

23 _____

24 _____

25 _____

26 _____

27 _____

28 _____

29 _____

30 _____

JULY

*The name of the Lord is a fortified tower;
the righteous run to it and are safe.*

—Proverbs 18:10 (NIV)

Therefore encourage one another and build each other up.... —1 Thessalonians 5:11 (NIV)

Janice, who runs an alterations shop out of her home, has helped me immensely over the years. So I was stricken to learn that her husband had passed away a month before without my knowing. I found out about Ed's death when I dropped off a skirt to be hemmed.

"I want to do *something*," I said. "How can I help you right at this moment?"

"Oh, nothing," Janice said. "It's just that it's so lonely these days, especially in the mornings. The worst thing of all is walking by his empty hospital bed in the living room."

I learned that the facility that issued Ed's bed still hadn't picked it up despite multiple phone calls to request the service. Every time Janice looked at the hulking piece of equipment, she saw her husband struggling in those terrible final days.

"Could I take care of that bed for you?" I asked. As soon as I spoke those words, Janice's features transformed from dismay to utter relief.

I'd often heard that one of the best things to do when someone loses a loved one is to propose a specific deed. But never had I witnessed the profound effect of such a gesture. In the future, I'm going to think beyond the usual flowers and food and probe for a practical expression of empathy, like the simple suggestion of returning a hospital bed.

Help me to make my love visible, dear Lord, through deeds that go straight to the heart.
—Roberta Messner

Digging Deeper: Proverbs 12:25, Ephesians 4:29, Hebrews 10:24–25

Sunday, July 2

All Scripture is inspired by God and profitable for teaching, for reproof, for correction, for training in righteousness. —2 Timothy 3:16 (NAS)

A remarkable thing happened to me this morning at the park near my house. I sat down at one of several tables under a large shaded shelter and saw a nice leather Bible on the table next to mine with a small card stuck between the pages. In neat block letters someone had written, "Free Bible."

Several minutes later a man walked up and sat down at the table. A park maintenance man, he was hot, apparently, and stopping to rest. He picked up the Bible, read the card, and blurted, "I always need one of these!"

Our eyes met, and he began to talk. He related how he had been an alcoholic since his teenage years and smoked three packs of cigarettes a day.

Eight years ago he realized he needed to conquer his addictions or die. Smiling, he said, "I picked up a Bible one day and just held it. Didn't know where to read. I closed my eyes and said, 'God, help me help myself. Please help me!' And, you know, I haven't had another drink. Can't explain it. Shouldn't have happened. But I never drank since. Got married and I'm buying a house now. I think I'll take this Bible with me. I never have enough."

The Bible is not magic. But this man had discovered that God's Spirit speaks and heals through Scripture, which came alive in front of me today.

Dear Father, thank You for Scripture that guides, inspires, consoles, heals, and feeds the spiritually hungry. Amen. —Scott Walker

Digging Deeper: Psalms 1:2, 119:105; Romans 10:17

Monday, July 3

So be content with who you are, and don't put on airs. God's strong hand is on you; he'll promote you at the right time. Live carefree before God; he is most careful with you. —1 Peter 5:6–7 (MSG)

I think that I can almost see God from here as I lie on my back in this grassy field. I have given myself twenty minutes to remain here, to simply lie here and do nothing of any value whatsoever.

Please don't tell my employer; it's the middle of the workday. Please don't look at the floors in my house that I'm supposed to be vacuuming. E-mail? Phone? I have left those devices in my office. They may be dinging and ringing; I don't know. There's the dog, too, probably waiting to be walked. Never mind. Not now. Things will get done later.

I hear a bird. Wait; I hear two. And now I see them flitting back and forth. Are they talking with each other? *Kee-kaw, kee-kaw.*

I've been here awhile. I know, because an inchworm has made it onto my pants leg. It is the color of the grass. How many others like it are all around me that I cannot see?

This day—this quiet moment of twenty minutes lying in the grass—I will pray for small creatures such as this inchworm, songbirds, and me. I'm too relaxed to worry. There are no "worry prayers" coming from me on this day, at this moment—only thanks for what has been given.

For the very gift of life today, I thank You, God.
—Jon Sweeney

Digging Deeper: Psalm 150:1, 6

Tuesday, July 4

Now the Lord is the Spirit, and where the Spirit of the Lord is, there is freedom. —2 Corinthians 3:17 (NIV)

My daughter Kristen and I headed over to a Fourth of July celebration in Fontainebleau State Park, situated on the north shore of Lake Pontchartrain. We spent the day listening to Cajun fiddlers, sharing a fried shrimp po'boy, and drinking cold, sweet tea while watching kids get tiny red, white, and blue flags painted on their cheeks.

"You know," I said to Kristen, "I'm free to vote, free to worship, and free to travel. I really do appreciate my freedom." She nodded. But it wasn't until later that I was reminded of a much greater freedom.

We were at the beach, waiting for the fireworks to begin. Boats were anchored in the shallow water, and one caught my eye. "Look!" I exclaimed, pointing to a boat festooned with hundreds of red, white, and blue flags.

A man seated nearby said proudly, "That's my boat!"

"It's awesome!" I replied.

"I love decorating it, though not just for the freedoms that come to mind for most. I had a rough childhood. I quit school as a teen. I used drugs. Then I got hired to do some repairs on a little church. It changed my life. I found Jesus Christ there—and a freedom from my sin."

At that moment, fireworks burst overhead. The man looked up, smiling. "And *that's* really something to celebrate."

Thank You, Father, for the priceless gift of freedom from sin and death that You give us through Your son, Jesus Christ. Amen. —Melody Bonnette Swang

Digging Deeper: Romans 6:18, Galatians 5:13

Wednesday, July 5

BEAUTY FROM ASHES
The Next Right Thing

"Eat something, because you have a difficult road ahead of you." —1 Kings 19:7 (CEB)

We were exhausted. The men of our family had moved Katie's heavy stuff into her new apartment and had gone home. The two of us sat in her den, surrounded by unpacked boxes. She looked at me, blinking back tears. I read her thoughts: *What do I do next, Mom, now that I'm getting a divorce?*

I didn't know the answer; I only knew that I didn't want to leave her alone. "Want me to make the bed? Set up the bathroom?"

"No, thanks. I'll do it later."

"Want me to spend the night?"

She shook her head.

Then an idea came: Katie needed a hot meal, nourishment. "Let's go out to eat," I said.

"I can't eat."

"We could rest for a few minutes."

"You know, that sounds nice. To relax and be still."

Twenty minutes later, we sat inside a candlelit booth at a nearby restaurant. We studied the menu, pretending to be hungry, and ordered the same thing: steak, baked potato, salad. Then something amazing happened. When our food arrived, we did the *next right thing*. We laughed and talked and ate.

"Mom, I cleaned my plate!" Miraculously, color had returned to Katie's cheeks. The unmistakable sparkle of possibility glowed in her eyes.

"You sure did. You're going to be okay."

**Father, when we don't know what to do,
You show us the next right thing…and the next.**
—Julie Garmon

Digging Deeper: 2 Corinthians 12:9,
1 Thessalonians 5:18

Thursday, July 6

**Dear brothers, warn those who are lazy, comfort those who are frightened, take tender care of those who are weak, and be patient with everyone.
—1 Thessalonians 5:14 (TLB)**

When my brother Joe, sister-in-law Linda, husband Jack, and I visited Ireland for three weeks, one of my favorite stops was Giants Causeway near Belfast in Northern Ireland. Forty thousand basalt columns from one foot to thirty-nine feet tall stand there, the result of an ancient volcanic eruption. Most of the columns are about six inches in diameter and are hexagonal in shape, although many have four, five, seven, or eight sides.

When we arrived, I could hardly wait to start climbing the jagged steps formed by the columns. Some led to a high perch where I'd be able to see a spectacular view of the Irish Sea. But with arthritis in both knees I was always in pain, and Jack was three months away from a complete knee replacement. So when we arrived at the site, he plopped down on a bench to wait for the rest of us. I wanted to climb those columns so badly that I started without thinking. Immediately, the pain slowed me down.

Just then Linda grabbed my hand. "Come on, I'll help you," she said. Together we struggled to the lookout point. At the top, I sat down on a smooth spot to enjoy the magnificent view of the sea.

Without Linda's strong hands and sweet helpful spirit, I would have missed one of Ireland's most amazing sights. From then on, when the walking was iffy or involved a bit of a climb, I grabbed Jack's hand and encouraged him at a slower pace.

Father, help me to be the one to offer my hand to anyone who needs a little boost. And thank You for the glorious places You have created on earth for us to enjoy. —Patricia Lorenz

Digging Deeper: Acts 20:28, 31–32; 1 Thessalonians 5:15–18

Friday, July 7

We are the clay, and thou our potter....
—Isaiah 64:8 (KJV)

When we first visited Zimbabwe, my greatest hope was that we might find the money to feed a few starving kids. If anyone had told me what would evolve, I would have laughed and said, "Impossible!"

House homeless children; buy a farm; create a community outreach that gives food, animals, seeds, and new farming techniques to an expanding rural area. Save the lives of abandoned babies; create a school lunch program for two thousand students; see once homeless children through school and into college; and build a preschool. "Find somebody else, God," I would have said.

The interesting thing is that God asks, but it's up to us to answer. He waits for our little *yes,* and when it comes, He turns it into an act that is far beyond our imagining.

Take Zimbabwe. Elizabeth Gold, a friend at Guideposts Books, said, "Write your story." That's all God needed. He touched hundreds of people with that article, and together their *yeses* became the foundation of a project that has saved the lives of countless children, lifted rural women living in mud huts, empowered unemployed men to provide for their families, encouraged thousands of children to go to school, and, indeed, changed the future of an entire rural community where three-year-olds now attend preschool. And on we go.

Life is quite a ride, don't you think? When asked, all we have to do is offer our little *yes*. God is with us and takes care of the rest.

Father, *yes!* —Pam Kidd

Digging Deeper: Proverbs 8:34, James 1:19

Saturday, July 8

A generous person will prosper; whoever refreshes others will be refreshed. —Proverbs 11:25 (NIV)

I said good-bye to one of my best friends. As Claire's car pulled out of my driveway, she embarked on her journey to a new life in California. I watched her Illinois license plate fade into the dusk. Emptiness crept across my chest while evening sucked the warmth out of the pavement.

This morning my phone rang. "Hello?"

"Logan, it's Kassi." I could tell from her muffled voice that my friend had been crying.

"Is everything all right?"

"No." Her voice caught. "My boyfriend and I broke up. I really thought he was the one, and now I…I need a friend."

I could have given her cliché words of sympathy, a quick verbal condolence. I could have just taken care of my own hurt. But I knew what I needed to do.

"What's your favorite Christmas movie and pizza topping?" It was an odd question, especially in the middle of summer, but Kassi didn't hesitate.

"*Elf* and pepperoni."

"Can you be here in an hour?"

Kassi and I spent the afternoon sprawled out on a picnic blanket in my living room. Sometimes we watched the movie. Sometimes I paused it while we talked or she cried. But somewhere in the middle of it all, the ache in my chest got a little bit smaller.

A couple of hours later, when we'd emptied the pizza box and gone through the tissues, it was time for her to go.

"I knew exactly whom to call," she said. "Thanks for taking care of me."

"No, Kass. Thank you."

Lord, thank You for pizza, Christmas in July, and friendship. —Logan Eliasen

Digging Deeper: Proverbs 11:24, 2 Corinthians 9:6

Sunday, July 9

"Why were you searching for me?" he asked. "Didn't you know I had to be in my Father's house?" —Luke 2:49 (NIV)

Visions of TV news headlines danced through my head as I frantically searched the church grounds yet again. My three-year-old son and his best friend, Joseph, were missing.

I picked up the phone and fingered the keypad, wondering how long I should wait before calling 911. The boys couldn't have gone far, unless... Well, I didn't even want to contemplate the freeway just three hundred yards away, the big city full of big-city problems that sprawled only yards from the quiet churchyard where I stood.

Finally, after a half hour of searching, it dawned on me to pray. "Lord, help me to find my son." The whispered plea seemed almost futile, as if it couldn't be enough, especially when things seemed so dire.

But then sheer relief came. "We found them! They were in the prayer chapel."

The prayer chapel? What in the world were Will and Joseph doing in the prayer chapel?

The story about Mary and Joseph losing Jesus on their way back from Passover flitted into my mind. They had also lost their son. They had panicked, searched, looked, done everything in their power to find Jesus instead of simply turning to the One Who has each of His children safe in His arms.

Why had I been in such a frenzy to do everything I could do to find my son, when the One Who knew exactly where he was hiding was just a prayer away? Why is it so hard for me to learn to rely on God when I so desperately need His help?

Father God, help me to turn to You first instead of trying to rely on myself. Amen. —Erin MacPherson

Digging Deeper: Psalms 20:1, 62:8

OVERCOMING LOSS
Healing through Generosity
"Deal loyally and compassionately with one another." —Zechariah 7:9 (JPS)

After my husband, Keith, died, I didn't think I could give away anything of his. I was wrapping his shirts around me to replace his embrace. I wanted to keep everything because the way things were before he died was the way things were supposed to be. I couldn't bear the thought of empty racks in the closet we shared and feared I would break down. In addition to the shirts, I was also wearing his pullover fleece, his rain jacket, and his wool socks. I became determined not to part with any of his stuff, even what I couldn't wear, like his suits or his jeans.

Then someone new began posting in one of the newsgroups I frequent online. He was from Oklahoma, and he and his wife had opened their house to a homeless family. He mentioned that he played the cello and had just been accepted into a local orchestra. "I'll have to see if I can find a tuxedo that doesn't cost too much," he wrote.

I didn't think twice before posting back: "What size do you wear? My husband's tuxedo is available, and I could send it to you for the cost of postage."

We worked out that it might fit him, and I felt not a moment's hesitation before finding the cummerbund, packaging it all up, and sending it. Alterations for the tux were minor, I'm told, but for me it was a huge change.

Thank You for making it possible for me to begin to heal, dear Lord. —Rhoda Blecker

Digging Deeper: Psalm 112:4–9

Tuesday, July 11

You have fixed all the bounds of the earth; you made summer and winter. —Psalm 74:17 (NRSV)

Why do people love summer? Especially in New York City, where it means sultry heat and sticky humidity?

I grew up in California, where humidity is unknown and summer means warm days, cool nights, and no bugs. Now that's a season to rejoice in!

"Let's go to the pool," I said to the kids. Kate was working, and we had the whole afternoon to ourselves. I packed a suit and towel, and we boarded the crosstown bus. Soon the kids were swimming and splashing around. I couldn't resist joining them. We stayed until just before the pool closed.

Inching home on the bus, we watched thunderheads gather. By the time we got to our street, the sky was almost black, the air tense. "Quick, before it rains!" I called. We sprinted to the door as the first fat drops fell. Inside, we huddled at the window, listening to rolls and cracks of thunder. Rain formed a river in the street.

"Wow, it never rains like this in California!" Frances exclaimed. "I love it!"

I had to admit she was right. Nor were trees and gardens in California so lush and green. Or the streets so alive with people reveling in the rain.

"The eyes of all look to you, and you give them their food in due season," says the Psalmist (145:15, NRSV). That's true. When my eyes look to God, every season is a gift—even summer in New York City.

Each new day, each new season, I have new reasons to thank You, Lord. —Jim Hinch

Digging Deeper: 1 Chronicles 16:28–34

Wednesday, July 12

"...When he had found one pearl of great price, went and sold all that he had and bought it."
—Matthew 13:46 (NKJV)

I had just promised my wife I would be more careful with our charge card when that vow was sorely tested. I was in a secondhand shop, and a large landscape painting took my breath away. It featured a field of red poppies with tall poplar trees in the background. I was transfixed, pacing back and forth, salivating over this masterwork.

Then I looked at the price. I would have to charge it. So began a conversation with my conscience: *Dan, don't do this. You shouldn't spend money you don't have for something you don't really need.*

I know, but this painting is so me—two of my favorite plants on one glorious canvas!

You are just infatuated, Dan. You will forget about it, if you just walk away.

My eyes fell. *I suppose you're right.* I started for the front door, praying as I went: "Lord, would it spoil some vast, eternal plan if I bought this one little ole painting?"

By the front door was a picture of a farmhouse with the words from Proverbs 24:3–4 (GNT): "Homes are built on the foundation of wisdom and understanding. Where there is knowledge, the rooms are furnished with valuable, beautiful things."

My study is now furnished with a valuable, beautiful painting of poppies and poplars. Some things in life are more important than thrift, like the inspiration this masterpiece, which I will pass along to my grandchildren when I die, gives me every day. And that time could be soon, if my wife does not let me back in the house.

"Honey, it's cold out here!"

Lord, help me to know when to be frugal and when to be "foolish." —Daniel Schantz

Digging Deeper: Proverbs 21:17–21, Matthew 26:6–10

Thursday, July 13

PARENTING ANEW: "You've Got the Stick"

Do not let any unwholesome talk come out of your mouths, but only what is helpful for building others up according to their needs, that it may benefit those who listen. —Ephesians 4:29 (NIV)

When my grandson Logan came to live with us, he was just three years old.

As my husband, Chuck, and I struggled with adjusting to having a little one in our home, our frustrations came out in our tone with each other. Part of the problem was making assumptions about who would watch Logan, bathe him, and wake him up. For example, I expected Chuck to watch him while I cooked dinner. Chuck expected me to watch him when he did yard work.

We wanted to give Logan a peaceful home, so we held our tongues to keep from arguing. As a result, this led to further misunderstanding. The harmony in our marriage was coming unraveled—something we definitely didn't want, either for us or for Logan. We realized we needed to improve our communication.

One day, out of the blue, Chuck said, "You've got the stick. I don't have the stick anymore."

I looked at him like he was crazy. "What?"

Chuck, retired from the US Air Force, explained this military jargon. "When a jet fighter pilot is going to give control of the plane to his copilot, he shakes the control stick and says, 'You've got the stick,' which means you've got control of the plane now. So what I meant was that I'm not going to be watching Logan now. It's your turn."

A simple solution, but we learned how to share the work by better communicating with each other, keeping our home safely on course.

Lord, may the words of our mouths and the meditations of our hearts be pleasing in Your sight, so we can demonstrate what a godly home should be.
—Marilyn Turk

Digging Deeper: Psalm 19:14, 1 Peter 3:10

For I consider that the sufferings of this present time are not worth comparing with the glory that is to be revealed to us. —Romans 8:18 (ESV)

My wife, Emily, and I spent our first two years of marriage living in a studio apartment. We loved being married, but sharing one room was not fun. At times we had no privacy and no space to do separate activities or make our own schedules. Being newlyweds brought enough challenges, such as learning to navigate our relationships with our in-laws, how to manage our money together, and law school and summer jobs. We certainly made it work, but it would have been nice to have a little extra acreage!

Just a week after I graduated, we packed up our belongings, of which we had far too many for our single closet to handle, and brought everything to a beautiful one-bedroom apartment just down the street. The night after we'd moved, Emily and I went out to dinner. As we were strolling home, we passed the old place. "Thank God we never have to step back in there again," I said.

Emily nodded. "But, hey, we'll look back on our tiny apartment and smile about when we were young and poor. It was the place where we learned to be married."

I could see she was right. I didn't want to go back, but I smiled when I thought of it. Through that little bit of unpleasantness and hardship, we learned how to transform from two people who happened to live together into a true partnership, independent but entwined.

Thank You, Lord, for the pleasures of life You have bestowed on us and also for the pains that help us grow. —Sam Adriance

Digging Deeper: Genesis 2:24, James 1:2–4

Saturday, July 15

Show me the right path, O Lord; point out the road for me to follow. Lead me by your truth and teach me, for you are the God who saves me. All day long I put my hope in you. —Psalm 25:4–5 (NLT)

"Ms. Ganshert, please come to the cash registers. Ms. Ganshert, please come to the cash registers."

It happened so fast, I barely had time to panic. One second, my son was lagging behind me and a friend, hiding down various aisles as he goofed around. The next, he was gone.

I had barely called out his name a second time when the announcement came over the intercom.

I rushed to the front and, sure enough, there he was standing beside a cashier with big tears in his eyes. As soon as he saw me, he ran over and hugged my waist. "I got lost!"

"Brogan," I said, hugging him back, "I told you that you have to stay by Mommy's side. As long as you're by my side, I promise you will never ever get lost."

The words left an impression.

Recently, I'd been struggling with some big decisions to make as a family, and I was terrified of stepping outside of God's plans. When I spoke those words to my son, it was as if God was speaking them to me.

He's not some aloof God wishing me good luck from afar; He is a loving Father. If I'm on my knees in prayer, if I'm studying His Word and begging Him to guide my steps, if I'm staying close to His side, He isn't going to let me get lost. I'm becoming more convinced of that when my heart's desire seeks His.

Thank You, Lord, for being close. Help me to remain in Your will today. I know from Your Word that this is a prayer You love to answer. —Katie Ganshert

Digging Deeper: Psalms 9:10, 27:8; Isaiah 45:19

Sunday, July 16

The Spirit and the bride say, "Come!" And let the one who hears say, "Come!" Let the one who is thirsty come.... —Revelation 22:17 (NIV)

A big storm had passed through town and knocked out the power. I was searching for a gas station, so I could fill my gas containers to run my generator to keep my refrigerator going. I passed by church, surprised to see cars in the parking lot. A large piece of plywood was propped up, spray-painted with the words *Come As You Are.*

I glanced down at my jogging pants and T-shirt. *Not today,* I thought. I drove past the entrance. Then, I turned the car around. *Maybe I can sneak into the back pew.*

There were no lights, no air-conditioning, and no microphones, yet the church was full. Wearing shorts, T-shirts, and tennis shoes, unshaven, and without hair styled or makeup just so, people had shown up.

I stood in the doorway and looked around. Despite no one wearing their Sunday best, the morning light streaming in through the stained-glass windows gave everyone a beautiful golden glow. I sat down and breathed deeply, feeling my worries disappear.

A fellow church member slid in next to me. "Isn't it wonderful?" she whispered. "Life doesn't have to be perfect and we don't have to look perfect to come to the Lord."

I nodded and reached over to squeeze her hand as we joined others in song:

Just as I am, without one plea
But that Thy blood was shed for me
And that Thou did bidst me come to Thee
O Lamb of God, I come.
("Just As I Am" by Charlotte Elliott)
—Melody Bonnette Swang

Digging Deeper: Isaiah 1:18, Joel 2:32

Monday, July 17

Finally, beloved, whatever is true, whatever is honorable, whatever is just, whatever is pure, whatever is pleasing, whatever is commendable, if there is any excellence and if there is anything worthy of praise, think about these things.
—Philippians 4:8 (NRSV)

"We'll get a cupcake afterward," I told Micah as we parked in front of the learning center. I'd resorted to bribing my daughter with a confection from the shop next door in order to get her to attend tutoring.

After driving half an hour each way from Edmond to Oklahoma City, four times a week, and waiting more than an hour, I wanted the reward as much as she did.

Micah needed to sharpen her math skills. With algebra looming on the horizon, I didn't want her to fall behind. I tried to remain upbeat but, truth be told, I was sick of driving her there and waiting. It was no way to spend the summer. We'd postponed our vacation to devote eight weeks to intensive math studies with the hope she'd catch up. Even then, the tutor warned that Micah might need to come during the school year to keep on track.

After errands, I went inside. In the lobby, on the bulletin board, was a white sign with red letters: *You get what you focus on.*

The words sunk in. I'd concentrated so hard on hating to come here that I'd missed the possibilities: *How awesome that this business exists! How fortunate that Micah has time to catch up! What luck having the best cupcakes in town right next door!*

I smiled and leaned back in my chair, thankful for my private tutorial.

Lord, help me see the possibilities in all situations instead of focusing on the negatives.
—Stephanie Thompson

Digging Deeper: Colossians 3:2, 1 Thessalonians 5:18

**I had fainted, unless I had believed to see the goodness of the Lord in the land of the living.
—Psalm 27:13 (KJV)**

A preacher I know says, "Be patient. Special orders take more time." I'd like to believe that I am patient, but the truth is I don't like to wait. So when I think of things to thank God for, making me wait is not very high on the list.

Right now I have that airport feeling where I'm excited about going someplace; where I've rushed to pack and get to the airport, only to find myself stalled by things I cannot see or control. Long security lines frustrate me. I don't complain because I know people are doing their jobs and working for my good. I smile and take deep breaths, but I'm thinking, *Hurry up!*

And that's how my life feels right now. I have no control and I'm waiting for career breakthroughs for myself and for my children; for godly spouses for my children and me; for grandchildren; for paychecks; for a house; for the perfect life!

So this morning as I pray, I don't like the thought that comes to me: *Thank God for waiting.* Tears come to my eyes. I am like a pouty child. I don't want to do it, but I pray anyway because I know the Lord loves me. And if I'm waiting, I know it is for my good.

Lord, I trust You. Thank You for making me
wait on You. —Sharon Foster

Digging Deeper: Psalms 27:14, 37:34, 69:6;
Proverbs 8:34

Wednesday, July 19

Give us this day our daily bread.
—Matthew 6:11 (KJV)

My husband, John, and I stopped in Allentown,
Pennsylvania, to have dinner with an army buddy
of his. The son of Russian immigrants, Kolya had
moved back to his parents' home after World
War II.

Dinner began with a spicy cabbage and onion
soup. "This is delicious!" John said. "What is the…?"

"*Yehst!*" The word exploded from Kolya's father
like a gunshot.

"That means eat," Kolya whispered.

Next Kolya's mother brought out a platter of little
dumplings stuffed with chopped eggs. "You'll have to
give me the recipe for…," I began.

"*Yehst!*"

Again that explosive syllable. Kolya's father
scowled at me, then turned back to his plate. There
was fried chicken, boiled potatoes, a lovely chocolate
pie—all of it eaten in tomblike silence.

"I should have warned you about my father," Kolya apologized as he walked us to our car. "Food is kind of sacred to him. Talking at meals is like chatting in church." In the village his father was from, people starved to death every winter. "Summers too, when the Czar's troops came through. He told me he went to bed hungry every night of his childhood."

I thought about my own childhood, how I complained when my mother made me finish everything on my plate. I thought about the billions who were hungry that very moment. A tomblike silence? No! A sacred silence. An acknowledgment of the supply that I'd always taken for granted.

Thank You, Father, for food! Show me how to respond to the world's hunger. —Elizabeth Sherrill

Digging Deeper: Matthew 25:34–35

Thursday, July 20

Now hope does not disappoint, because the love of God has been poured out in our hearts by the Holy Spirit who was given to us. —Romans 5:5 (NKJV)

We're gathered in the backyard. The smaller boys are bathing our Labrador pup in a plastic pool. The water they've hauled from the house is too warm, so they grab the hose. When the spray hits the water's surface it makes frothy, white bubbles.

Rugby, our pup, dives under and bolts out the other side. This looks like fun, and the younger boys climb in. Their laughter hangs in the thick summer air. My husband and the older boys stand by. They're captivated too.

I sit still for a moment and appreciate the goodness of it all. Four months before, our beloved greyhound, Sissy, passed away. There were days of tears, mournful nights, boys with hearts that longed for something they couldn't have.

But things have changed. The wound has begun to heal. Now our home brims with crazy, playful, new-puppy life.

Our family continues to wrestle with some tough issues. There's been struggle and strife and a shadow that seems to never move. But I believe that one day it will. Just like our time of grief, this time of hardship will pass.

"Look, Mom," someone shouts, "it's a man spa!"

My two little sons are wearing bubble beards. They recline, and just shoulders and smiles poke above the water. The puppy is between them. He has a bubble beard too.

A carefree day in the sun—it shines with every hope.

Lord, thank You that even the hardest seasons come to an end. Amen. —Shawnelle Eliasen

Digging Deeper: Psalm 30:5,
Song of Solomon 2:11–13

Friday, July 21

For our citizenship is in heaven, from which we also eagerly wait for the Savior, the Lord Jesus Christ. —Philippians 3:20 (NKJV)

The coffee plantation sloped down ahead of us on the flanks of a mountain on Hawaii's majestic Big Island. The turquoise Pacific Ocean spread out in the distance while a misty cloud protected coffee berries and our heads from the midday sun. Conditions were perfect here, our tour guide explained. Volcanic soil, daily cloud cover, ideal elevation, and the grower's care conspired to produce the world's finest coffee beans.

Our family sipped their sample cups. We had to agree. It was the best coffee we'd ever tasted: smooth, rich, flavorful, not a hint of bitterness. The guide bragged about winning both local and international coffee "cupping" contests with these beans. Margi and I were hooked. We splurged on a pricey bag of coffee beans to take home to California.

A couple of weeks later, we broke it open for our own special experience. We ground the beans, poured them into the French press, and added water. Four minutes later, we were sipping memories of Hawaii. It was a disappointment.

The coffee was still *good,* but it wasn't *as* good. Not as strong, perhaps. Not brewed by the exact method as those sample cups that won our hearts.

"It's not quite the same," Margi said. "Not as good as being there." I nodded my agreement.

Later that evening, I read my Bible, only to be reminded that nothing will ever taste as good here as it will in that perfect land I'm journeying toward. And I'm not talking about the Big Island.

Heavenly Father, though life on earth offers its blessings, nothing compares to the inexpressible delight of being home some day with You. Help me keep my eyes fixed on heaven, even as I enjoy tastes of Your grace here on earth. —Bill Giovannetti

Digging Deeper: Ephesians 2:11–13

Saturday, July 22

The Lord is my strength and my shield; my heart trusts in him, and he helps me. My heart leaps for joy, and with my song I praise him. —Psalm 28:7 (NIV)

There was a stack of them. Bills, bills, bills.

I started making payments, able to see our bank balance actually shrinking in real time online. *Can we put off this bill? Can that one wait till the next pay period? Should we just pay a partial amount on our credit card?*

Millions of Americans go through this every month. Most don't have the options my wife, Julee, and I do, even if we were short on breathing room this month. But nothing causes me greater anxiety than finances. And I know enough by now to say that the existence of great anxiety is a very reliable indicator of a lack of faith and trust.

God promised us manna from heaven. He didn't promise us cushy bank balances. In fact, Jesus seems to have frowned on excessive wealth. I detest feeling like this about money, but I dislike it more that I feel this way. Where is my trust? Where is my faith that I will be watched over and loved? Why does that faith disappear when it comes to finances even though God has always provided one way or another?

I got to the final bill. We weren't broke. We might have to cut back on a few things for a while. What I couldn't afford to cut back on, though, was my faith.

Lord, in a perverse way, I put money ahead of You when I lose sleep over bills. Yes, I have financial obligations that must be honored. But before them and all things earthly, I must honor You with my trust.
—Edward Grinnan

Digging Deeper: 2 Samuel 7:28, Psalm 37:3

Sunday, July 23

Wisdom cries out in the street; in the squares she raises her voice. At the busiest corner she cries out; at the entrance of the city gates, she speaks.
—Proverbs 1:20–21 (NRSV)

The girl was about seven years old and dressed in a sweet cornflower-blue dress with ribbons in her blonde hair. She'd been annoying during the entire Mass.

Clearly, her grandmother was at her wits' end trying to control the child without losing her temper. The girl had no such concern about keeping her own temper as she whined, repeatedly dropped her prayer book, asked for gum, pouted, mocked the choir, and yanked the ribbons out of her hair. The poor woman kept glancing at the rest of us with embarrassment. I *almost* felt sorry for her, if only she'd taken the child outside.

For what seemed the twentieth time, the grandmother bent low over her charge and urgently whispered yet another admonition. The little one shouted back, "Don't tell me what to do!"

With a collective gasp, we all had the same thought: *What a thing to say in church!*

Then again, wasn't she saying what we all say to God?

The mail includes a solicitation for a missionary group. *Spread My Word,* Jesus asks. "Don't tell me what to do!"

A local soup kitchen needs canned goods and pasta. *Feed the hungry,* Jesus asks. "Don't tell me what to do!"

Your spouse has a bad day, but so have you. *Love one another,* Jesus asks. "Don't tell me what to do!"

Your neighbor knocks over your garbage bin—again. *Forgive repeatedly,* Jesus asks. "Don't tell me what to do!"

The little girl and I were right where we were supposed to be this Sunday.

Jesus, please teach me to be more patient with others as You are with me. Amen. —Marci Alborghetti

Digging Deeper: Mark 10:13–16

Monday, July 24

Behold, children are a gift of the Lord....
—Psalm 127:3 (NAS)

"Why rent if I can own?" became our son's motto. Elba and I didn't take Paul too seriously because he needed time to save. Unbeknownst to us, he had already explored his options and found a property he was serious about purchasing.

On the one hand, we were happy for him. And I won't lie: the idea of reclaiming the finished basement as my man cave made me happy. On the other hand, feelings of concern flooded us. We had worried about Paul since his birth. He was born with medical complications and already had four corrective surgeries. The doctors had given him only a 50 percent chance of survival, but Paul had beaten the odds. Years later he was involved in a horrific car accident. Miraculously, he again overcame the odds.

We experienced feelings of loss, concern, and separation as Paul pursued his dream of owning a home. Elba especially struggled with her baby leaving. But once the realization that Paul needed to go sank in, we knew it was time to let go and let God. We would tell each other, "We raise them in love and then send them out in faith."

Our home without Paul has been different, but the nest doesn't feel as empty as we thought it would. He and his sister still find their way back home for a good meal and love from their mom and dad.

Lord, thank You for the gift of parenting and the spiritual lessons we learn through our children.
—Pablo Diaz

Digging Deeper: Proverbs 17:6, 20:7

Tuesday, July 25

Send me your light and your faithful care, let them lead me.... —Psalm 43:3 (NIV)

Charlotte redeemed a long overdue high school graduation present: a mother-daughter trip abroad.

One week in London and a second, I suggested, somewhere less overwhelming. Charlotte consulted guidebooks and chose York.

London was stressful, because while I liked to wander around and happen upon delights, Charlotte had a rigid schedule of sights, restaurants, and stores. Worse, upon arriving at Heathrow Airport, she announced she was the navigator. "You always get lost," she explained, which is true.

It was a misery new to me: in the tow of a sightseeing despot half my age. I felt as my mother-in-law probably did, being propelled through supermarkets and doctors' offices in her last years. "This way!" I roared in those days, seeking to combat her unwillingness and deafness simultaneously. Then I'd take her elbow to hurry her along. Now remembering my mother-in-law, I felt more remorseful.

York was a relief after London. Charlotte and I sat in parks and tearooms, friendly again, her crocheting, me reading. Then it was back to the airport and home.

Heathrow Airport was on high alert when we left London. I had no idea where to go or stand but somehow Charlotte did. What an unexpected sense of calmness to be steered by my elbow through the chaos to our gate. I hoped—and somehow knew—that my mother-in-law had felt taken care of, too, in the end.

Father, take my elbow; lead me in the right way.
—Patty Kirk

Digging Deeper: Genesis 50:15–21, Romans 8:28

Wednesday, July 26

"Or what woman, having ten silver coins, if she loses one coin, does not light a lamp and sweep the house and seek diligently until she finds it?"
—Luke 15:8 (RSV)

This story is family lore. About fifteen years ago I came home from work to find my wife in tears, inconsolable. I braced myself for the worst news possible, trying to imagine whose funeral we'd be attending.

Between sobs, Sandee said, "I lost my engagement ring!"

"Oh, thank God," I said. "I thought it was something serious."

This, it turns out, was *not* the thing to say at that moment. Apparently, Sandee had taken off her ring for an instant, only to hear it clink down the basement steps. We turned the house upside down, even brought in a metal detector ... nothing.

Last week I was not thinking about our engagement; my mind was engaged in something less positive. I had been redoing our basement with every spare second and not feeling particularly appreciated, especially by my bride of thirty-plus years. It wasn't a fight; more like a slow burn on its way to the powder keg.

Then the ring appeared in a far corner, half-buried in dryer lint. I was so stunned I sent my daughter Grace on a secret mission to get a jeweler's confirmation that the diamond was real and with strict instructions to text me in code in case Sandee picked up my phone. (Grace texted me: "The eagle has landed. Or something.")

I am already plotting when I'll give it to Sandee: our upcoming anniversary. Somehow my previous black mood was erased by this serendipitous find. I thought, *Did it really take this miraculous discovery to make me realize what I have?*

Lord, let me understand what losses are serious and care for the things that truly matter.
—Mark Collins

Digging Deeper: Luke 15:9, 11–32

Thursday, July 27

When I consider your heavens, the work of your fingers, the moon and the stars, which you have set in place, what is mankind that you are mindful of them...? —Psalm 8:3–4 (NIV)

I do a good deal of thinking in my backyard. I talk with God there a lot too. It's hard not to, especially at night, when the sky is intensely black and the stars incredibly bright. I feel the Creator right there.

One night, as I sat outside engrossed in cosmic wonder, I experienced something I find hard to describe. I felt a palpable sense that God was yearning for me, for all of us, to know Him and to love Him as He loves us. I sensed a magnetic pull toward His open arms. I listened with heightened senses. Coyotes howled in the distance. A breeze caressed my face. Bare cottonwood branches etched the air. A sliver of moon perched vividly above the horizon.

I've felt God's love countless times, but this was the first time I'd felt His longing for closeness, His passionate desire to be known, adored, seen as essential. *You are my masterpiece*, He seemed to say. *In this boundless universe, you are my special creation. I want you to seek Me, know Me, love Me. You are Mine. I am your God.*

For a few matchless moments, time stood still as I felt the profound and fervent hunger of my heavenly Father for us, His creation, to come to Him.

"I need You, Lord," I whispered, embraced by God's love.

Father God, I am in awe that You want me so much
that I can feel it. —Kim Henry

Digging Deeper: Matthew 23:37, Luke 19:41–42

Friday, July 28

"Ask and it will be given to you; seek and you will
find; knock and the door will be opened to you."
—Matthew 7:7 (NIV)

Before I left home to enter the air force soon after
college, my mother gave me a small notebook with
twenty-two of her favorite Bible verses. I loved this
collection of Scripture. They guided me through
many challenges and a few storms too. Even
more, they were from my mom—Scripture in her
handwriting, anchors from her journey.

But after surviving my many relocations, a decade
of living overseas, and countless trips, the notebook
was missing. I searched through the house numerous
times over several months without ever finding it.

One day, I was reading a devotion in *Daily
Guideposts* by Debbie Macomber, who told of her
pursuit to find a lost gold cross that she treasured. Not
finding the cross, she asked God to help her and was
led to locate it. Inspired by her experience, I, too, asked
God for help to find the notebook that I treasured.

A few days later, I was moved to search once again. In a drawer I had looked through many times before, I was attracted to a small box tucked beneath some clothes—a box I hadn't noticed before. Inside was my mother's collection of Scripture. How had I missed it? I thanked God for showing me what I thought was lost forever and for reminding me, through Debbie's story, that none of my struggles are too small to take to Him.

Dear God, thank You for those who share faith experiences from their journey. Help me connect with them and apply the lessons they have learned in my own walk with You. Amen. —John Dilworth

Digging Deeper: Jeremiah 33:3, Mark 10:27, Acts 17:28

Saturday, July 29

"Stay here and keep watch with me."
—Matthew 26:38 (NIV)

I've been a doodler for as long as I can remember. I'd always viewed my habit as a silly distraction until I attended a daylong retreat. We were invited to bring our Bibles and some colored pencils or markers, so off I went in hopes of finding a new way to experience God.

When I arrived, I was handed a packet of notes and a schedule, indicating several hour-long segments of silence and full-page designs suitable for adult coloring. "This is your time alone to spend in silence," the retreat leader said. "Don't worry about looking for the presence of God. You are already in His presence. Don't feel like you have to be productive by reading bunches of Scripture. Try to unhook your rational mind and take it down into your heart. Doing something with your hands like doodling or coloring or even knitting often helps. Simply watch with Jesus."

So off I went to sit on a rock and started doodling on a blank sheet of paper. Soon I flipped it over and tried sketching the mountain and lake and trees in front of me. I didn't let the quality of the work distract me. Instead, the simple experience of drawing drew me into a rich and focused awareness of God's presence and creation.

I brought home many spiritual nuggets from the retreat, but the most freeing was the defense of doodling, which brings me nearer to God.

Lord, I'm thankful for the many ways to more deeply experience Your promised presence.
—Carol Kuykendall

Digging Deeper: Psalms 39:5–6, 46:10

Sunday, July 30

Humble yourselves in the sight of the Lord....
—James 4:10 (KJV)

Though I haven't seen her for years, I still "see" my friend Patti in my mind, always in the same pose. We're rehearsing music with our liturgical folk group, and she sits on the carpeted altar slightly apart from the guitarists and fiddlers. She sings her throaty alto harmony and smiles. Throughout the song, she mends a rip in the crimson carpet with a curved needle and waxed thread. The tear probably isn't even visible from the congregation, yet Patti knows it's there and will eventually grow large enough to trip someone. She sings and sews and smiles.

After rehearsal, I compliment her sewing project.

She shrugs. "Oh, it just needed doing."

No one asked her; she simply saw a modest need and filled it.

Mother Teresa of Calcutta knew that service shines through small tasks. She acknowledged that most of us cannot do big things but can do "small things with great love." Patti sewed the carpet. Robin takes home a pile of linens to wash after Sunday coffee. The "lay weeders" keep the church's memorial garden tidy and blooming. Small things. Yet the cumulative effect of so much loving effort makes our world a sweeter place.

So I consider what small things I can do today.
Teach my granddaughter to roll out dough for pizza?
Phone a friend recuperating from a hospital stay?
Drive forty miles to spare my daughter a round trip?
The task is less relevant than the love I pour into it.

**Father, thank You for the blessings of those who
quietly tend to the small things. They teach me love.**
—Gail Thorell Schilling

Digging Deeper: Micah 6:8, Luke 16:10

Monday, July 31

I keep the Lord always before me; because he is at
my right hand, I shall not be moved. Therefore my
heart is glad, and my soul rejoices; my body also rests
secure. You show me the path of life....
—Psalm 16:8–9, 11 (NRSV)

"Did you hear that?" I said to the kids. We were
all making dinner together in the kitchen after
a stressful week, which featured one child in the
emergency room and another in detention.

We looked at each other, puzzled, when we heard
a strange hissing noise. A few seconds later, we all
started looking up.

"It's coming from above," I said. "Joe, go outside
and check if you see something!"

My son ran on to the porch. Through the family room window, I saw him looking at something in the air. He didn't say anything but just stood there, looking up. So the rest of us ran outside too.

"Wow!" we all exclaimed.

There was a large, beautiful, purple and blue, star-speckled hot air balloon directly over our house!

Within minutes, the balloon landed in our yard. Thank goodness we had a large space and the dog wasn't outside! He probably would have attacked the mysterious "creature."

"Where did you intend to land?" I asked the captain as soon as I could get there. "And are you okay?"

"We are fine," he said.

"You must be way off course. We've never seen a balloon here before."

"Sorry," he said. "But when the wind pushes us, we can only push back so much until it is smartest just to land." Then they packed up and left.

Finally we sat down to dinner. "I think the balloon guy was right," my daughter said. "Let's call this our landing, and start again."

Show me today, Lord, how to ride Your gracious wind. And please tell me when to push, when to let go, and when to land. —Jon Sweeney

Digging Deeper: Nehemiah 9:19–20

IN GOD'S HANDS

1 _____

2 _____

3 _____

4 _____

5 _____

6 _____

7 _____

8 _____

9 _____

10 _____

11 _____

12 _____

13 _____

14 _____

15 _____

16 _____

17 _____

18 _____

19 _____

20 _____

21 _____

22 _____

23 _____

24 _____

25 _____

26 _____

27 _____

28 _____

29 _____

30 _____

31 _____

AUGUST

"Peace I leave with you; my peace I give you. I do not give to you as the world gives. Do not let your hearts be troubled and do not be afraid."

—John 14:27 (NIV)

Tuesday, August 1

PRODIGAL HOMECOMING
Sweet Gift of Forgiveness

Be kind to one another, tender-hearted, forgiving each other, just as God in Christ also has forgiven you. —Ephesians 4:32 (NAS)

Walking through the grocery store, I tried to forget that my son Jeremy and I had had an explosive argument. Sometimes speaking before we think, if we really push each other, we shout. This time it happened in his front yard as traffic drove by. We leaned into each other, fists clenched, mouths wide open—almost like cartoon characters. A "rage bomb" seemed to go off in us at the same time.

I wasn't interested in groceries, and God seemed far away. I wondered what Jeremy was doing and longed to make things right. My heart hurt. I was sorry for my outburst.

Waiting to check out, my eyes landed on a display of giant chocolate candy bars. *Get him one.* The thought didn't seem to come from me, although Jeremy and I both adore candy bars. I bought one.

Driving home, I passed his house, pulled into the driveway, turned off the motor, and sat there. Jeremy burst out the front door. I rolled down the window and reached for the candy bar. At the same moment, he presented me with an identical bar.

"How could this be, Jeremy?"

"Beats me."

God seemed to whisper, *I'm in this.*

I want to learn, precious Jesus, more about the sweet gift of forgiveness. —Marion Bond West

Digging Deeper: Mark 11:26, Luke 6:37

PRODIGAL HOMECOMING: Small Steps

I have made the Lord God my refuge....
—Psalm 73:28 (NAS)

If I'd have known that I would have a son who'd be homeless, I would have certainly fallen apart. But it happened bit by bit, like erosion. Tremendous disappointments in life, addictions, prison, no place to call home.

Now Jon had agreed to meet us at a fast-food place in a nearby city. Would he really show? My husband, Gene, my daughters, Jennifer and Julie, Jon's twin, Jeremy, and I prayed so. We'd just parked when we saw him at a distance. He smiled and waved first.

"Can I hug you, Jon?" He hadn't wanted to hug me at the brief encounters I'd had with him in the past.

He put down a tattered black sports bag and reached for me. I had to make myself release him and remembered that homeless people carry all their belongings, so they don't get stolen.

Settled snugly in a booth, it was a bit like old times. Our family had eaten here on many occasions. Jon ate slowly. Perfect manners. Napkin in lap. Smiling. No complaints. Even made us laugh with his extradry wit, like always. He permitted me to take his picture with my new smartphone. I now study the snapshot daily when I pray for him.

After our meal, we gathered in a sorrowful clump, watching him disappear back into the life he's chosen...for now.

Father, "it is much easier to do something than to trust in God" (Oswald Chambers). I choose to trust.
—Marion Bond West

Digging Deeper: 2 Chronicles 20:20, Hebrews 2:13

Thursday, August 3

PRODIGAL HOMECOMING: Recovery
Bring forth the best robe, and put it on him; and put a ring on his hand, and shoes on his feet...and let us eat, and be merry. —Luke 15:22–23 (KJV)

My son Jeremy has battled bipolar disorder and addictions for decades. When he recovers and walks the straight and narrow, it's the most wonderful thing. I've celebrated quite a few times...and learned to spot evidences of heading in the wrong direction again. Only recently have I told myself, *Marion, it's not your battle. He has a right to make life choices.*

His latest recovery seemed like Christmas and the Fourth of July, blended with the unmistakable sweetness of answered prayer. He was shabby when my husband, Gene, and I brought him home from jail. Not guilty. Mistaken identity. At first. They'd had to Taser him twice.

Jeremy slept uninterrupted for a day and a night at our home. With him back on his prescription medications, I surprised him with a new red Georgia Bulldog shirt, jeans, tennis shoes, and socks. And I cooked his favorite meal: roast beef, carrots, potatoes, asparagus, and banana pudding. Later that week in church, he noticed our pastor's ring— gold with a cross in the center. I couldn't find one anywhere, so a jeweler suggested making one. I liked the idea and splurged. Giving it to Jeremy was one of the most satisfying experiences of my life.

"I'm just like the prodigal son in the Bible, aren't I, Mom?"

I nodded and beamed. "That makes me the parent of the prodigal."

Father, I guess being a parent hasn't changed that much in the last two thousand years.
—Marion Bond West

Digging Deeper: 2 Samuel 1:27, Psalm 146:7

Friday, August 4

PRODIGAL HOMECOMING
Ask and Receive

Some have entertained angels without knowing it....
—Hebrews 13:2 (NAS)

My twin sons' birthdays were coming up. Jeremy would be easy: a banana pudding and a sporty shirt. But Jon, who was homeless, insisted, "I'm *fine*" when any family was able to make contact with him. He had ceased making calls to me, but he'd talked to one of his sisters recently.

"Jennifer, y'all can send me a gift card, if you want to. Don't go to any trouble. Love everyone. Bye."

The shelter where Jon slept didn't give out information about residents or have mail service. We weren't even sure he was still there. I dragged the heaviness around with me.

I'd done a bit of shopping one day and stopped by a fast-food place. I spotted a homeless fellow at the counter who'd asked for a cup of water. "Hi," I said. He smiled at me. "Would you join me for lunch?"

Conversation came easily. He, like Jon, was *fine*. (There was that word again.) Suddenly, I blurted out that none of us knew how to get Jon's gift card to him. He didn't want to see us, and I didn't think I should call the shelter.

When I was silent, the man looked at me with ocean-blue eyes and said softly but emphatically, "Call the place. Ask. The Bible says to ask and you shall receive." His instructions seemed ethereal, as though they hadn't come from a stranger at all but from a Voice I knew.

I gathered my courage and called the mission. Yes, they'd make an exception for Jon's birthday.

Oh, Father, praise You for dear people who care for and love the homeless. —Marion Bond West

Digging Deeper: Psalm 91:11, Hebrews 1:14

Saturday, August 5

**"I am not being unfair to you, friend....
Are you envious because I am generous?"
—Matthew 20:13, 15 (NIV)**

"It's not *fay-uh*!" my four-year-old grandson, Cam, told me several times when I spent the weekend caring for him and his older brother and younger sister. The response was triggered by sibling comparisons, which are the first places we recognize that life isn't fair.

I found myself repeating Cam's phrase, half-amused and half-surprised by how many times it fit my own feelings. When our dog woke me up at 6:00 a.m. while my husband slept, "It's not *fay-uh*!" When a friend in aerobics class gushed that her pounds were melting off, "It's not *fay-uh*!" When someone else got credit for an idea that was mine, "It's not *fay-uh*!"

I certainly should have outgrown this Cam–like response because I know better. Jesus talked about it in the parable of the workers in the vineyard. The ones who worked the least got the same pay as the ones who worked the most. The ones who worked the most grumbled to the landowner, "It's not *fay-uh*!"

This parable shows that God doesn't keep score or make comparisons like Cam and I do. God is totally fair and equal in giving out what matters most: His lavish, grace-filled love. I want to let that truth seep into my thoughts and responses, so someday I may encourage Cam to understand what "fay-uh" really means.

Lord, I want to live in a way that encourages my grandchildren to know that You are both loving and fair. —Carol Kuykendall

Digging Deeper: Luke 15:11–32, John 21:20–22

Sunday, August 6

For the Lord Most High is awesome, the great King over all the earth. —Psalm 47:2 (NIV)

My earliest memories of experiencing sacred mystery were formed in Saint Nicholas Chapel while attending Brent School in Baguio City, Philippines. Brent School was founded in 1909 by Bishop Charles Brent. Saint Nicholas Chapel is a small and intimate place of worship that survived the ravages of World War II. Nestled high in the Cordillera Mountains, yet only seventeen nautical miles from the South China Sea, Baguio City and Brent School now seem, for me, a Shangri-la.

Primarily a boarding school for American children, all one hundred students—kindergarten through twelfth grade—gathered for worship at seven thirty each morning. Father Alfred Griffith, our headmaster, would don his vestments and lead us in hymns, readings from the prayer book, and a short homily.

The hymns are what remain with me sixty years later. As I drove home late one night, I mused on the plight of our world. It seems that peace can never be gained among nations and religions and cultures. Suddenly, I realized that I was quietly singing the final verse of "This Is My Father's World" by Maltbie Davenport Babcock, a hymn I learned at Brent School:

> *This is my Father's world*
> *O let me ne'er forget*
> *That though the wrong seems oft so strong,*
> *God is the Ruler yet.*

What a gift to learn in early childhood that it is God Who is in charge. Such faith becomes the ballast in the ship that brings stability in the midst of a global storm.

**Father, may I never forget that
You are the ruler of all. Amen.** —Scott Walker

Digging Deeper: Psalm 22:28;
Isaiah 41:10, 45:6–7

Monday, August 7

Your fellowship with God enables you to gain a victory over the Evil One. —1 John 2:14 (MSG)

Proverbs is the only book of the Bible with thirty-one chapters, so on the seventh day of the month, I read the seventh chapter. The verses warn young men to run from sexual temptation and not to go near a prostitute's house or even peer into her window.

This doesn't apply to me, I thought and closed my Bible. But when I stood up from my prayer chair, I sensed the Holy Spirit tapping on my heart: *Read the verses again, Julie.*

The nudge was so soft, I almost ignored it but sat back down and whispered a few verses: "Say to wisdom, 'You are my sister,' and call understanding your intimate friend; that they may keep you from an adulteress, from the foreigner who flatters with her words" (Proverbs 7:4–5, NAS).

I couldn't shake the notion that God had a message in these words for me. *Okay,* I decided, *I'm ready to listen. Are You talking to me?*

I'm Your first love, God pressed on my heart. *There are many ways to cheat in your relationship with Me.* I glanced out the window at the strong wind bending the thin Georgia pines. *You've doubted Me.*

True. And worry had been my temptress. I'd given in over and over.

At times, you've lusted for control.

That settled it! Proverbs 7 was definitely for me. I jotted a note beside the life-changing verses: "Lord, forgive me. I've cheated on You. Temptation comes in many forms."

Father, whenever I'm ready to get honest,
You are right there to teach me. —Julie Garmon

Digging Deeper: Exodus 20:2–3, Revelation 2:4

Tuesday, August 8

"From one man he made all the nations, that they should inhabit the whole earth; and he marked out their appointed times in history and the boundaries of their lands." —Acts 17:26 (NIV)

I was making a quick stop to pick up some half-and-half I'd forgotten the night before for my wife's coffee. I was jumping back into the car when a neighbor waved and said, "Millie stopped by to see Bosco the other night. That was sweet of her."

I smiled through gritted teeth. "It sure was," I answered as I drove away. Bosco was the neighbor's new puppy.

Back at the house I took my golden retriever aside and looked her in the eyes. "What have you been up to?" I asked. Millie tilted her head innocently.

We have an underground electric boundary fence that is supposed to keep our dog safely on our property. We've had it for years, and Millie, I assumed, had long since internalized her boundaries. The electric collar we put on her when she was out was more of a formality. Or so I thought.

I got the boundary fence guy over right away. He checked the system; everything was fine. We just needed to put a fresh battery in Millie's collar, which was done immediately. Next time she was out, I heard a tiny yelp. Yep, she'd been testing her boundaries all right, even at age eight. I had to laugh because suddenly I saw the lesson in it.

A minute later she marched into the house and gave me what, I swear, was a look of supreme indignation. "It's for your own good, Millie, because we love you." Then I made everything right with a treat.

Father, Millie is not the only one who tests boundaries. I test my own with You when I lose sight of Your direction, when I am prideful or petty or self-centered or simply wander from Your grace. Help me keep my own spiritual battery fresh.
—Edward Grinnan

Digging Deeper: Acts 17:25–27

Wednesday, August 9

Even though I walk through the valley of the shadow of death, I will fear no evil, for you are with me....
—Psalm 23:4 (ESV)

Back in the late 1990s I wrote the first book in the "Cedar Cove" series, which was a TV series on the Hallmark Channel. In setting up the story line, I introduced Judge Olivia Lockhart and her family. The turning event in their lives was the death of Olivia's son at age thirteen in a drowning accident. Everything changed after Jordan died; the ramifications rippled through the family. Right away I started a story manual and entered the date of Jordan's death. I wasn't sure why I chose that day. In retrospect, it was likely the date I wrote the chapter.

Years later my husband and I lost our youngest son at age thirty-six to suicide. Dale's death ripped out our hearts, and like it had in my fictional family, his three siblings, his father, Wayne, and I were deeply affected in one way or another. The pain was all-consuming, all-encumbering. For months, we stumbled from one day to the next, dealing with our grief.

It wasn't until recently that I happened upon the story manual for the Cedar Cove series and noticed the date of Jordan's death. It was the same day our son decided to end his own life—the same day.

I believe there are no coincidences with God. He knew and, perhaps, in some way He was preparing me for the future.

My comfort comes in knowing that our son is at peace and rests, Lord, with You.
—Debbie Macomber

Digging Deeper: Psalm 62:1, Matthew 11:29

Thursday, August 10

OVERCOMING LOSS: The Lord Gives
You will turn and comfort me.... —Psalm 71:21 (JPS)

Keith wore jeans and T-shirts every day to work as a pool man when we were in Los Angeles and also during retirement once we moved to Bellingham, Washington. So the collection of T-shirts my husband left behind after he died was extensive. Everywhere we traveled had produced more of them, and there were a multitude of shirts from the Grand Canyon, our favorite vacation spot.

When I finally got around to looking through his dresser, I found two types of T-shirts: those that didn't have holes and those that looked like imitations of Swiss cheese. Keith had been raised by his father in a tiny apartment; there had never been enough money. Keith always said he had "poor boy syndrome." He couldn't bear to throw away anything because he might need it again someday.

I moved his intact T-shirts to my own drawer. I didn't want to wear the holey ones, but I wasn't willing to throw them out either; they were so much a part of my memories of him.

Then, Keith's granddaughter took up quilting. When she and her mom asked for scraps of material, I gave them the T-shirts with the holes. A year later, a package from them arrived. It contained a quilt made of the T-shirts, most from the Grand Canyon. The letter said everyone in the family had participated in the project so that when I wrapped myself in the "Keith Quilt," I would be wrapping myself in their love as well.

You find ways to remind me, Lord, that when You take away, You also give. —Rhoda Blecker

Digging Deeper: Jeremiah 8:18

Friday, August 11

When I was in distress, I sought the Lord; at night I stretched out untiring hands, and I would not be comforted. —Psalm 77:2 (NIV)

Tonight, *Survivor* is on TV. I'm a little embarrassed to admit I've watched the reality show since it began. My sons love it. We sit together on the couch, eating popcorn and talking over who might win.

The only year I didn't really watch was the year my sister died. The title of the show took on a new meaning, and no matter how hard I tried I couldn't get lost in the episode. As the season aired, I replayed the tragedy of losing Maria. I'd think about writing her obituary and how the last paragraph stumped me—"survived by." It made the gap between us vast and deep, earth versus heaven, now versus then.

While the *Survivor* cast dwindled down and competed in strange and sometimes silly challenges, all I could think about was the reality of my grief and that being a survivor was overwhelmingly hard.

Over the seasons, my grief has transformed at a painfully slow pace, the way a cut heals, turning from weakness to strength. Tonight I realized the show had truly become just a show again. Being a survivor doesn't separate me from heaven; it connects me.

Dear Lord, You are my constant Source of strength, an ever-present Healer helping me through life's losses.
—Sabra Ciancanelli

Digging Deeper: Psalms 30:5, 48:14; Isaiah 25:8

Saturday, August 12

"... That your joy may be complete."
—**John 15:11** (NIV)

I was on a getaway, hoping to escape—even temporarily—some unhappy circumstances. As I walked along the beach, I felt sad, remembering happier days here with my family.

My eye caught a stick shaped like a *y* that was about twelve inches long. I picked it up. Could God be spelling something? I looked around the sand. There was very little driftwood and a few small shells. It was unlikely I'd find any more letters, much less any in scale with this stick. But, lo and behold, farther up the beach, I found a stick just the right size shaped like a *j*. The word *joy* popped into my mind, and just then I noticed the shell of a horseshoe crab. It wasn't really round, but it was close enough.

Oh, I thought, *I'd been thinking that all of the letters to spell joy had to be sticks. Have I been missing out on the ingredients of joy because I'm trying too hard to put together my vision of what it should be made of?*

My heart felt lighter—even a little joyous—over the thought that God could speak to me in such a fun way through two sticks and one crab shell! How gleefully my Creator must have tossed these treasures on the crest of a wave for me to find.

Lord, open my eyes, my heart, and my imagination today to the surprising components that can spell joy. Amen. —Karen Barber

Digging Deeper: John 16:24, 1 John 1:4

Sunday, August 13

The Lord is my strength and my shield; my heart trusts in him, and he helps me. My heart leaps for joy, and with my song I praise him. —Psalm 28:7 (NIV)

I had to laugh to keep from crying. Sitting in a pew with a twenty-two-month-old and an eight-week-old and trying to listen to the service was like brushing my teeth while eating cookies: useless and messy.

Weeks went by. The toddler grew more verbal. "Look, Mama!" she'd exclaim as she gazed at the stained glass. The baby grew less sleepy, always seeming to fuss during the homily. All this effort to get us bathed, dressed, and to church at least close to on time and I'd leave the sanctuary having gained nothing except more drool on my clothes.

I packed busy bags, took turns with my husband going outside, and did my best to be an example for my daughter, telling her about Communion and helping her onto the kneeler. Still, we'd end up leaving right after because someone was absolutely *done*, even if the service wasn't.

One Sunday as we drove home, the car heavy with hungry sobs and my frustration, I felt Someone write on my heart that mothers of young children shouldn't worry about what they're *getting from* church but rather what they're *bringing to* church: the next generation to love our wonderful God.

It seems simple, but that moment transformed my Sundays. I was able to share my daughter's joy over the stained glass instead of shushing her exclamations. When my son cried, I told him stories, whispering God's truths into his ears. We still leave after Communion; we know our limits, after all. But now we leave with great rejoicing.

Lord, remind me that church is about praising You, not appearing perfect. Help me to raise children who run to Your home on earth with a happy heart.
—Ashley Kappel

Digging Deeper: Psalms 98:4, 100

Monday, August 14

When Jesus saw her weeping, and the Jews who had come with her also weeping, he was deeply moved in his spirit and greatly troubled. —John 11:33 (ESV)

A friend of mine was struggling. She was passing through a desert season—a waiting, grief-soaked spell. I wanted to be a merciful ear, a safe place, a voice of encouragement.

It felt satisfying to step outside of my own parched land for a little while and focus on somebody else's pain. You see, I was in the thick of my own desert season: an impossibly long wait for our daughter, who was stuck in her birth country behind a slew of bureaucratic red tape. For reasons we couldn't see, the Lord was tarrying and my husband and I were bone-weary.

As my friend and I were talking, I brought up the story of Lazarus. I love that story. "When Jesus finally showed up, He wept with Mary and Martha, knowing full well that in a little bit, He'd call the dead man out," I said. "They wouldn't just know Him as Healer, they'd know Him as the Resurrection and the Life."

This friend, whom I was trying to console, said, "And before that, they knew Him as Comforter and Companion in their pain."

Because He wept with them. He didn't scold them for not trusting. He didn't tell them to have hope or that His timing is perfect. No. He didn't offer platitudes or admonishments. Jesus wept.

I've read that verse a hundred times, but this time it fell on fresh ears. This time it was new and profound. Because that is what Jesus did with me throughout our two-year wait—He sat with me and wept. He never left my side. Not once.

Thank You, Jesus, for weeping with us.
Thank You for being our Comforter and
Companion in times of pain. —Katie Ganshert

Digging Deeper: Isaiah 41:10, John 16:33,
2 Corinthians 1:3–4

Tuesday, August 15

"The grass withers, the flower fades, but the word of our God stands forever." —Isaiah 40:8 (NKJV)

I looked over our landscaped gardens with sadness and pride. Pride, because they were beautiful; sadness, because something had to die.

Every plant had been selected by my wife and me. Every shrub, every tree, every flower had been placed strategically. Each one told the story of design and labor. In our rocky soil, these extensive plantings required a rented jackhammer to dig a hole big enough for each root-ball. It was backbreaking work, but it was worth it. After years of sweat equity, our planting areas looked beautiful.

In our first year in northern California, it rained every day for a month in the winter and then we had hot, dry summers. The pattern continued, which made for verdant landscaping.

But now it was time to decide which plants would have to die. We're facing a major drought. We're several years into it with no end in sight. Water restrictions now require us to turn off the irrigation, to rethink our landscape, to say good-bye to that hard-won beauty.

As I walked through our yard for early morning devotions, God whispered His reminder—that all things on earth will pass away, that I'm a pilgrim here. This brief sojourn will give way to heavenly glory, where the rivers of God never run dry, where the beauty lasts forever.

Father of Mercies, teach me to hold all earthly things lightly and to fix my mind on a realm where Your grace will never fade. —Bill Giovannetti

Digging Deeper: 2 Corinthians 4:18

Wednesday, August 16

Judge not, that ye be not judged. —Matthew 7:1 (KJV)

I was combing the sale rack in my favorite clothing shop when my least-favorite salesclerk appeared at my side. She touched my arm and smiled. "Tomorrow's your surgery, isn't it, Roberta?" she asked. "I'll be praying. All day."

Her comment took me aback because my surgery had been rescheduled. I had long since forgotten the original date. Carla (as I'll call her) went on to say that she had marked my surgery date on the calendar in the break room, "so all the staff would remember and either think positive thoughts or pray."

Carla did that for me? Not Marty or Twila or Annette—the clerks I chatted up when I shopped? The ones I secretly hoped would check me out?

You see, I had Carla figured out as being snooty. You know, someone who really didn't care for anyone outside of her own inner circle. But I was wrong. It turns out the whole world is Carla's inner circle. I've since learned she has a deeply spiritual life that includes praying for just about anyone who crosses her path.

That day's sale merchandise didn't hold much attraction for me. I left the shop empty-handed but with a full heart.

Dear Lord, who else have I been wrong about?
—Roberta Messner

Digging Deeper: Matthew 7:3–5, Luke 6:37, John 7:24

Thursday, August 17

Let the sea roar, and all that fills it; the world and those who live in it. —Psalm 98:7 (NRSV)

When we heard the storm was coming our way, we didn't think much about preparing for it. We lived in Vermont, after all. A hurricane hadn't affected our town in any serious way for more than a century. That was Tuesday evening when the rain started. On Wednesday morning it was still pouring down hard, and by noon I joined our neighbors in trying to build a wall of sandbags to stop the river from flooding our backyards. Three days after that the regional director of FEMA was having his picture taken in what was left of our front yard.

You can imagine the destruction and the mess. A friend gave me Scripture to ponder: "Let the floods clap their hands; let the hills sing together for joy at the presence of the Lord" (Psalm 98:8–9, NRSV). *He's kidding me, right?* I thought.

But five weeks later, when autumn arrived and the hills were more colorful than I ever recalled seeing them before, I remembered the verses. Could it be that the glorious colors were there to remind us of something? The hills, seas, and floods were both exhilaratingly beautiful and potentially frightening, but all somehow evidence of God's presence.

"I wasn't trying to be funny," my friend said when I reminded him of the Scripture. "I knew that you'd rebuild things, that the difficulties were only for a time. No one was hurt. God is good. I figured you'd see all of that clearly again."

May I see the unexpectedness and surprises of life today, God, as Your handiwork and call them beautiful. —Jon Sweeney

Digging Deeper: James 4:13–14

Friday, August 18

Many are the afflictions of the righteous, but the Lord delivers him out of them all. —Psalm 34:19 (NKJV)

It was the perfect day trip, until we climbed back into our SUV for the long drive home. I turned the key and nothing happened. The battery was dead and the alternator was not charging.

I found someone to give us a jump start and was headed for a dealership, when I heard a loud crash behind me. I had left the hatch door open, and my big toolbox had fallen out into traffic. I watched in disbelief as a huge truck ran over it.

I was able to salvage some tools, and then we drove to the dealership. "I'm sorry," the dealer said, "but I can't get an alternator until tomorrow."

We had to stay in a motel and buy some meals. In the end, our "fifty-dollar day trip" took two days and cost over a thousand dollars.

"Where is God when you need Him?" I muttered to my wife. "It's hard to see His hand in this situation."

"Well," Sharon replied, "don't forget about that elderly woman who gave us a jump start. She was so gracious!"

"Yes, she was a sweetheart. And there was that salesman who called all the motels, looking for the best price, and then took us there in his car and picked us up this morning."

"Right. And don't forget the man who directed traffic, so you could pick up your tools. That was a brave thing to do." Sharon paused and then added, "And wasn't it wonderful of that mechanic to come in extra-early today just so he could get us on our way?"

Suddenly, I felt rather sheepish. I decided that next time I would show a little more appreciation for the friends God sends to deliver me from my afflictions.

**Forgive me, Father, when I don't recognize
Your hand at work in my life. —Daniel Schantz**

Digging Deeper: Psalm 116:6

Ye shall see, and not perceive. —Acts 28:26 (KJV)

"Don't just glance and walk on," a stern-looking Englishwoman said, wagging a finger at me at the Louvre Museum. "Stand and look! Stay with a painting half an hour, till you begin to see it."

I stationed myself before a huge Nicolas Poussin canvas titled *The Triumph of Flora*. Cupids pulled a chariot bearing the goddess of flowers while revelers cavorted around her. After two minutes I was sure I'd seen everything. I kept standing though. After what seemed like a long time, I looked at my watch. Two more minutes had passed.

Looking is work! I rented a folding stool and sat before the tiresome spectacle for ten minutes. Then ten more. Gradually, little by little, I saw Roman sculpture come alive and dance, saw hidden colors, saw symmetry, saw the painting.

Two days after I got home to Massachusetts, I ran into a neighbor from down the hall, a talkative woman I always tried to avoid. "Welcome home!" she said.

"Thank you! Got to get these groceries into the freezer."

I was in the kitchen when, in as near to an audible illusion as I've ever had, I heard a peremptory

English voice: *Don't just glance and walk on. Stand and look until you see.*

People, I thought suddenly, *are God's artworks!* How much I was missing by rushing past. I went down the hall and knocked on my neighbor's door. "I'd love to show you the photos I took."

What masterwork of Yours, Father, will You show me today? —Elizabeth Sherrill

Digging Deeper: Psalm 39:6–8

Sunday, August 20

"But I say to you, love your enemies and pray for those who harass you so that you will be acting as children of your Father who is in heaven...."
—Matthew 5:44–45 (CEB)

After dinner at a popular restaurant, my daughter Rebecca and a friend stopped at a service station to pump up a low tire. While they waited their turn for the air hose, another car pulled in front of them, scraping their bumper. When they got out to inspect the damage, they were confronted by a man brandishing a gun and a knife. He fled in their car, taking Rebecca's purse, phone, identification, and keys.

Although no one was harmed, we all had a harrowing night. It was a huge relief when the police phoned the next day to say Rebecca could pick up her belongings. The carjacker had left them with the car when he abandoned it. He then committed several other crimes before being captured and hospitalized with severe injuries.

On Sunday, I requested prayer for the victims, police, and bystanders. Our pastor prayed for them and then offered a prayer for the thief. I was about to be outraged when she explained: "I know it seems wrong to pray for those who hurt others. But Jesus tells us to pray for our enemies. And perhaps this criminal is the person who most needs to experience God's saving grace."

They were hard words to hear and harder to follow. I can't say I felt much compassion for the man. But thinking of the many times that I have needed forgiveness allowed me to add prayers for his life and soul to my prayers for those he had harmed.

Father, "forgive us for the ways we have wronged you, just as we also forgive those who have wronged us" (Matthew 6:12, CEB). —Penney Schwab

Digging Deeper: Matthew 18:21–22, Luke 23:40–43, Romans 5:8–11

Monday, August 21

Do not say, "Why were the old days better than these?" For it is not wise to ask such questions. —Ecclesiastes 7:10 (NIV)

"Hi, Sam." It was my mom on the line. I could hear she was close to tears. "Everything's fine, but I just wanted someone to talk to. We're starting to pack everything, and I'm getting sad thinking about it."

My parents sold the home they'd lived in for twenty years and were moving to a smaller house. She was sad to be leaving the place that held so many memories, and when I talked to my dad, his thoughts were the same.

I came down from Connecticut to New Jersey to see them. (It took weeks to pack up twenty years' worth of possessions.) It wasn't home to me anymore, but it was to my parents, and I kept hearing about how they were going to miss this house.

I wanted to see the new house so we got in the car, and after a scenic, winding drive through the hills, we arrived. "Wow," I said unthinkingly, "this is an upgrade!" The setting was gorgeous, isolated in a wooded clearing, with a garden path up to the front door. The house was smaller, yes, but big enough for a married couple whose children had moved out. It was old but renovated on the inside, a perfect combination of classic and modern beauty. I loved it!

A few weeks later, after the move was complete and they'd settled in, my mom called again. "You know what? You were right. This place is an upgrade. I still love our old house, but I love this one too.

I was just so sad about leaving all that behind that I couldn't see it."

Thank You, Lord, for freeing us from attachment to our past and preparing us for the new things that are always around the corner. —Sam Adriance

Digging Deeper: John 14:1–2, Ephesians 4:22–24

Tuesday, August 22

Those who know your name trust in you, for you, Lord, have never forsaken those who seek you. —Psalm 9:10 (NIV)

I peeked out the window to see my daredevil toddler standing on the top beam of the swing set, holding onto a trowel in one hand and a watering can in the other. I resisted the urge to scream for fear he would be startled and take a tumble. Instead, I took a deep breath, stepped outside, and said, "William, honey, that's really unsafe. I'm going to stand underneath you and I'd like you to climb down."

"Don't worry, Mommy. I'm holding the can and rake very tight."

Oh, of course! As long as you are holding tightly to the gardening tools, then carry on.

Okay, so I didn't say that, but once my son was safe in my arms and the rules were clearly laid out— that the top bar was to hold the swing's chains, not little boys—I had to laugh at my son's thought process. In his three-year-old innocence, he had found safety in gripping the things that afforded him no protection at all and had ignored the security that my arms would bring.

It's funny, but how often do I respond to God in the same way?

Father, I pray that when I am in danger, I will be willing to drop that trowel and watering can and tumble confidently into Your waiting arms. Amen.
—Erin MacPherson

Digging Deeper: Psalm 37:4–6, Mark 5:36

Wednesday, August 23

But God demonstrates his own love for us in this: while we were still sinners, Christ died for us.
—Romans 5:8 (NIV)

I ran my hand along the edge of the desk I had just bought. Heavy oak, dark stain, mission style—it was exactly what I was looking for, and I had gotten it for a steal at the auction.

But the next morning, when the sun crept onto my desk, I was horrified by what I saw. What had seemed like the perfect purchase now revealed itself to be a rip-off. The desk wasn't oak; it was cheap wood with a faux finish. Even worse, it was scratched and scraped, crisscrossed with lines and gouges.

"How could I be so stupid?" I said out loud.

I lugged the desk out of my room and into the garage, so I would no longer have to look at my mistake. Then I listed it on the Internet.

Over the next week, several people came to look at the desk and pointed out its flaws. Each time I felt more ashamed of my naïveté. Then a woman arrived. "It's perfect!" she said, her smile breaking wide. "I'll just put a table runner over these scratches, and it will look beautiful in my living room."

Her appreciation tugged at something inside me. I had passed heavy judgment on the desk and on myself. So I didn't have the scrutiny of an antiques dealer, nor had I made the best purchase, but the Lord valued me in spite of my shortcomings—scuffs, scrapes, and all.

Lord, thank You for looking past my flaws and seeing my worth. —Logan Eliasen

Digging Deeper: Ephesians 2:8, Titus 3:5

Thursday, August 24

The Lord said, "I will surely return to you in the spring, and Sarah your wife shall have a son".... Sarah laughed to herself.... —Genesis 18:10, 12 (RSV)

Life had been going well for my friend and his girlfriend. But then there were silences and petty fights. Finally, she showed up at his doorstep, returning things given to her.

"You were a great boyfriend," she said tearfully, "but as you know—we've talked about this many times—I just can't stop thinking about Derek."

"Here's the thing," my friend told me as he recounted this story. "I have no idea who Derek is. She never mentioned him."

My friend wasn't just thrown a curveball; he was waiting to hit the next pitch and the pitcher threw a football. Or threw a fit. Or a hockey game broke out.

I tried to read his face; no reaction . . . at first. Then there was a small crack, followed by a wider grin, a chuckle, then gales of laughter, both of us convulsed, tears streaming down our faces.

"I'll bet she's talking to Derek right now," I said between gasps of air, "and Derek's thinking, *Who's this other guy she's talking about?*"

In the Bible, Sarah laughed when God predicted her pregnancy at such an advanced age because sometimes all you can do is laugh at the absurd. Sarah's ironic snort at the Almighty wasn't punished but rewarded with her son, Isaac, the Hebrew word for laughter.

My friend is now happily married, loaded with a great story to tell. There's no word on Derek. I'll let you know what I hear.

Lord, thank You for laughter, the salve of the human condition. —Mark Collins

Digging Deeper: Genesis 17:19, 21; 21:4–5

Friday, August 25

For the Spirit God gave us does not make us timid, but gives us power, love and self-discipline. —2 Timothy 1:7 (NIV)

Sid was one of those people who came into my life for a short time with a significant purpose. He was a seasoned businessman who was about thirty-five years older than me, and he helped me start a nonprofit that offered community services through my church.

I had hit a vocational crisis, a spiritual slump, and I wasn't sure about my call to ministry. I considered becoming a funeral director, thinking it might be a great way to combine pastoral skills with business. Sharing my struggle with another person wasn't easy, especially since I was the pastor.

Sid sensed something, but he never approached me. It was his respectful, nonintrusive, caring presence that opened the way for me to confide in him. I shared how the everyday challenges of leading a church had worn me down and how my passion for ministry had hit rock bottom.

"Pablo, the passion does come back," he said after carefully listening to me. "God will renew your energy. The fire will return for ministry."

I didn't believe him. After all, Sid and I were worlds apart in age, education, and background. But whenever I was at my lowest, his words replayed in my mind, giving me something to hold on to and hope for.

**Lord, let me be a caring presence for others
as others are to me. —Pablo Diaz**

Digging Deeper: Isaiah 41:10, Galatians 6:9

Saturday, August 26

"He must become greater and greater, and I must become less and less."—John 3:30 (NLT)

My wife, Pat, and I recently visited our son, Johnny, who serves in the US Air Force in Honolulu. As we drove from the airport, Johnny pointed out a sticker on the car in front of us with the symbol in bold, black letters: HE>i.

"Do you understand the message on the sticker?" he asked us. Not having seen this symbol before, neither of us knew what it meant. *"He is greater than I* expresses the message of John 3:30: 'He must become greater and greater, and I must become less and less,'" Johnny explained.

I was intrigued by the symbol and researched it to find out that HE>i was developed in 2003 by a group of young folks near the North Shore of Oahu. They were looking for something clever to put on the main screen of their smartphones. They came up with this symbol to represent one of their favorite Bible verses. While in Hawaii, we saw the sticker often.

Back home, I ordered a few of them in varying sizes. The smallest size fits perfectly onto the back of my smartphone. HE>i prompts me to step aside and let God play through—a reminder I need throughout every day. The symbol celebrates God's greatness in a powerful and personal way to me, especially now when I'm embarking on a new journey—retirement! It's a bright beacon I can look to whenever I'm unsure of the way.

Thank You, God, for the new and different ways You remind me not only of Your greatness but also of Your presence! —John Dilworth

Digging Deeper: Matthew 11:28–30, Mark 9:35

Sunday, August 27

Let each of you lead the life that the Lord has assigned, to which God called you....
—1 Corinthians 7:17 (NRSV)

Could you check my address book and give me my cousin Kathy's ZIP code?" I call to my husband. I'm sending a note to Kathy and am too lazy to get up and look. After a minute I ask, "Did you find it?"

Charlie appears in the doorway, paging through my tattered, ancient book, a bemused look on his face. "Why are there dead people in this?"

"Because I don't like to scratch them out."

"If you had a smartphone, it'd be easy to just delete the names."

"Exactly." I return to my correspondence.

Charlie, who has been trying to drag me into the twenty-first century for some time, sighs and returns to his desk. But the truth is that keeping dead people, and, for that matter, people who are no longer in my life, in my address book has nothing to do with my technophobia. I like seeing their names and remembering why God brought them into my life. There's the older gentleman with whom I corresponded for years until I received a note from his son, informing me of his death.

There's the college friend I lost touch with because I wasn't patient enough to listen to a regular recital of all her troubles. Years later, after I had cancer and many people listened to *my* litany of problems, her name became a bittersweet reminder of God's lesson in compassion.

I keep listings of old beaus so I remember to thank God for Charlie every time I see one of their names.

I rise now and follow my husband into the office. "Here's why," I begin.

**Lord, thank You for every single person
You have brought into my life. Amen.**
—Marci Alborghetti

Digging Deeper: Ecclesiastes 3:11–15

Monday, August 28

Pride goes before destruction, and a haughty spirit before a fall. —Proverbs 16:18 (NRSV)

"Mom, no!" screamed Micah from the driveway.

Home from her third day of school, she'd gotten out of the car to throw away some garbage. My tire thudded. I shifted into reverse. "My backpack!" She grabbed the strap and dashed inside.

Unbeknownst to me, she'd dropped her new designer backpack in front of the car. I'd never sprung for an expensive book bag before, but Micah was starting middle school and I wanted her to look nice.

Cross-legged in the entry hall, she sat sniffing. I lifted the fabric satchel. White lining peeked through the blue flower pattern. The side cup holder had two holes. The strap looked like someone had run over it.

"Why did you drop it in front of the car?" I asked. She ran to her room in tears. I was angry. "If you want another, you'll have to pay half!"

The next morning, Micah took an old backpack to school. At home, I stroked the fancy fabric and heard a voice: *For whom did you buy this backpack?*

My mind flashed to the back-to-school photos I'd taken: Micah holding the backpack on her lap that first day. She and her friends looking over their shoulders with their backpacks. I'd counted the students with the same designer backpack. Yep, I was proud of it—a little too proud.

Guilt washed over me. Micah needed something to carry her books in, but I'd placed both our senses of self-worth inside a backpack that wasn't even mine! So I drove to the mall. Now we both have matching book bags, but mine has a tire mark to remind me of a lesson I needed to learn.

When I try to build myself up with nice things, help me remember, Lord, that You're all I need.
—Stephanie Thompson

Digging Deeper: Jeremiah 49:16, Romans 12:3

Tuesday, August 29

Be kindly affectioned one to another with brotherly love; in honour preferring one another.
—**Romans 12:10** (KJV)

I stood at the airport curb, watching my brother's car as he drove away. He'd dropped me off, confessing he was nervous about finding his way home through the streets of Portland, Oregon, where I'd just helped him move from California. He'd be starting law school.

For Ben, my younger and only sibling, this was a lifelong dream come true. It had taken him a while to get to college, and then he'd worked for several years at a grocery store. Finally, he'd taken the LSAT. And now here he was. On scholarship, even.

I was so proud of him. But I felt heavy and anxious too. Ben and I had been close all through our chaotic childhood. We talked by phone several times a week. We were anchors for each other.

I knew that would change once classes started. The first year of law school is intense. Ben wouldn't have much time for long conversations. And he was scared he wouldn't measure up. Ben wasn't a churchgoer. But, of course, I prayed for him every day.

We'd had a terrific road trip together. Hours and hours of talk were enough to last through dry patches when Ben was pulling late nights in the law library. The more I thought about it, the more I saw God's imprint all over this moment. God had given us exactly what we needed. I waved and headed into the airport. Plenty of time to pray and give thanks before my flight.

In our love for our family, we catch a glimpse of Your love for us, Lord. Today I will pray for my family.
—Jim Hinch

Digging Deeper: 1 Peter 2:17

Wednesday, August 30

So then, just as you received Christ Jesus as Lord, continue to live your lives in him, rooted and built up in him, strengthened in the faith as you were taught, and overflowing with thankfulness.
—Colossians 2:6–7 (NIV)

I pulled up to the tollbooth plaza and started digging for my wallet. I took out a one-dollar bill. *Oh no, I thought this was a five!* I dug in my cup holder for change. I dumped my purse on the passenger seat, hoping to find some coins in the bottom of my bag. All that and I still came up a quarter short.

"I don't have enough money for the toll." The ticket taker sighed and started to direct me over to the side, so I could park. I would have to go into the plaza and deal with nonpayment. But then he waved me through.

"What? I thought I had to pay now."

"The truck behind you is going to pay for you. Move it, lady. You're good."

There was no way to say thank you to the truck driver. I crossed the bridge, and by the time I got to the other side he was lost in traffic.

I feel the same way about the gift of life everlasting. I want to thank God, but I know my attempts are insufficient. It is not a gift I can pay back. But just as the truck driver who paid my way, God does not want thanks. He wants me to be on my way, to live a full life here and now. The praise and thanks due are in the act of my living for Him.

Dear Father, there is no way to thank You for the gift of life, so I will do my best to live with joy as my praise to You. Amen. —Lisa Bogart

Digging Deeper: Psalms 107:1–3, 115:1; Luke 17:9–10; 1 Thessalonians 5:10

Thursday, August 31

"He will wipe away all tears from their eyes, and there shall be no more death, nor sorrow, nor crying, nor pain. All of that has gone forever."
—Revelation 21:4 (TLB)

Death slapped me in the face with a cold hand a few years ago. Between June and December, eight friends and neighbors and my husband's brother died.

In July, my dad, about to celebrate his ninety-fifth birthday, broke his back, causing some in our family to fear that the end was near.

In January, I was admitted to the hospital with what the doctors said was a life-threatening case of swine flu and a serious lung infection, forcing me to ponder the possibility of my own death. (After five days I was discharged.)

The following April, Jeana, a vibrant fifty-two-year-old woman we'd had lunch with the first day of our European cruise, died suddenly in her cabin from diabetes and kidney complications. Death was on my mind every week during that stretch of time. One minute we're here enjoying life; the next minute we don't exist on this earth.

The only way I could reconcile the grief was to remind myself that, with the Lord, death equals heaven and heaven equals pure joy with God. The equation brought me peace and I began to refocus on a life-centered equation. Life equals challenge and opportunity, and challenge and opportunity equal accomplishment and peace.

So there's really nothing to fear, either here on earth or in the afterlife. It's all good.

Heavenly Father, thank You for life here and in heaven. Bless all those I love and care about. —Patricia Lorenz

Digging Deeper: 1 Corinthians 13:11–13, 15:50–58; Revelation 21:5–8

IN GOD'S HANDS

1 _____

2 _____

3 _____

4 _____

5 _____

6 _____

7 _____

8 _____

9 _____

10 _____

11 _____

12 _____

13 _____

14 _____

15 _____

16 _____

17 _____

18 _____

19 _____

20 _____

21 _____

22 _____

23 _____

24 _____

25 _____

26 _____

27 _____

28 _____

29 _____

30 _____

31 _____

SEPTEMBER

*Those who know your name trust in you, for you,
Lord, have never forsaken those who seek you.*

—Psalm 9:10 (NIV)

Friday, September 1

"And you will feel secure, because there is hope; you will look around and take your rest in security."
—Job 11:18 (ESV)

The roller-coaster car shuddered as it began its ascent. I was taking my little brother Isaiah on his first coaster ride. His small hand gripped mine.

"Are you okay?" I asked.

"Yep," he said. He bit his lip.

The car ticked as we rose higher. "Are you sure?" I asked him again.

"I'm good," he said. We crested the track's peak, and the drop loomed before us.

"I'm not okay!" he shouted. "I'm scared! Please stop it!"

But it was too late. We were committed. Dozens of other screams drowned out Isaiah's as we whooshed toward the ground. I wrapped my body around his and moved my mouth near his ear. "I know this is scary, but you are completely safe."

In Isaiah's little-boy mind, the track continued forever. But I could see the big picture. I knew that soon we'd slow down, our lap bars would rise, and I'd buy him some cotton candy.

As I held Isaiah, I understood how he felt. It was a shaky time in my life. I was embarking on my last undergraduate semester and anticipated upcoming struggles with classes, grad-school applications, and student loans. The uncertainty terrified me. But God could see the big picture; I trusted that.

The car slowed down, and Isaiah's breathing steadied. "We're okay," he whispered.

"Yes, we are."

Father, thank You that despite life's twists and turns, my future is secure. —Logan Eliasen

Digging Deeper: 2 Corinthians 5:1–5, Revelation 22:3–5

Saturday, September 2

"He will lead them to springs of living water. And God will wipe away every tear from their eyes." —Revelation 7:17 (NIV)

We had done all we could for our beloved eight-year-old golden retriever, Millie, but the cancer had progressed too far. Now, on this beautiful God-given morning, it was time to do the kindest and hardest thing of all. Dr. Maddie would be out to the house at eleven o'clock. A few minutes before, I logged onto my work e-mail account with my password to tell a few friends what we had finally decided for Millie and to ask for prayers. Millicent Johanna was her registered name, and Julee and I often called her Millie Jo for fun or Millicent when we wanted her undivided attention. By any name, we would miss her terribly.

Right after Millie had breathed her last gentle breath, with Julee and me stroking her head, I went back inside to log on again and let friends know. Access denied. My password had expired without notice. Now my tears were tears of fury. I could not reset the password remotely; I was locked out. I fired off an angry e-mail to the IT team via my private account. How could they do something like this?

All day I veered between grief and rage. I am not a complete fool. I knew the two overpowering emotions were intertwined, like a riptide just below the surface of consciousness. But these were emotions beyond my control.

That night I tried once more to log on, typing my password: Millicent. It finally struck me. The password had expired mysteriously at virtually the same moment my beloved dog had. I understood the message: Don't be angry. Let go. Move on.

Lord, I was angry and heartbroken at losing Millie so young—angry at cancer, angry at the IT guys, angry at You. But really I was confused and overwhelmed at loss and death and the failure of my love to save our dog. But Your love has saved me, and it will heal my heart. —Edward Grinnan

Digging Deeper: 1 Corinthians 15:53–55

Pray in the Spirit at all times and on every occasion. Stay alert and be persistent in your prayers for all believers everywhere. —Ephesians 6:18 (NLT)

I sent a text message to my daughter Misty, asking her to pray for a friend at a job interview.

However, I didn't receive the usual "Sure!" Instead, she texted: "Lord God, I lift him up to you this morning. You are the God of our past, present, and future. If it is Your will, make this job happen. But, ultimately, I pray that Your will be done. Cover him with confidence and peace as we pray with abundant expectation. Amen. Love you, Mom!"

I wrote back, "Thanks, honey! I didn't expect to receive a prayer from you!"

"Whenever someone asks me for prayers, I try to pray and send it to them at that moment," she replied.

"Great idea, honey!" I texted back.

Just then, I heard the *ding* that signaled another incoming text. It was from my son Kevin. "Hey. I'm waiting to speak with my boss. Asking for a raise. Prayers needed."

I texted back, "Lord, please give Kevin the confidence, courage, and words to speak what is on his mind and heart. And may his boss see him for the hardworking employee that he is. Amen."

Kevin texted back, "Thanks! I'm praying your prayer as I sit here. U r awesome."

I had to smile. It's just like a quote I read: "You can write and read about prayer, but sooner or later you need to pray."

Thank You, God, for the opportunities that come my way all day long to not just talk about praying but to text it too! —Melody Bonnette Swang

Digging Deeper: Colossians 4:2, 1 Thessalonians 5:17

Monday, September 4

But prove yourselves doers of the word, and not merely hearers who delude themselves.
—James 1:22 (NAS)

Today I received an e-mail from Rebecca, who is a Service First volunteer in Thailand. Service First is a program I direct through the Institute of Life Purpose at Mercer University. Rebecca is an honors graduate in biology and chemistry, but she is translating her love for others this year by teaching young children in a rural Thai village how to speak English. Because of Rebecca, many of these kids may have the opportunity to attend college or secure a job with a good company. The knowledge of English is, increasingly, a survival skill in today's global culture.

Rebecca also attached some photographs to her e-mail. She jokingly labeled one: "My new electric dryer." It was a picture of her clothes flapping in the wind on an outdoor clothesline. As I gazed at the image, I could clearly read the writing on one of her T-shirts. It was a quote from Mahatma Gandhi: "Be the change you wish to see in the world."

I smiled, thinking, *Rebecca is being the change she wants to see in the world. Her example is an inspiration. We cannot control life, but each of us can resolve to personally embody the change we feel is most desperately needed.*

What is the change you most want to see?

Dear Lord, You required of Your disciples one thing: "Come, follow Me" (Mark 10:21, NAS). May I follow You this Labor Day and always, and allow You to show me the change You wish me to address in my world. Amen. —Scott Walker

Digging Deeper: 1 Corinthians 13:1–13, James 2:14–17

Tuesday, September 5

Some trust in chariots, and some in horses: but we will remember the name of the Lord our God. —Psalm 20:7 (KJV)

My daughter, Lanea, and I were delighted when we learned that my son, Chase, was chosen to sing the role of Mingo in *Porgy and Bess* at the Lyric Opera. Though finances were tight, we were determined to attend one of the performances.

Chase planned to drive his battered car from North Carolina to Chicago. He'd put a lot of work into it, but it still made a loud wheezing sound when he drove it. The flivver just didn't sound or look reliable, unlike Lanea's much newer vehicle.

She and I were horrified, imagining his car wheezing up the West Virginia mountains on his way to rehearsals in Illinois. But Chase was insistent. "I'll be fine."

So my daughter and I hatched a plan: we'd follow Chase. We planned our own visit to family and friends just around the time his rehearsals began. We'd depart a few days behind him, just in case his asthmatic car left him stranded along some highway.

We prayed and then Chase took off as planned. Three days afterward, Lanea and I began our own adventure. However, not even two hundred miles from home, her car, enveloped in a cloud of smoke, died and left the two of us stranded and praying for help. Chase, on the other hand, had arrived safely, and his wheezer is still running strong.

Lord, thank You for keeping us safe and reminding us to trust in You and not in our cars. —Sharon Foster

Digging Deeper: Psalm 28:7; Proverbs 3:5–6, 16:20

A friend loves at all times....
—Proverbs 17:17 (NRSV)

It was time to pick up the kids from their first day at PS 163, the public school around the corner from our house in New York City. I pictured them coming home, sad and anxious, telling us how out of sorts and lonely they felt. I could practically hear Frances's voice: "I'll never make friends!" I waited on the playground for her class to emerge. Kate was at Benjamin's kindergarten classroom.

I spotted Frances walking onto the blacktop with her second-grade class, smiling and holding hands with another girl. "Daddy!" she cried, running up to me when the teacher dismissed the class. "This is Ella. She's new like me. She's from France!" Ella smiled shyly.

"Nice to meet you, Ella," I said.

A man approached and extended his hand. "I'm Jopi," he said. "Ella's dad." Ella, her younger brother, Kian, Jopi, and his wife, Helene, had arrived from Paris. Helene's work had transferred her to New York, just like our family.

"Ella is a little shy," Jopi said. "But she and your daughter seem to get along very well."

The girls scampered around the jungle gym. I spotted Kate and Benjamin approaching from the kindergarten class. "There's Helene and Kian," Jopi said, pointing toward another kindergarten classroom.

Somehow, I knew Benjamin's first day would be as happy as Frances's.

You give us friends, Lord, to remind us of Your ever-present love. Today I will reach out to my friends.
—Jim Hinch

Digging Deeper: Psalm 25:12–15

Thursday, September 7

I consider everything a loss in comparison with the superior value of knowing Christ Jesus my Lord. I have lost everything for him, but what I lost I think of as sewer trash, so that I might gain Christ. —Philippians 3:8 (CEB)

I picked up the flyer that had been slipped under our front door and groaned. "They want us to recycle our kitchen garbage," I said to my wife. We were already sorting our plastic, glass, cans, and paper; now a new citywide program was encouraging us to throw our food scraps into a special bin for composting.

"It's all about making something useful out of what we throw out," Carol explained.

Over the next few weeks we got into the habit of throwing food scraps in a bag in the freezer, which I'd take down to the bin in the basement every four days. I'd see lemon rinds, apple cores, coffee grounds, potato peels, carrot stubs, cauliflower stems, artichoke peels, broccoli trunks, tea bags. *It'd be amazing if something could be made of my own personal garbage*, I thought. *My pigheadedness, selfishness, anger, jealousy.*

The city picked up the composting once a week, and the recycling became a habit. One day I was walking through the park on my way to work and saw a city truck dumping a dark, moist pile of fertilizer next to a clump of trees. *Is that what came of our garbage?* I wondered. I walked closer to inspect. It had that satisfying loamy feel to it; it didn't even smell. Whatever had happened, it had been transformed.

I headed toward the subway where I would settle into my prayer time. Maybe I needed to think of it as a sort of spiritual composting, turning my garbage over to God, trusting in His forgiveness and mercy and powers of transformation.

Lord, thank You for the fragrance of forgiveness You leave in Your wake. Forgive me for all the wrongs I've done. —Rick Hamlin

Digging Deeper: 2 Corinthians 5:17

Friday, September 8

OVERCOMING LOSS: Death Can Be Kind
A gift in secret pacifieth anger.... —Proverbs 21:14 (JPS)

I kept Keith's voice on the phone machine so that I could continue hearing him speak. Every time I heard his voice, I had trouble making myself believe that someone so strong, so vital, so funny and tender was not alive any longer. It made no sense to me, and I hated the whole idea of his being gone.

One day, almost two years after Keith died, I was on my way down our long driveway toward the mailbox when, in a towering pine tree, there was a sudden crashing of needles and limbs. I stopped walking just in time to avoid being struck by the body of a rabbit and looked up to see the huge wingspan of an eagle as it flew away.

I stared at the rabbit for a long moment and was grateful it was dead. If it had been still suffering, I wouldn't have known what to do to help it. I felt for the first time an acceptance that death could be the right thing, a cure for pain and affliction.

The eagle circled back overhead, and I went on down to the street. When I headed back up to the house with my mail, the rabbit was gone.

The next time I heard Keith's voice answering the phone, I thought about those last few days of his life. He had been suffering, struggling to breathe, and now that was over. I was still grieving, but I wasn't angry anymore.

> **Thank You, Lord, for showing me that death can be kind.** —Rhoda Blecker

> **Digging Deeper:** Ruth 2:20

Saturday, September 9

See if I will not open the windows of heaven for you and pour down for you an overflowing blessing. —Malachi 3:10 (NRSV)

A few years ago I was wiped out, spent. My tank was empty, and I was at the end of my rope, totally burned out. It was a long road back for me.

What's been most important is not so much how I refueled my tank but the practices I learned to help me to never get that low again—things I now try to do every day. I'd like to share a few of them with you:

- Schedule two or three activities that give you energy each and every day. Call someone to say thanks. Pray through a portion of your prayer journal. Take a short walk. What you do isn't as important as doing it regularly, whether you think you need it or not.
- Commit yourself to using only positive language for an hour or a morning or even a whole day. It makes a huge difference.

- Write yourself a note at the end of the day, affirming three positive things you did that day, and leave it in a place where you'll read it first thing in the morning. It's a great way to finish one day and start the next.

Have these simple changes made a difference in my life? Profoundly so. Today, it's my faith that helps to make me well. And just as important, these practices have allowed me to better use my God-given gifts—ones I came close to losing—to make a difference for others.

Fill my cup, God. Let it overflow—not for me but that I can serve You with all the good gifts You have given me. —Jeff Japinga

Digging Deeper: Psalm 116, Luke 17:11–19

Sunday, September 10

Be strong in the grace that is in Christ Jesus. —2 Timothy 2:1 (KJV)

I was stopped at a red light when I felt a tap on the rear of my vehicle. As I got out to meet the offender, an elderly man with a gentle demeanor held up his insurance card in surrender. "I'm so sorry, ma'am," he said. "I'll take good care of you. Me and my insurance company, that is."

That sure was music to my ears. Last year, I spent nearly fifteen thousand dollars in out-of-pocket medical expenses. I could rub out the black smudge on my spare tire cover and keep the insurance money. One of those babies was sure to cost several hundred dollars.

But wait a minute! That was exactly what a woman did to me a couple of years ago. I'd barely tapped her bumper, and she took my insurance company for a long, expensive ride.

Choose grace, a Voice I've long known spoke to my heart. *You won't get any money, but it's the better path.*

The man looked at me. "My truck's okay," he said. "It's just a work truck. I'll do whatever you need, but I think that little place on yours will wax out."

I'd been wearing my seat belt and felt absolutely fine. I smiled. "You know what, sir? I do too."

Grace never felt so good.

Teach me, Lord, to walk in Your ways, even—and most especially—when it's hard. —Roberta Messner

Digging Deeper: Isaiah 40:31, John 1:16, 2 Timothy 4:22

Monday, September 11

Be strong and of a good courage; be not afraid, neither be thou dismayed: for the Lord thy God is with thee whithersoever thou goest. —Joshua 1:9 (KJV)

Ever hear the story of Welles Crowther, the man with the red bandanna? Welles was a kid from New York who carried a red bandanna everywhere he went from the age of six until the day he died. He wanted to be a firefighter so badly, he volunteered for his local firehouse the first day he legally could, at sixteen. A terrific athlete, he went to Boston College and played lacrosse. After school, he got a job in New York City as a trader in the South Tower of the World Trade Center on the 104th floor. He was pretty good at it, but one day he called his dad and said he wanted to switch careers and be a firefighter.

He was chewing over this decision when murderers flew an airplane into his building. One woman saw a young man with a red bandanna helping people escape the carnage. He led people to the stairs and accompanied them down forty floors, and then he went back upstairs again and rescued more people. Then the tower collapsed, and everyone in it was atomized. Welles died.

His mother showed his photograph to two of the survivors, who said, "Oh yes, that's the young man with the red bandanna. That's the young man who saved twelve people from death."

He was twenty-four years old. God was with him when, during hell on earth, he tied his bandanna on and saved people from death. God was in

Welles. Now Welles is in God somehow. Welles is in us somehow also. You cannot kill defiant, adamant, roaring grace and courage. Don't ever forget that.

Dear Lord, there is, by Your right hand, a young man named Welles Crowther. Could You give him a message from many millions of people here? We admire that young man; we honor his courage and selflessness; we will sing his song for centuries and so put to rest those who thought his murder would inspire fear and terror. Not so. Not at all so.
—Brian Doyle

Digging Deeper: Proverbs 28:1

Tuesday, September 12

How sweet are Your words to my taste, sweeter than honey to my mouth! —Psalm 119:103 (NKJV)

It's a curious sensation being a student again after fifty years. I missed the mental and social stimulation of college, so I am taking a class in Old Testament poetry at Central Christian College, where I was a student in 1965 and later a professor.

This time I am not pursuing a degree or a career. I am learning the way a child learns, for the sheer joy of it. My hand is often in the air: "Why would a loving God allow a good man like Job to suffer such afflictions?"

The professor of this class was a student of mine twenty years ago. Now Chad has several diplomas and a unique teaching style. Wise, funny, and in constant motion, he holds our attention well: "The women of Song of Solomon were probably like the women in Renaissance paintings—pleasingly plump."

When I was a teacher, I often wondered if my work really mattered. Now I can see just how invaluable a teacher can be. Chad is not just presenting data; he is helping us to find the poetry in our own afflictions.

This class is a welcome break from my daily chores. For ninety minutes I have no aches and pains, no allergies, no worries, no regrets. I am infatuated with Lady Wisdom in Proverbs, and I am charmed by the ballads of King David.

The other students here are just kids to me, but they are fun and friendly: "Hey, Mr. Schantz, sit by me and I'll share my cheddar crackers with you."

As I drive home, I am thinking that there is "a lot of sugar in the bottom of life's cup" if I am willing to keep on learning.

Father, I am glad You made life so rich and complex that we can never master it, no matter how much we learn. —Daniel Schantz

Digging Deeper: Psalm 71, Ecclesiastes 8:1

I wait for the Lord, my whole being waits, and in his word I put my hope. —Psalm 130:5 (NIV)

Every morning I drive my husband to the train station, joining all the other commuters. In the long line of traffic headed into town, I can see the stoplight as we approach.

On Monday, we didn't make it through the stoplight and were the first car in line. Tuesday, the timing was wrong again; we were the first car waiting at the light. Wednesday, same thing. In fact, all week long we were the first car in line at the light!

I am not good at waiting, and so on Monday and Tuesday, it made me feel like I'd been singled out for punishment. It was irritating. But by the third day, it got to be a joke. "Here we are again," I said to my husband. By Friday, we felt like we were going for the record. It surprised me how an annoyance actually turned into a fun challenge: "Can we have a clean streak of five days being first in line?" We did, by the way.

I am not going to tell you that waiting suddenly became easy for me. But I will say I look at times of waiting with a different perspective. Now I try to find something I can focus on that makes the challenge less of a struggle. Seeing small steps of progress helps: one more day checked off the calendar, one more chore taken care of, one more verse of encouragement. In these ways, I give myself the opportunity to find spiritual growth in waiting, which is probably why I have been asked to wait in the first place.

Dear Father, help me find the good in waiting. I know it's there somewhere. Amen. —Lisa Bogart

Digging Deeper: Psalm 18:29, Hebrews 6:15

Thursday, September 14

"Blessed are you who weep now, for you will laugh." —Luke 6:21 (NIV)

I spent the wee hours of the morning searching for a poem for my thirteen-year-old son to read in front of his class. We got up way before our normal waking time, as agreed the night before when Solomon pleaded with me to help him with his English assignment.

With an hour of searching behind me and time running short, I can attest that it's not an easy task to find a poem for a boy on the edge of manhood to read to a class of his peers and not sound silly or like he's trying too hard. The chore got even tougher with the assignment restrictions, length, tone, similes, and allusion.

I was lost in thought, my nose in a book, when Solomon looked over at me and said, "Mom, you're crying."

I looked up from the poem, and he shook his head. "I'm definitely not reading that one!"

I laughed and cried at the same time.

Right on the very next page, I stumbled on a perfect poem for him to read. With the assignment behind us, his lunch made, and time to spare before the bus came, Solomon asked, "Mom, can I read the poem you were reading before? Not for my class. I just want to read it."

I watched him take the words to heart—not crying because he's a boy and most likely his years haven't given him enough experience to give the poem teeth, or maybe a million other reasons that are only for him to know. But for a blessed moment, we shared something sacred, probably the very thing his poetry assignment was meant to teach.

Dear Lord, thank You for unexpected moments that bring laughter and tears and the grace that transforms a task into a blessing. —Sabra Ciancanelli

Digging Deeper: Numbers 6:24–26, Galatians 6:10

Friday, September 15

"Do not be afraid...," says the Lord, " for I am with you...." —Jeremiah 42:11 (NKJV)

Just a few days until the big move. Our house is in boxes. Frances has finished her last gymnastics practice. Benjamin has bid good-bye to his kindergarten classmates. Soon we'll be three thousand miles away, in the middle of New York City, about as different from our quiet suburban life as you could imagine.

We walked in Santa Cruz, California, breathing cool, salty Pacific Ocean air. We were certain God was calling us East. We trusted He had good reasons for the move. Or did we? I had an indelible memory of the morning when, out for a run in the predawn dark, I felt God say, *Go. I will be with you.* Yet, still, I wondered.

Suddenly, we noticed everyone on the bluff-top stop and point out to sea. We shaded our eyes and gazed west. "Daddy, a whale!" cried Frances. Sure enough, a pod of gray whales was passing close by the shore. A spout of water shot from a blowhole, and a murmur rose along the sidewalk.

Then—something I had never seen before—the whale closest to us, just a few hundred yards from shore, lifted its fin and waved it up and down in the air.

We looked at one another. "It's waving!" exclaimed Benjamin.

I thought I heard the words *Go. I will be with you.* Then the whale lowered its fin and slipped beneath the water.

Wherever we go, You are already there, Lord.
Help me to remember that. —Jim Hinch

Digging Deeper: Exodus 23:20–21

Saturday, September 16

"For your Father knows the things you have need of before you ask Him." —Matthew 6:8 (NKJV)

I was on my hands and knees in the garden, pulling weeds. It was a hot morning. I stopped for a moment to wipe my brow. I'd hoped that if I started early enough I'd escape some of the heat and humidity. But even at this early hour, I was sweltering under the blistering sun.

Sure wish I'd remembered to grab my bandanna! I thought. It was a special one designed to cool you off. All you had to do was insert a couple of ice cubes into a compartment sewn inside, tie it around your neck, and voilà!—the ice would melt and drip down your back.

I should get it, I thought. I looked down at my clothes covered in dirt. *Maybe not.*

I got up and walked over to the tall, dense patch of ginger growing alongside the house under the shade of a big oak tree. I plopped down and immediately felt a trickle of cool water run down my back. Startled, I turned quickly and laughed out loud. I'd sat in just the right spot under a tall green ginger leaf still cradling its morning dew. The water trickled down my back, cooling me off just fine.

Lord, thank You for those tiny moments in life that remind me how much You care for me.
—Melody Bonnette Swang

Digging Deeper: Psalm 37:23, Luke 12:31–32

Sunday, September 17

"Give...an understanding heart...."
—1 Kings 3:9 (NKJV)

"Help!" I half-whispered as I got out of bed.

My son, Harrison, had started high school, and I knew all of the temptations and possibilities for poor decisions that lay ahead. How could I help him?

At the other end of the spectrum, our daughter Mary Katherine had just turned three and our youngest, Ella Grace, was one. Between diapers and fevers and toddler tantrums, my wife, Corinne, and I were often overwhelmed. *Help!* I thought again as I brushed my teeth.

My career was hitting its stride and business was great, but success came with more responsibility and longer hours. And I had recently said yes to chairing the board of a start-up school for some of the poorest children in Nashville, Tennessee.

"Am I in over my head?" I whispered as I hurriedly showered for church. "Help!"

We dropped off the girls in the nursery, and Harrison, Corinne, and I quickly slid into the pew. Our pastor was explaining, "Today, we're going to talk about Solomon." Next came the familiar story of how God appeared to Solomon in a dream, offering him the gift of his choice. Solomon, surprisingly, asks for wisdom rather than wealth or power.

I thought of my earlier pleas. In my distress, I'd forgotten where to go that would allow me to tackle life's problems. The answer was and would always be God.

Church wasn't yet finished, but already a calmness had settled over me. Whatever lay ahead, if I, like Solomon, looked to God for wisdom, help would be on its way.

Father, stay by me; give me wisdom. —Brock Kidd

Digging Deeper: Proverbs 2:6, James 1:5

Monday, September 18

Pray for kings and everyone who is in authority so that we can live a quiet and peaceful life in complete godliness and dignity. —1 Timothy 2:2 (CEB)

I've never been particularly interested in politics. I study candidates' positions prior to elections, and

I always vote. But I rarely express my opinions on issues.

Last year was different. Kansas state legislators made cuts to funding that could have forced some schools to close and others to eliminate summer school or increase the student/teacher ratio. There was also a move to drop an early childhood program that had proven effective in increasing parenting skills, kindergarten readiness, and early detection and treatment of developmental delays.

I e-mailed about thirty-five representatives, thanked each person for serving our state, and gave reasons why I supported full funding for both programs. To my surprise, one legislator replied. He served an urban district across the state from my rural western home. We were affiliated with different political parties, and I had never met him. He didn't promise to support my position, but he did promise to carefully consider the points I had made. What a contrast to the legislator who publicly complained that e-mails from constituents had clogged her in-box!

In the end, the school cuts stood. But funding for the early childhood program was restored, in large part because of support from hundreds of people from all walks of life and all parts of the state. I kept a copy of the e-mail I received because it reminds me that every voter's voice counts. I also now pray for legislators on a rotating basis, by name, because every one of them counts too.

Lord God, You alone have wisdom to govern perfectly. Help me pray with compassion for those with whom I agree and disagree. —Penney Schwab

Digging Deeper: Isaiah 9:6–7, Titus 3:1–2

Tuesday, September 19

"What is gained if I am silenced, if I go down to the pit? Will the dust praise you?..." —Psalm 30:9 (NIV)

"Are you safe?" I ask my son gently. This is code for *Are you feeling suicidal?*

"I am now," John answers. "Yesterday wasn't so good."

I nod and give his shoulder a pat. Touch is important. Empathy is important. A lot of things are important, but most of them aren't in my power to provide.

John had been enjoying college and doing well until he was hit hard by depression. It's tough to go to class if you can't get out of bed. Eventually, he withdrew on a medical leave of absence. Now the lack of structure in his days is making it difficult to get back on track. Deep down I want to howl, *Get up! Do something! Go somewhere!* I bite my tongue; saying what I feel would make John feel worse.

The situation is exacerbated by my husband Andrew's depression and our daughter Maggie's. Their withdrawal has triggered our younger son Stephen's anxiety too. Running the household falls on my shoulders, as does the monitoring of behavior, managing of therapy schedules, and coaching them through oppressive emotions.

I'm pretty sure it's not possible to do all this, but I plug along anyway. I do what I can, pray often, cry at night. In the midst of my massive to-do list, one item stands out: I need to love my Lord. Without that, nothing else is possible.

Father, I want to love and serve You all my days, no matter how hard that may be. —Julia Attaway

Digging Deeper: Deuteronomy 7:9, 11:1

Wednesday, September 20

With good will render service, as to the Lord, and not to men, knowing that whatever good thing each one does, this he will receive back from the Lord.... —Ephesians 6:7–8 (NAS)

It's not the kind of letter you expect in the mail. I'd been working with Zina, a Russian immigrant in her sixties, on the cemetery marker for my mother. She'd quoted me the price for a bronze plate to match my father's. It would be inscribed "Ever True to God." I mailed her a check.

A few days later I received a handwritten letter, which read in part, "Dear Carol! I want to apologise for mistake and misunderstanding about quote for your mom's marker. I ask someone in company about price for bronze marker. So I have been told that price including foundation. When I received your check and write order they tell (accounting department) me that base (foundation) extra $190 + tax $16.53 = $206.53. So Carol! I offer to you that I will pay $206.53 (myself). This is my mistake and I want to fix it. Please, forgive me for this mistake. Respectfully, Zina S."

Zina's letter touched me to the core. The company had misquoted a price to her. Yet she was willing to make it up from her own earnings to someone she didn't even know. I later learned she commutes a long distance to her job, stays all week with a friend, and returns home for the weekend. The amount of money she wanted to pay would have filled her gas tank multiple times.

I couldn't accept Zina's financial gift. But I did accept her concern for me in a time she knew was hard. I accepted her willingness to sacrifice. Her generosity. Her humility. Her beautiful spirit. The offer she made is best explained in those words from Mom's marker: "Ever True to God."

There are many ways to be true to You, Lord, and they all begin in the heart. May it be my joy to keep a true-to-You heart. —Carol Knapp

Digging Deeper: Matthew 25:31–40, 1 Timothy 6:18–19

Thursday, September 21

"Lord, let our eyes be opened."
—Matthew 20:33 (RSV)

I keep the letter in a folder labeled GBGFB (God brings good from bad). It's filled with letters, articles, scribbled notes that I pull out as an antidote to the negatives in my life.

I chose this particular letter after getting a discouraging report from my eye doctor about my worsening macular degeneration. The letter was dated March 9, 1993. The writer was a retired medical missionary who'd worked for many years in Congo/Zaire, where blindness caused by a river parasite was an all-too-common malady.

"There's no cure," she told me. "All we could do in these cases was try to help them cope." Then two years before she and her husband retired, a young German couple with the Christoffen Blinden Mission came to Zaire. They introduced farming techniques developed specifically for the blind and brought Braille Bibles in the local language and began teaching them to read.

"The most wonderful thing is happening!" she wrote. "Of course there's no electricity in these remote villages. Nights are long and dark. But blind people can read anytime! A whole village will gather around one or two of them to hear the Scriptures read aloud. Nights aren't long enough for all the stories and questions and excited conversation."

I'd picked that letter because eyesight was on my mind. But it's about so much more than a disability turned to good! It tells me there's no darkness too thick for God's light to enter.

Loving God, shine Your light on my path today.
—Elizabeth Sherrill

Digging Deeper: 2 Samuel 22:29, Psalm 139:12, 2 Corinthians 4:6

Friday, September 22

For I have no one like him, who will be genuinely concerned for your welfare. —Philippians 2:20 (ESV)

My husband Michael's grandmother called me. "Come speak at our Friends of the Library meeting. Bring your books."

I had a story in a compilation book and welcomed the chance to sell copies, but Nana and

Grandpa lived more than two hours away. Even though I'd been in the family a few years, I felt like an outsider. It wasn't because of anything they did; it was just because we didn't share a history. But how could I say no?

I met Nana at the Love County Library in Marietta, Oklahoma. She showed me to the conference room with thirty-six chairs and an old card table in the front corner.

"We usually put the books by the door, so people can look before they leave," I said.

Nana shook her head. "Not enough room."

I shrugged it off. *Perhaps we'll get better acquainted this time*, I told myself.

Typically authors sell one book for every ten people in attendance. Still, I unloaded my boxes.

One-third of the people there were Nana's relatives. It was fun talking to her sisters and their family members. By the time I started speaking, I was glad I'd come, and when I finished, applause erupted from the group, who then turned toward the exit.

"Y'all aren't leaving yet." Nana's five-foot-four frame blocked the doorway. "My granddaughter drove here from Oklahoma City. Get to that table and buy her books!"

Thanks to Nana, I sold all twenty-eight books. But the best thing I gained was that Nana was no longer "Michael's grandmother" but mine.

Lord, thank You that love connects us when we don't share the same blood. —Stephanie Thompson

Digging Deeper: Philippians 1:3–4, 1 Thessalonians 5:11

Saturday, September 23

God shall supply all your need....
—Philippians 4:19 (KJV)

One of the first things I learned as a volunteer guide at Bok Tower Gardens in Lake Wales, Florida, is that Spanish moss is neither Spanish nor a moss. "It's an epiphyte, an air plant," explained my wise mentor, Sarah. "It lives not just on air, but on the moisture and nutrients in it." This rootless marvel floats through the air and attaches to trees that keep it off the ground where it sways in the lightest breeze. It draws no nourishment from soil or the host tree, yet these silvery-green strings of tangled life produce tiny blossoms. The utter simplicity and freedom of the air plant's existence fascinates me.

And I reflect on the many times God has supplied all my needs when I, too, felt I was living on air. How about the years when I raised four children alone and often received anonymous cash in the mail? Other times I found vegetables or boxes of gently used clothes on the porch. How about the unknown benefactor who paid my pediatrician's bill? I never did figure out who it was. Or the semester I couldn't pay preschool tuition and they let me bake snacks for several months. My dentist accepted home-baked birthday cakes as payment for two crowns. Back then, our little family seemed to live on air but lacked for nothing.

More recently, I lived like the free-floating Spanish moss: house-sitting to save enough money to travel. Over the course of two years, jobs meshed one right after another, sometimes several at a time. I always trusted that I would have a bed. After all, God has provided for my needs for decades. He keeps His promises because He loves me.

Gracious God, even when I feel rootless and living on air, I am secure in Your hands.
—Gail Thorell Schilling

Digging Deeper: Matthew 6:31–34, Luke 12:15

Sunday, September 24

How lovely on the mountains are the feet of him who brings good news.... —Isaiah 52:7 (NAS)

Roque and Nancy and my husband, Gene, and I had been in the same Sunday school class for years. Roque was a sharp dresser and quite distinguished-appearing with his Ernest Hemingway beard, soft voice, and quick laughter. He'd been born in Cuba but lived most of his life in the United States.

I was drawn to Roque's uncompromising bold faith and ready wit. He had a deep love for the down-and-out and had helped me deal with having a homeless son.

One day he came to class wearing the most fascinating woven, chocolate-brown shoes I'd ever seen. I have a thing about shoes. I decided they looked like Palm Beach attire and slipped across the room to tell him. He laughed his slow, low, rumbling laughter and said he didn't know where Nancy had gotten them. Later, she told me they were Cuban shoes that she'd ordered online.

When Roque's health began to decline, he rolled into class in a fancy electric wheelchair. Some of us had to jump out of his path. He still wore his happy expression and marvelous shoes, and right up to the end Roque maintained his devotion to the down-and-out.

Several weeks after his funeral, Nancy handed me a sack. "Roque wanted Gene to have these."

Now my husband walks around in Roque's Cuban shoes, continuing to share God's love…and Roque's too.

Father, help me to walk with quick laughter and deep love for those in my path. —Marion Bond West

Digging Deeper: Luke 1:77–79, Acts 8:25–40

Monday, September 25

You will keep in perfect peace all who trust in you, all whose thoughts are fixed on you! —Isaiah 26:3 (NLT)

I stood on my lawn and lobbed the bright green tennis ball for Sunrise, my golden retriever. While she raced away, my thoughts drifted to a situation where I felt I'd been wronged. *God, they never should have done that!* Over the past couple of days, I played the memory over and over in my head until it became a menacing movie. Worse still, I lost my peace.

With the ball in her mouth, Sunrise galloped back, handed it to me, then shifted her weight side to side with her eyes fixed on the ball. I winged it—hard. Sunrise was hot after it, and I grimaced as I watched the ball settle among my tomato plants. She dove into the garden and chomped down with gusto. When she turned around, I saw that, instead of the ball, she had a green tomato in her mouth. Suddenly, she stopped midstride, puckered her brows, and spit it out. Then she stalked around the tomato, cocking her head and making faces at it.

I chuckled as I walked toward her. "Tomatoes might look like a ball, but dogs aren't supposed to bite into them." When those words spilled out of my mouth, instantly I thought, *And bad memories are like green tomatoes. Don't bite them!* By choosing to continually replay the menacing movie, I was wasting my brain space and creating torment.

I picked up the green tomato and threw it in the trash can, along with the bad memory.

Thank You, Lord, for free will. Help me to make choices that bring me closer to You. Amen.
—Rebecca Ondov

Digging Deeper: Deuteronomy 30:19–20, Amos 5:15

Tuesday, September 26

"Blessed are the peacemakers, for they will be called children of God." —Matthew 5:9 (NRSV)

This past spring my favorite avenue underwent construction work. A project that was supposed to take two months stretched into winter. My walk was disrupted by torn roads, ragged sidewalks, and grit-filled air. Daily, I passed police officers sitting in running patrol cars and workers milling around or watching me. It was worse for residents of the avenue, known for its lovely homes and meticulous yards. Curbs were heaved, chunks of soil and grass strewn everywhere, flower beds ruined. Entire houses were covered with grime.

I worked myself into a righteous fury as September approached. This neighborhood was known for colorful autumn displays: rows of asters and mums; porches decked with Indian corn, pumpkins, and gourds; sprays of bittersweet; and sheaves of hay. But I just knew that this year, with all the mess, no one would bother.

Except they did. Almost overnight, the neighborhood adorned itself in all its autumnal glory. A friend was on her porch as I walked by in amazement. "Why bother?" I asked.

She smiled wryly. "We got together and decided if we couldn't do anything about the disaster of this project, we could at least do something about how we reacted to it."

For the first time in months, instead of steaming in anger, I spent my walk admiring the yards, thankful that God had shown me how to see the beauty in the mess.

Father, teach me to do and find what good I can and to leave the rest to You. Amen. —Marci Alborghetti

Digging Deeper: Psalm 37:7–8, Matthew 5:43–45

Wednesday, September 27

Do not worry about it. —Luke 12:29 (NIV)

I sat at the table after breakfast, worrying about my son's depression, while staring out over the trees in the backyard. As I looked at the skeleton of a dogwood, my eyes were drawn to the only leaf still clinging to it. The leaf wasn't much—gray and about the size of a quarter. But there must have been a very slight breeze because it was quivering, calling attention to itself by quaking against a whole landscape of stillness and tranquility.

I identified that forlorn leaf with my constant "what if" worries. Then, suddenly, the leaf stopped quivering and I lost sight of it. I never would have seen it if it hadn't been stirring from the slightest breeze.

The leaf was small and insignificant in the context of the whole tree. I noticed the moss and lichen on the trunk and the buds on the fingertips of the branches. Look how tall, beautiful, and strong the tree was! The leaf was irrelevant to it as a whole. In fact, the leaf was already dead and would soon fall.

I saw what God was trying to tell me.

Dear Lord, is what I'm worrying about today really that significant? Enable me to see Your big-picture view of it. Amen. —Karen Barber

Digging Deeper: Matthew 6:25–33, Luke 21:14

Thursday, September 28

Now may the Lord of peace himself give you peace at all times in every way.... —2 Thessalonians 3:16 (ESV)

I sat beside nine-year-old Gabriel. His fingers curled around his pencil, and frustration colored his face. Long division wasn't a favorite.

"Divide. Multiply. Subtract. Bring down," I said.

Gabriel sighed. I was frustrated too. The day's to-do list was long, and my mind ran fast. Teach lessons. Run Gabriel to a piano lesson, Samuel to swimming, and Isaiah to soccer. Deliver dinner to a friend. Take Rugby to the vet. Wash sports uniforms. Meet a work deadline after the boys are in bed. Stress settled on my shoulders.

"I can't get this, Mom. It's too hard," Gabriel said. His jaw set, and his freckled nose scrunched.

I took hold of the pencil. "Okay, let's see. How many times does eight go into fifty-eight?"

Gabriel looked to the ceiling and drummed his small fingers on the desk. "Seven," he said.

"Then put the seven on top like this. Now multiply."

Gabriel and I worked through the problem, and when the right answer came, a smile brightened his face. "Thanks, Mom. It's easier to take it one step at a time."

I thought about Gabriel's words: one step at a time. Maybe I could break down the hours of my day in a similar way and focus on, find peace in, the task at hand. After all, worrying about the next ten things on my agenda could rob me of the present moment's joy, like when my little boy triumphed over long division and his green eyes shone bright with pride. "Good job!" I said. We clapped a high five.

Step-by-step—it works for math and for life.

Lord, help me to claim the peace You offer today. Amen. —Shawnelle Eliasen

Digging Deeper: Psalm 55:22, John 14:27

Friday, September 29

No good thing will he withhold from those who walk along his paths. —Psalm 84:11 (TLB)

With mounting medical bills, it had been a trying month financially. I had more month left than money. "Lord, I give my situation to You," I prayed. "Totally. I'm going to put You first and trust You with everything."

Not long after, I felt a strong urge to purchase some men's dress shirts at the local thrift store. The shirts were brand-new and still wearing their tags from a fine men's store. Five shirts could be had for ten bucks, so I used the money I would have spent on a take-out meal and donated the shirts to a local resource center that serves homeless veterans.

Time passed, and I ran into one of the social workers at the center. "I need to tell you about those shirts you brought in, Roberta," she said. "Right after that, a young vet who served in Iraq dropped by. I could tell he'd been crying. 'You wouldn't happen to have a nice shirt a guy could wear to his mother's funeral, would you?' he wanted to know." The social worker fixed him right up with a white cotton, no-iron button-down, and the vet left, so grateful for the gift.

Of course, the real winner in this little faith exercise was me. There had been more money than month after all. There always is when you trust the Giver.

You keep every one of Your promises, Lord.
Help me to always walk along Your paths.
—Roberta Messner

Digging Deeper: Jeremiah 29:11, Matthew 6:26, Philippians 4:19

Saturday, September 30

"What is the price of two sparrows—one copper coin? But not a single sparrow can fall to the ground without your Father knowing it."
—**Matthew 10:29** (NLT)

We'd hoped and prayed for this moment for two years—our daughter from the Democratic Republic of Congo was finally home. We were a family of four, not just on paper but in real life. God had made a way. He'd performed a miracle that had family and friends praising His name. It felt like our happily-ever-after had finally come.

Yet real life was only just starting. And let me tell you, it was overwhelming. Parenting is hard. Parenting a toddler who has been through significant trauma, doesn't know the meaning of trust, and can't understand English was a whole new brand of hard.

On top of doctor appointments and lab work and evaluations and tantrums, we quickly discovered that Salima has special needs. I felt ill-equipped, unprepared for this particular journey. I felt like I was drowning. I felt like I had to swallow my complaints. In my lonelier moments I felt isolated, like nobody could possibly understand.

Then, about a week into this new crazy life, I opened my Bible and found Matthew 10:29. It was like a whisper to my heart. The same God Who sees every sparrow is the same God Who brought my daughter home and the same God Who will equip me to parent her through the tough times. He is the God of the miraculous and the God of the everyday and the God of the unseen.

He sees. He cares. He knows, even when nobody else can.

Thank You, Jesus, for caring for the sparrows. Thank You that with You, we are never misunderstood or alone. —Katie Ganshert

Digging Deeper: Psalms 61:2, 103:12

IN GOD'S HANDS

1 _____

2 _____

3 _____

4 _____

5 _____

6 _____

7 _____

8 _____

9 _____

10 _____

11 _____

12 _____

13 _____

14 _____

15 _____

16 _____

17 _____

18 _____

19 _____

20 _____

21 _____

22 _____

23 _____

24 _____

25 _____

26 _____

27 _____

28 _____

29 _____

30 _____

OCTOBER

But I trust in your unfailing love;
my heart rejoices in your salvation.

—Psalm 13:5 (NIV)

Now faith is the substance of things hoped for, the evidence of things not seen. —Hebrews 11:1 (KJV)

I have a friend who is right there when the chips are down, the kind of guy you would trust to take care of your kids if you died—that kind of great guy. But he is obsessed with God and religion and spirituality; he hates, denies, and can't ever stop bitterly complaining about all of the above. But recently I realized the nut of the problem for him: he cannot go past sense. Sense and reason and logic are the frontiers of his country; anything that does not make sense for him is silly or a lie.

Whereas for me it is the very unreasonableness of God that allows me to believe. Because I cannot understand, count me in. If God was reasonable, logical, sensible, God would be within reach of my limited human understanding. Because God is a verb, a mystery, a force, an energy, a Something far beyond even my wildest imagination, therefore I believe. *I am with you.*

I can only believe in the unbelievable; I can only totally trust that which is beyond understanding, like marriage and democracy and the final victory of light over darkness. "But that doesn't make sense!" *Exactly.* "That's ridiculous!" *Absolutely.* "That's unreasonable and illogical and silly!" *Yes, yes, yes.*

Because I cannot make sense of it does not mean it is not so; that is why it may very well be so. The Mercy, the Creator, That which set the stars to spin—I cannot understand what I will call God; therefore, count me in.

Dear Lord, totally weird prayer of the day here. Can I ask politely that You never let me believe even for a second that I understand You? Can You always gently remind me that You are unimaginable and limitless, and my brain is the size of a penny? In other words, protect me from arrogance, which leads to greed and blood. —Brian Doyle

Digging Deeper: James 2:14–26

Monday, October 2

He looked for a city which hath foundations....
—Hebrews 11:10 (KJV)

"I'm so tired of playing scales!" my sister told me. "I want to play Bach, Schubert, Chopin!" Yet her teacher kept assigning finger exercises. "Major scales, minor scales. She says I'm not ready for more!"

I wasn't thinking about Caroline's frustration as I walked a nature trail at the North Carolina Botanical Gardens in Chapel Hill. "The long-leaf pine thrives in the Coastal Plain," I read, "where porous sand hills make a dry climate with frequent forest fires."

But where was this tree? All that was growing near the descriptive label were a few tufts of grass. A guide explained. "We had a fire four years ago." He gestured at the wisps of green. "As you can see, the long-leaf pines survived fine."

"Those are trees?" I asked. "Why, if that's all they've grown in four years, it will be decades till they mature!"

"Oh no," he said, "they've just been laying the foundation, putting down roots so they can grow tall. If you come back next year, they'll be three or four feet high."

Slow, almost imperceptible growth at the beginning—like practicing the piano. Today, as I watch Caroline's fingers skimming swiftly over a Schubert prelude, I think about the early stages of any skill worth learning: music, sports, cooking, language. Laying foundations takes time. Without them, nothing grows tall.

In today's world of instant gratification, Father, teach me the wisdom of Your patient timing.
—Elizabeth Sherrill

Digging Deeper: 1 Corinthians 3:10–11

Tuesday, October 3

My heart leaps for joy, and with my song I praise him. —Psalm 28:7 (NIV)

Kathy knocked on my back door. My golden retriever Sunrise raced to the sound. She bounced straight up and down like a pogo stick. "Stop that!" I commanded. The previous week I'd entertained friends and fought Sunrise's exuberance. I was at my wit's end.

"Go to bed!" I growled and pointed to Sunrise's bed. But she jumped up and down, over and over again. I grabbed her by the collar and yelled through the door, "Come in!"

As Kathy stepped in, I steered Sunrise out the door, shut it, leaned against it, and blurted, "Some days I get so tired of her!"

Kathy was a doggie guru; surely she'd give me some sage advice.

"Maybe she's just happy," Kathy said.

Her words stunned me. *What is wrong with Sunrise being happy?* I wondered.

Kathy continued, "I've always appreciated that saying 'You don't get the dog you want. You get the dog you need.'"

Instantly, I knew. I was taking life too seriously. *It wouldn't hurt to lighten up and take on a bit of Sunrise's exuberance. It's just what I need!*

Please show me, Lord, how to live a life filled to the brim with joy. Amen. —Rebecca Ondov

Digging Deeper: Psalm 16:9–11,
1 Thessalonians 5:16

"For the Lord your God will be with you wherever you go." —Joshua 1:9 (NIV)

I climbed into a van laden with containers packed with baked chicken, mustard greens, and corn bread. I was heading out with Yvonne, the volunteer driver of a local food ministry, to distribute meals to shut-ins.

After a couple of hours, she said, "Just two more stops" and turned into a street littered with trash. Most of the homes were in disrepair. "Make sure your door is locked. This isn't a safe part of town."

We parked in front of a rundown house. I glanced over at the faded address scrawled on the mailbox. We delivered the lunch and drove out of the neighborhood. Yvonne looked at me. "You okay?"

I nodded.

She handed me a map. "We've got a new place on our route. Let me know where to go."

I looked at it. "Take a right at the red light. Then left." I hesitated for a moment. "You know that house we just left? I lived there as a child."

"In that part of town?" she asked, surprised, and squeezed my hand. "No shame, baby," she said. "You know that big storm we had a few years ago? My house flooded badly. My favorite piece of furniture—my momma's armoire—was left with a waterline on it. And you know what? I didn't refinish that piece of furniture. No, I didn't. I kept it just the way it was."

We pulled up to the last stop. She reached over to put away the map. "It might be important to know where you're going, honey, but it's just as important to remember where you've been."

Thank You, Lord, that whether I look back on the past or forward to the future, You are always present.
—Melody Bonnette Swang

Digging Deeper: Psalm 139:7–12, Isaiah 43:2

Thursday, October 5

"Go assured. God's looking out for you all the way."
—Judges 18:6 (MSG)

The day hadn't started out well. I was rushing to an appointment and had skipped my early morning devotional. Singing Frank Sinatra songs, I passed through several hamlets en route. Then I heard a siren and looked in my rearview mirror—blue flashing lights.

Oh me. This is what I get for not having my devotional study this morning. I said a quick prayer and pulled off the highway. The officer strode up to my car. "Hi," I said blithely with a smile. Surely, he'd made a mistake. Perhaps one of my tires needed air.

"I like to know who I'm talking to. May I see your license?"

I fumbled through my billfold and handed it to him. I wondered if I should tell him I'd gotten only one ticket before and the judge didn't make me pay.

"Here's what you did," the officer said, handing back my ID card. "You were speeding. Did you know that?"

I didn't. "By how much?"

"Seventeen miles over the limit." His face looked like a statue carved in stone.

I sighed, smile gone, and decided to come clean. "I didn't have my worship time this morning, but I asked God to watch over me in my car and keep me safe."

"I'm an answer to your prayer, lady." He smiled suddenly and stuck his yellow ticket pad back in his pocket. "Go on, but slow down."

Father, please protect police officers. Keep them safe. Thank You for them. —Marion Bond West

Digging Deeper: Isaiah 31:5

Friday, October 6

PARENTING ANEW: "Yes, You Can"
I can do all things through him who strengthens me. —Philippians 4:13 (NRSV)

Computers and I have a love-hate relationship. I've never been a technical person and don't enjoy pressing keys to see what happens. When I do, I end up erasing something valuable. But, thank God, I have Chuck, a patient husband.

It was time to replace my old laptop, but the upgrades meant learning new versions of programs I was comfortable with. One updated program that I use to write with didn't work the way the old one had. Soon I became frustrated as I tried to do things in a different way. "It's too hard!" I wailed. "I can't do it!"

My husband sat down at the keyboard and calmly figured out how to accomplish what I'd been unsuccessful at. "Yes, you can. Come over here, and I'll show you what to do," he said, pointing to a nearby chair. I obeyed like a sulking child and watched, amazed that he had figured out the technique.

A few days later, I was working with my grandson, Logan, on his spelling words from kindergarten. He was having a difficult time writing the letters with his chubby little fingers, spacing the letters correctly, and knowing when to use capitals. Irritated, he threw down his pencil and said, "It's too hard! I can't do it!"

My own words echoing through my mind, I knew how to respond.

Lord, sometimes life is hard. But thank You for being there and showing us what to do. —Marilyn Turk

Digging Deeper: Psalm 30:10, Hebrews 13:6

Saturday, October 7

"Fill the earth and subdue it. Rule over the fish in the sea and the birds in the sky and over every living creature that moves on the ground." —Genesis 1:28 (NIV)

For almost three months, I've prayed for Rock Hudson, a rescue dog on the Web site where we found our dog Soda. A senior Chihuahua with cloudy eyes and a snaggletooth, Rock Hudson is a hard case. Finding him a home will take time.

I visit the rescue's Web page a few times a day even though we're not looking for a dog. I read the descriptions of the animals recently rescued from a Georgia shelter, big and small, old and young, some easy to place, others with special needs. A few have known histories, owners who moved or went on to heaven. Some, like Soda, were found wandering the streets.

My heart breaks for each and every one, so I adopt them in prayer. I ask God to send His love and comfort, to help them find just the right family.

I guess it started with Soda. I couldn't get over how much I love him, how effortlessly he filled a void I didn't know existed. A cat lover for most of my life, I never wanted or thought about owning a dog until my son Henry insisted we get one. Soda surprised me by being an answer to prayer I hadn't thought to pray.

Today is Rock Hudson's lucky day. "Home at Last" reads the headline.

Dear Lord, thank You for answered prayers and humans who do Your work here on earth. Please send Your comfort to all the animals in need and guide us humans to open our hearts and homes—and let in love. —Sabra Ciancanelli

Digging Deeper: Proverbs 12:10

Sunday, October 8

The night cometh, when no man can work. —John 9:4 (KJV)

I was visiting a friend in the hospital when I overheard the staff talking about a woman who was staying with another patient down the hall. "Oh, she's only a sitter," one of them remarked.

My thoughts traveled back to a night in 1976 when my grandfather was dying in that same hospital. As Papaw gasped for breath, I held his hand and thanked him for all he had meant to me. One of my fondest memories was on Fridays when I was growing up. After he and my grandmother finished their weekly grocery shopping, Papaw would be sitting across the street from my house in his bright turquoise pickup truck. He always had a chocolate bar and a five-dollar bill for my college fund waiting for me.

But there in the hospital, Papaw had been pulling at his tubes and intravenous lines, so we had hired a sitter to stay with him when our family couldn't be there. That night, his faithful Lula said to me, "Don't be so sad, Roberta. Your Papaw is going to Gloryland. Yesterday, I prayed with him and he invited Jesus into his heart."

Only a sitter? I don't think so. Some of the most heavenly work is done by these angels who keep watch at our bedsides.

No work is menial, Lord, if it's done for You. Thank You for every worker who labors for Your kingdom.
—Roberta Messner

Digging Deeper: Exodus 35:35, Matthew 9:37

Monday, October 9

"Consider the lilies, how they grow: they neither toil nor spin; and yet I say to you, even Solomon in all his glory was not arrayed like one of these."
—Luke 12:27 (NKJV)

I'm gazing at a close-up photo of a daylily that my father grew, raindrops beaded like quicksilver atop the ruffled petals, the same exuberant orange as a Gulf of Mexico sunset. It's all I have left to remember Dad's lush gardens now. He died seventeen years ago, and both his home and the gardens he lovingly landscaped have been sold.

Daylilies like these often grow wild in New Hampshire. Many once grew alongside old cabins and farmhouses that succumbed to fire or collapsed over the centuries. Deep in the woods, it's not unusual to find lilies blooming around the stone foundations and cellar holes overgrown with weeds. How little they need in order to thrive!

So here in my new empty apartment, I consider the lilies and the rest of Jesus's teaching: *Take no thought for your life.* I believe this.

During my past four years of house-sitting, traveling, and writing, I found that I needed very little to thrive. God took care of my needs then so that I could continue my creative work. Now, as I rebuild a more settled life in a home of my own, I marvel how once again God has uniquely provided for my needs through my friends. I see Kathy's lamp, Diana's drapes that match Ruth's sofa, Jill's shelves, and my son-in-law Steve's daylily photo. And that's just the living room.

My father's daylily will always be a part of my decor. It reminds me that my heavenly Father will care for me forever.

Gracious God, how little I need if I have You!
—Gail Thorell Schilling
Digging Deeper: Matthew 10:29–31

Tuesday, October 10

"Thus says the Lord of hosts..., 'Build houses and live in them; and plant gardens and eat their produce.... Seek the welfare of the city where I have sent you....'" —Jeremiah 29:4–5, 7 (NAS)

Mercer University has a beautiful law school building, which is a replica of Independence Hall in Philadelphia. It's perched on the summit of the highest hill in Macon, Georgia, which is a favorite place for strolling.

Recently, I walked past the beautiful wrought-iron fence that surrounds the school and noticed an oak sapling growing out of the top of a sturdy brick fence column. Amazed, I pondered how a small acorn could land on top of a ten-foot structure, wedge itself into a crack, and take root. One day this determined oak sprig will likely be trimmed away, but for now it is a symbol that life can bloom in the most tentative situations.

There have been moments in my life when I have taken root amid stressful circumstances. When I was fourteen, my father and maternal grandmother died within a three-month period. There was no choice but to leave my childhood home in the Philippines and take root in my mother's hometown of Fort Valley, Georgia. I spent my high school years planted in small-town America.

Now, fifty years later, I look back and understand that being rooted temporarily in this rich soil was a gift. Fort Valley was comfortable, manageable, and filled with friendly and hospitable people. It was a place to rest before moving on.

Father, give me courage to be rooted wherever life may place me. Amen. —Scott Walker

Digging Deeper: Jeremiah 29:11, Romans 8:25, Hebrews 6:15

Wednesday, October 11

OVERCOMING LOSS: Climbing Up
You have captured my heart....
—Song of Songs 4:9 (JPS)

There was a time after the initial shock of Keith's death, the funeral, and the emptied house of visitors when I could not cry. I could feel the pressure in my chest, swelling upward until it threatened to make my throat close, and I knew that tears might relieve it, but they would not come.

I was moving in limbo, doing things on my to-do lists, showing up for appointments, feeling only the emptiness of my husband's absence, as sharp as an amputation. I tried to pray, but it was mere lip service. I could sleep only if the TV was on all night, and if I had dreams, I didn't remember them. I tried reading books about loss, but looked at the same sentence five or six times without comprehension. Other times I picked up a book and put it down without reading a word.

One day I dusted bookshelves, the next item on my to-do list. I picked up the books one by one, and a pale blue sticky note fell to the floor. I recognized Keith's handwriting. He'd tucked the note into my suitcase on a package of sugared almonds when I left for a business trip. "Here are some sweet nuts for a sweet, loving nut. Have a safe and happy trip. I love you with all my heart and miss you very much."

I burst into tears and cried for what seemed like hours. When I exhausted the pent-up reservoir, all I was thinking was, *Thank You, thank You, thank You.*

I am so grateful, Source of Healing, that You helped me to begin climbing out of the pit. —Rhoda Blecker

Digging Deeper: Proverbs 16:24

Thursday, October 12

He said to them, "Why are you troubled, and why do doubts rise in your minds?" —Luke 24:38 (NIV)

"A problem never leaves you where it found you," intoned Rev. Robert H. Schuller. I was listening to an old motivational cassette tape I found after moving off the ranch where I'd raised cattle for twenty years.

I grimaced. After rupturing a disc in my back, my full-time ranching days were over. Where was I? Happily married, yes. On another ranch, yes. But what good was I? Raising cattle had been my life, my passion, my identity. Now what?

Just then my neighbor called. "I hate to bother you, but..." Ann's heifer was calving.

"How long has she been in labor?" I asked.

"Twelve hours."

It had been too long for the calf. I wasn't sure we could save the cow. I rushed to the corral. The cow's pelvis was malformed; no calf would ever fit through there. I grabbed the foot of the unborn calf and gave it a gentle tug. It pulled back. "It's still alive! Call the vet. She needs a C-section. Now!"

I fretted as we waited. Fortunately, the vet was able to perform the surgery in time, saving mama and baby.

"Thank you so much," Ann said, giving me a hug. "If you hadn't been here, those two wouldn't be here."

Here—right where my back problem left me, where there's less stress, more love, more peace, and more opportunity to help others with the skills I've learned.

Lord, You took me from where I thought I wanted to be and led me to where I really belong. Why do I ever doubt You? —Erika Bentsen

Digging Deeper: Deuteronomy 31:6–8, Joel 2:21–22

Friday, October 13

I know the plans I have for you, says the Lord, plans for your welfare and not for harm, to give you a future with hope. —Jeremiah 29:11 (NRSV)

"Daddy, is today tomorrow?" My three-year-old said this to me one morning while she still lay in bed, within minutes of opening her eyes.

"What, honey?" I had no idea what she meant. It took me less than a minute. Then I remembered. The afternoon before, we had the following conversation:

"Can I watch a movie, Daddy?"

"No, not today. Not now. We have friends about to come over for dinner."

"But, Daddy!"

"Tomorrow, hon. Tomorrow. There is no school tomorrow. You can watch that movie tomorrow. I promise."

Gracefully, she let it go, but clearly she did not forget.

So the following morning, about forty seconds after she asked if today was tomorrow, it occurred to me what she meant.

"Ah yes!" I said. "Yes, hon, today is indeed tomorrow!"

"So I can watch my movie?"

"Yes, you may."

In my daughter's amusing way of relating only to what is "today" and what is "tomorrow"—there is no distant, troublesome past and no fretful future—it seems to me that she completely gets the idea of discipleship and eschatological hope.

May I live for You in the present today, Lord? Oh, and I look forward to tomorrow too! —Jon Sweeney

Digging Deeper: 2 Chronicles 20:16–17

Saturday, October 14

Comfort, comfort my people, says your God. —Isaiah 40:1 (NIV)

I was having a medical test—routine but involving sedation. Yet when they wheeled me into the room for the procedure, I found I couldn't stop shaking. Fear gripped me. What if I didn't wake up? What would my daughters do without me?

My nurse anesthetist, Errica, is the wife of a former student of mine. Just seeing her friendly face that morning had made me less anxious. But now she looked concerned. "Are you cold?" she asked.

I felt silly but admitted the truth. "I'm scared," I answered.

Errica took my hand. "It's okay. I get emotional every time I have to be sedated. It's perfectly normal." She let me talk about my daughters and my love and concern for them. Errica has little girls of her own, so she could relate. What a sweet blessing to be understood and reassured!

I'd been reading about a missionary who gave up everything to move far away and help people. I'd prayed about whether I was about God's business enough, here in my safe Southern hometown. Maybe someday I would go afar and do mission work, but Errica's kindness reminded me that I could minister to others right where I was.

I said a prayer of thanks for Errica before I drifted off. When I awoke, my family was there. I could hardly wait to get back home to my own little mission field.

Lord, thank You for the kindness of others. Help me extend that same kindness to those I encounter today.
—Ginger Rue

Digging Deeper: Matthew 7:12, Galatians 6:2

Sunday, October 15

"See, I am sending an angel ahead of you to guard you along the way and to bring you to the place I have prepared." —Exodus 23:20 (NIV)

Let's go around and share something about your experience of working with Lindsay," the hostess suggested.

I had no idea what I was in for when I took my seat at a celebration for my daughter, who was ending several years of volunteering as director of the women's ministry at our church.

One by one, people began speaking about Lindsay's leadership and depth. But many picked up on a word that surprised me.

"You were pretty *pushy* sometimes and you wouldn't let me get away with just doing things the way I always had."

"I experienced your *pushiness* too, but you *pushed* and stretched me in the right direction."

"You are *pushy*, but it's a good *pushy*. You've made me think deeper."

I felt something stirring inside me: the memories of all those years of mothering a strong-willed, *pushy* child. Feeling frustrated that a five-year-old could totally baffle and boss me. That an eight-year-old could rule over her older brother and younger sister. That a teenager could threaten my way of thinking with the passionate expression of her opinions.

When it came my turn to speak, my tears surprised me. "I used to faithfully pray the promise of Exodus 23:20 for my children, and today you have given me an affirmation of that promise. God sent an angel to protect Lindsay from a mother who tried to change her strong-willed personality. Yet He kept growing her into the person He created her to be… in preparation for the places He'd planned for her. Your words today have blessed me."

Lord, I'm grateful for the way You grew Lindsay, and I pray You give other parents the trusting hope and patience they'll need while You grow their children for Your purposes. —Carol Kuykendall

Digging Deeper: Proverbs 22:6, 1 Corinthians 13:11

Monday, October 16

A merry heart does good, like medicine, but a broken spirit dries the bones. —Proverbs 17:22 (NKJV)

I read an article by a doctor who doesn't believe there is a causative relationship between a good attitude and good health. It is on my mind today because I feel a cold coming on.

The doctor's concern is if people's minds have power over their bodies, then wouldn't it stand to reason that they are in part to blame for their physical ailments? My wife suffers with lupus, and it is very hurtful when people think that if only Julee had a more optimistic outlook she would get better. It is hard to be positive when you're sick.

With all due respect to the good doctor, I think the jury is still out on whether a person's thinking can directly affect health and healing. It makes sense to me that optimism is a key advantage to staying healthy. A positive person is more likely to eat right, exercise, take medicine, get rest, and follow through on physical therapy and other medical advice. Her health is more likely to improve than that of the negative, fatalistic person who is less motivated toward these beneficial behaviors.

Maybe there's no escaping this cold, but more studies than not say that a faithful and prayerful person is more likely to get better sooner. Or at the very least to feel better about being sick. I'll take that outcome.

Lord, You must have endured a cold or two during Your thirty-three years on earth. You share in all our suffering. Help me to always keep a positive attitude about my health. —Edward Grinnan

Digging Deeper: Proverbs 16:24, 3 John 1:2–4

Tuesday, October 17

"With God are wisdom and might; he has counsel and understanding." —Job 12:13 (ESV)

In my work, I often sit around a table with a lot of smart people, wrestling together with tough issues, the kind where really good, constructive answers can be pretty hard to come by.

So what do you do when you're facing a challenge that's truly got you stymied? I've begun using an idea I learned from a three-year-old at my church. He was down in front for the sermon, as he always was, neither sitting still nor paying attention, as he never did. At one point he approached the pastor, tugged on the sleeve of her robe, and asked, "When is God coming?"

There was laughter in the congregation, but I just marveled. This three-year-old had asked the question that every single human being who has faced a daunting decision or a busted-up family or a hurting friendship or a shocking diagnosis or a messy world thinks: *When is God coming?*

So I tried it at my next meeting and then at another. What I discovered is that often the most brilliant answers are revealed by simple, clear, concise questions that help us refocus on what's most important. Here are five that I use: (1) When is God coming? (2) Is that really true? (3) What is our real purpose? (4) What is my heart's desire? and (5) How can I help you?

What do you need from God today? Maybe the answer is in your question.

May the simple questions of my heart, God, reveal Your profound presence in my life today. Help me to listen for Your answers. —Jeff Japinga

Digging Deeper: Proverbs 4, James 1:5–8

Wednesday, October 18

Give thanks to the God of heaven. His love endures forever. —Psalm 136:26 (NIV)

I have a new strategy for nudging my students to revise their work. While collecting papers, I remind them of my specific expectations for that assignment and how I plan to grade it. "Anyone wish they'd done something differently?" I ask. Hands go up, and we discuss the corrections they'd like to make.

I used to say, "Okay, give me a revision and I'll grade that." Maybe two students would show up at the next class, revisions in hand.

"Why didn't the rest of you revise?" I'd ask.

"I forgot to." "No money in my printer account." "I forgot what I wanted to change."

So this semester I've been giving them less time to forget—only till midnight that same day—and I have them e-mail me their revisions. Before going to bed I send the class a reminder, and in the morning my in-box overflows with new work. The majority of the students revise, and their writing demonstrates they've genuinely learned something.

One student sent not only his revision but also a thank-you for the reminder: "Professor Kirk, I just wanted to let you know it makes me happy when you call us *sweet ones* when you e-mail us!"

My students teach me so many things. Lesson one was that the less time we take after noticing a fault to correct it, the likelier we are to get the job done. And lesson two? How wonderful God must feel when we notice and appreciate the constant reminders of His love. Truly, we are His sweet ones.

Father, I just wanted to let You know how happy it makes me to be called Your beloved. —Patty Kirk

Digging Deeper: Deuteronomy 33:12

Thursday, October 19

This is the message we have heard from him and proclaim to you, that God is light, and in him is no darkness at all. —1 John 1:5 (ESV)

We're driving home from swim team practice, and it's quiet because my soul is under a great deal of distress. There's worry, uncertainty, about a circumstance with a son.

"You okay, Mom?" my twelve-year-old, Samuel, asks. He's riding in the passenger seat. His hair is wet from the pool. His profile is young-man strong.

"Yes," I say. But Samuel has a tender spirit. He's sensitive to my heart.

We ride along in silence. The night is cool, and as we move down the road that runs by the river, there's the scent of burning leaves.

I'm thinking, courting worry, conjuring fear, injecting my family into the world of what-ifs. But Samuel's voice pulls me from all that's spinning in my head. "Look, Mom," he says. He points out the window. "It's so beautiful. Full and bright."

I look to the sky, and the moon is like a pale paper cutout against black velvet. It's striking, luminous, and strong, as though it has torn through the darkness. Something about it hits me in the deepest place. Suddenly, my throat is tight. I swallow hard and press back tears. "Do you mind if I pull over?" I ask Samuel.

"No," he says. "That would be nice."

And so we sit. The river flows outside my window. Nighttime folds around the van. My son, strong and compassionate and kind, sits beside me. He takes my hand. Together we watch the moon.

Life can hold all kinds of darkness, and darkness can be overwhelming. It can try to tug and pull and swallow and steal. But it won't win. I'm a follower of the Light.

Lord, thank You for being the Light of my world. Amen. —Shawnelle Eliasen

Digging Deeper: Isaiah 42:16; John 1:4, 9:5

Friday, October 20

When you are full, you will refuse honey, but when you are hungry, even bitter food tastes sweet. —Proverbs 27:7 (GNT)

When my bronchitis wouldn't go away, the doctor put me on stronger medicine whose side effect was a loss of appetite. All the foods I usually crave became almost repulsive, including spaghetti, soups, fruit—even popcorn, my pièce de résistance. I just nibbled at my food and excused myself from the table.

"You have to eat something," my wife, Sharon, insisted. "You can't get well without nourishment."

I lost fifteen pounds in two weeks. It sounds good, losing weight, but I wouldn't go through that again for anything. It was scary. For the first time in my life I could see that appetite is a friend, a great gift from God to protect me. I have to control it, of course, but without it I would soon be dead.

I have other appetites: a taste for beauty, for music, for fine automobiles. All of these have their downside, but each of them adds a certain zing to my life. What would my life be like without the beauty of grandchildren to charm me? How could I stand the monotony of freeway driving without beautiful music in the background? And without the hope of a new car every so many years, I might lose interest in life altogether.

I am learning to appreciate my appetites because they indicate that I am alive and healthy, and without them, life would be unbearably dull.

I thank You for hunger pangs, Father, which drive me to seek manna from heaven. —Daniel Schantz

Digging Deeper: Matthew 5:6; Luke 6:21, 25

Saturday, October 21

BEAUTY FROM ASHES: Don't Quit
Let us run with determination the race that lies before us. —Hebrews 12:1 (GNT)

Katie's divorce was finalized in April. In August, she had double hernia repair surgery. While recuperating, she told me about her plans to run a half-marathon in October, six weeks post-op.

"This sounds dangerous. Are you sure?"

"It's something I have to do. It's important to me. Running is a part of who I am—or at least who I used to be."

I remembered her high school years of running track. She'd been a sprinter and had never run a half-marathon.

On race day she texted at 7:55 a.m. "Say a prayer that I finish strong."

I texted the same Scripture I'd given her years ago before every track meet: "Those who trust the Lord will find new strength. They will... run without getting tired" (Isaiah 40:31, CEV).

Soon, I got another text: "Pray. Mile 8. This is hard."

"Praying. I love you!"

"Mile 10. Can barely move my legs. Pain in my sides. Keep praying."

I wanted to text, "Just quit!" Instead I wrote, "I'm praying. Text me when you finish!"

Shortly after 10:00 a.m., a picture flashed of Katie crossing the finish line. She called and cried happy tears. "Thanks for praying, Mom. When I wasn't sure if I could keep going, I knew you and God wouldn't let me quit."

Lord, when the road ahead of us looks impossible, You cheer us on. You alone are our strength.
—Julie Garmon

Digging Deeper: Psalm 59:17, 2 Corinthians 12:10

Sunday, October 22

Peter knocked at the outer entrance, and a servant named Rhoda came to answer the door. When she recognized Peter's voice, she was so overjoyed she ran back without opening it and exclaimed, "Peter is at the door!" —Acts 12:13–14 (NIV)

My granddaughter Maddy was born on my birthday, the very best birthday gift of my life! My daughter Jenny Adele went into labor in the morning and phoned to let me know she was heading to the hospital. There have been few times when I have been more excited.

I rushed out the door, jumped in the car, and started for the hospital. On the way, I remembered I had a nail appointment that morning, so I swung by the salon and explained why I had to cancel. The salon was in the mall and I knew several of the business owners, so naturally I stopped by to tell them my good news.

As I left the mall, I passed the bank where one of my friends was manager; I hurried inside to let Betty know. I even stopped strangers on the street and blurted out my joy.

Long story short: I missed Maddy's birth. I was too busy spreading the good news.

As I read the story of Rhoda, who left Peter standing at the door, knocking, while she rushed to let everyone know their prayers had been answered, I thought, *Yup, that would have been me!*

Father God, I love Your surprises and the wonderful excitement You bring into our lives.
—Debbie Macomber

Digging Deeper: Proverbs 15:30, Luke 9:6

Monday, October 23

So God set another time for entering his rest, and that time is today. God announced this through David much later in the words already quoted: "Today when you hear his voice, don't harden your hearts." —Hebrews 4:7 (NLT)

After two days of heavy winds, I noticed an abundance of leaves floating in the swimming pool. *I'll skim them out tomorrow*, I told myself.

The next day, the leaves were no longer floating. They were resting on the bottom. I'd let them become waterlogged, and they now formed a dark brown carpet across the pool's bottom. I shouldn't have waited. The easy job of skimming had just morphed into the exhausting task of scraping and lifting. It felt like shoveling sludge.

As I pushed the heavy basket across the bottom, chasing leaves that didn't want to be caught, I thought how much easier life with God was when

I didn't procrastinate over spiritual things. I'd let some bitterness build up in my heart. Unkind intentions floated on its surface. There were Bible readings to catch up on and some attitude adjustments to make, a relationship to reconcile, a thank-you card to write. I shouldn't wait.

Now's the time, I thought to myself, *before these issues become heavy, spiritually waterlogged. Before they sink and double in difficulty.*

I finished my pool duties, grateful for a reminder to listen to God's voice today.

Dear Father, may I never resist the promptings of Your Spirit and Your Word. Spare me from letting my troubles grow needlessly difficult simply because I put them off. —Bill Giovannetti

Digging Deeper: Ephesians 4:22–24

Tuesday, October 24

"For six years you shall prune your vineyard...."
—Leviticus 25:3 (ESV)

While my wife, Beth, and I are not skilled gardeners, we enjoy nurturing potted plants. The column-lined porch of our old Southern house is draped with hanging ferns and filled with tropical hibiscus— my favorite plants native to my childhood home in the lush Philippine Islands. Hibiscus grow to be large shrubs and produce red, orange, and yellow trumpet-shaped flowers. Framed by dark green leaves, the flowers make me smile each morning to see the new life that has bloomed overnight.

As winter approaches, however, Beth prunes our hibiscus to a smaller size. I wince to see the branches shortened as we bring these plants into the warmth of our house. I do not like the pruning process. But my wife assures me it is the winter pruning that allows the plants to erupt into new and vital rejuvenation when spring arrives. Then the hibiscus explode with growth, and flowers of astonishing beauty reappear.

Pruning is necessary for vitality. So it is with my life. Sometimes I have to be cut down to size by a change in circumstance in order to be prodded into new growth and creative activity. It usually comes with the change of seasons. I became a youth minister in my young adulthood, a pastor during middle age, and a professor in my senior years. Each required a pruning process, and all led to new growth, new beauty, and new fruitfulness of labor and creativity.

Father, may I not dread Your pruning process. Amen.
—Scott Walker

Digging Deeper: John 15:2

Wednesday, October 25

"You haven't tried this before, but begin now. Ask, using my name, and you will receive, and your cup of joy will overflow." —John 16:24 (TLB)

At eight in the morning I asked my husband, Jack, to take me to the emergency room. Normally, I believe the body heals itself, given enough time, but something wasn't right. The hospital staff admitted me with a severe case of swine flu and a serious lung infection. For the next five days, I lived in a quarantine room with no visitors except Jack. He came the first two days, wearing a mask, but the chair in my room was uncomfortable and I didn't feel like talking, so I sent him home.

Alone in my room, I kept wishing I had some flowers to look at. I thought of the wedding at Cana where Jesus performed His first miracle. I thought, *If Mary could ask Jesus to provide more wine, and He turned big vats of water into wine, then I could surely ask my husband to bring me some flowers.*

The next time Jack called to see if I needed anything, I said, "Flowers. Something small, not expensive, but cheerful." A few hours later, he brought me daisies, carnations, chrysanthemums, and baby's breath in a yellow flower pot. It was perfect!

It's okay to ask for what we need. And often our request is a gift to the person we're asking. Jack was delighted to bring me something he knew I would appreciate just as I'm sure Jesus was happy to do something that would bring joy to His mother and the bride and groom.

Lord, You know my needs before I do. Thank You for the courage to ask for what I need and for providing loved ones who do Your work. —Patricia Lorenz

Digging Deeper: John 2:1–11, 4:43–54

Thursday, October 26

"You must not covet...." —Exodus 20:17 (NLT)

Lust isn't merely of the flesh; it tempts the mind with the impulse: I must have this at once."

I set down the book, chuckling. *That sounds like shopping in town.* I live on a remote cattle ranch. Because of the long drive, going to town is an all-day event. I make extensive lists and only go when I have to. Stores in town are small and unpredictably stocked, so getting everything on my list often proves difficult. The town motto ought to be "I'll have to order that."

During the next town run after I finished the book, a new chore coat pulled me like a magnet inside the farm supply store. Amazingly, they even had my size. *It's meant to be*, I rationalized. *If I don't buy it now, I'll never get another chance.*

Two aisles over, I loaded buckets of trans-hydraulic fluid into my cart and checked my list: lag bolts, barbed wire, T-posts. Things I needed. I looked at the coat. *The coat I have isn't worn-out, but I want this…*

Wait. Was this lust in the farm supply store? I fought the impulse and reluctantly hung the coat back on the rack.

I regretted it for a while. As predicted, my size was gone the next time I was in town, but the urge had passed. I knew I'd done the right thing when I unearthed a truly needed hydraulic floor jack on sale for the same price as the coat.

Lord, You provide for my real needs. Give me strength to overcome life's temptations, even the little ones.
— Erika Bentsen

Digging Deeper: Proverbs 14:30, Matthew 26:41

Friday, October 27

Rejoice in the Lord always; again I will say, rejoice. —Philippians 4:4 (ESV)

Ordering school portraits for my children has always been frustrating. Finding the right outfits and styling my children's hair can get hectic, but that's not the part that bothers me. The challenge is completing the order form. Packages are designed for "intact" families: two parents; two sets of grandparents; and a host of aunts, uncles, and cousins.

This label doesn't quite fit our family. Loving, supportive, and beautiful? Yes. Intact? No. With one set of grandparents divorced and remarried, our family hasn't fit the mold for over a decade.

I usually end up purchasing a school portrait package and at least one add-on picture. So when I opened my son's order form, I expected that same annoyance. Then I remembered: my parents passed away earlier this year.

This portrait season, our family fit the traditional mold. My children have only two sets of grandparents now. This time my usual frustration was replaced by overwhelming sadness. Ironically, I longed for the complicated planning and adding on of previous years. I wished I could turn back the hands of time.

I'm learning now to be grateful for all that life brings. After all, I never know when I might be faced with a longing for yesterday.

Heavenly Father, may I learn to rejoice today and every day, no matter what challenges may come my way. —Carla Hendricks

Digging Deeper: Habakkuk 3:17–19, 2 Corinthians 6:4–10

Saturday, October 28

PARENTING ANEW: Finding Ways to Fish

There is a time for everything, and a season for every activity under the heavens. —Ecclesiastes 3:1 (NIV)

The red tips are blooming. That means the pompano are running," my husband, Chuck, remarked, his voice tinged with regret.

Becoming parents to my three-year-old grandson was not in our plans when we got married as empty nesters just a few years ago. But when Family Services asked us to take in Logan because he couldn't stay with his mother anymore, we said yes. Logan's father, my youngest son, single and working two jobs, wouldn't be able to care for his son either...at least not yet.

The free lifestyle that Chuck and I had enjoyed was suddenly curtailed by a child's schedule, so we needed to make sacrifices in our personal time. One of the things we had to give up was fishing. We live in an area surrounded by water, and fishing had been integral to our relationship. Chuck introduced me to this activity while we dated and even proposed to me when we were in our boat. We loved getting out on the water early, basking in the first rays of sunlight, and enjoying the peace and tranquility of nature.

But fishing was no longer possible for us to do together. We tried taking Logan with us, but having a youngster poses many challenges—from keeping him busy to making sure he is safe all the time while he is jabbering.

I hated to take the joy of fishing away from Chuck. So for Father's Day, Logan and I bought Chuck a kayak, allowing him to easily go off by himself.

I miss going with my husband, but I'm happy he's happy.

Lord, thank You for giving Chuck a chance to fish again. Help us to find other ways to be together.
—Marilyn Turk

Digging Deeper: Psalm 65:8, Ecclesiastes 7:14

Sunday, October 29

Greet all God's people in Christ Jesus....
—Philippians 4:21 (NIV)

My husband, Gordon, didn't consult me when he signed us up to be greeters for church once a month. I wasn't happy about it. The last thing I felt like doing was acting cheerful when I was the one needing some cheering up because of the long, emotionally draining journey we'd been on with our son who'd gone through a divorce and was depressed.

There was plenty to complain about. We had to be there by 8:00 a.m., so I lost thirty minutes of sleep! We started in the dead of winter, and I froze every time the door opened. Plus, there wasn't much action at my entryway at such an early hour. I whiled away time watching the woman who sets up the coffee near the entrance. Then, as I finished my shift, I was told I was supposed to be stationed at the door *after* the service to say farewell to people too!

When I returned to my post, I was surprised to find the area buzzing with activity. Who knew that coffee could draw so many people? Suddenly, a friend came up and hugged me. A woman from my prayer group whispered in my ear that she was praying for me. More folks warmly shook my hand and beamed smiles at me. By the time I left, I realized that even though I had been a reluctant greeter, it hadn't stopped God from being an unsparing generator of good people bringing good cheer, even when I was personally fresh out of it.

Dear Lord, open up my heart to welcoming others today so that I might be filled with Your hospitality. Amen. —Karen Barber

Digging Deeper: Mark 9:15, Acts 15:4

Monday, October 30

For it is by grace you have been saved, through faith—and this is not from yourselves, it is the gift of God. —Ephesians 2:8 (NIV)

I was irritable. My two boys were annoying me as I tried to get them ready for school. They played when they should have been getting dressed, dragged through breakfast as they talked more than they chewed, and had a sword fight with their toothbrushes instead of brushing their teeth.

"Hurry up!" I shouted through each task. I nagged as I pointed to their shoes, mumbled under my breath as we walked to the elevator, and then plodded through the gray morning to school. I couldn't wait to get there. I needed to be child-free, and the sooner we got there, the sooner that would happen.

We arrived. I shooed them through the gate to the school entrance without my customary kiss and hug. My older son, Brandon, got to the door but then turned back to give me a hug. Then he stopped my younger son, Tyler, in his tracks, and whispered in his ear.

"What are you doing?" I barked. "You're late! Get inside!"

Tyler walked toward me with that "obedient little brother" mug on his face. That's when I realized what Brandon was telling him to do: "Go hug Mom."

My heart crumbled. I didn't deserve my sons' hugs or their compassion. But I humbly accepted the love, the grace, and the lesson my sons extended to me that day.

Lord, You give Your grace for the very reason that I'm not worthy of it. Thank You. —Karen Valentin

Digging Deeper: Ephesians 2:9–10

Tuesday, October 31

"See, I have tattooed your name upon my palm...."
—Isaiah 49:16 (TLB)

We'd had a fun-packed weekend with our grandchildren Olivia and Caden and our great-nephews Derek and Dominick. Tuesday morning I felt unwell, but I thought I was just tired. By suppertime, though, I was in too much pain to eat. At four o'clock Wednesday morning, my husband, Don, drove me to the emergency room. Five hours, three doctors, and multiple tests later, I was in the ICU, where I received antibiotics and pain medications while waiting for a surgeon to review test results.

It was late afternoon before the surgeon finished his scheduled procedures and examined me. He was "98 percent sure" it was appendicitis; it was. The surgery was uneventful and my recovery smooth. The only thing that wasn't routine was my attitude. I usually have a problem with letting go and letting God.

From the time I walked though the hospital door until my release, I didn't have a single moment of panic, fear, or worry. I didn't care that I met the surgeon less than one hour before he operated or that I hadn't checked the credentials of the nurses who managed my IVs. I trusted them to provide everything I needed for a full recovery.

Now, when a worry pops up, I take a deep breath and remember that experience. I was safe with people I didn't know. Why wouldn't I be far safer with my heavenly Father, Who has my name written on the palm of His hand?

"Lord, I would place my hand in thine content, whatever lot I see, since 'tis my God that leadeth me." ("He Leadeth Me" by Joseph H. Gilmore)
—Penney Schwab

Digging Deeper: Psalm 23, Luke 12:6–7

IN GOD'S HANDS

1 _____

2 _____

3 _____

4 _____

5 _____

6 _____

7 _____

8 _____

9 _____

10 _____

11 _____

12 _____

13 _____

14 _____

15 _____

16 _____

17 _____

18 _____

19 _____

20 _____

21 _____

22 _____

23 _____

24 _____

25 _____

26 _____

27 _____

28 _____

29 _____

30 _____

31 _____

NOVEMBER

*Let the peace of Christ rule in your hearts,
since as members of one body you were
called to peace. And be thankful.*

—Colossians 3:15 (NIV)

Wednesday, November 1

"The seed sprouts and grows, though he does not know how." —Mark 4:27 (NIV)

Ever since I drew pictures of them in second grade and labeled them "sedes," I've been fascinated by seeds. I could never figure out how a tiny, dried-up brown speck might be buried in the dirt and then emerge green as a bean or a flower just about the time I had given up on it. Yet even as a child, I knew God had a hand in the process.

For years, I shared with my children the miracle of sprouting seeds on a wet paper towel in the garden and in pots on the windowsill. Later, my granddaughter Hannah was delighted when marigolds popped through soil in a paper cup and when an avocado pit, suspended in water, sent down roots and turned into a skinny tree. Nowadays, my children and granddaughter continue gardening traditions on their own.

So when I wintered in Florida and nearby Bok Tower Gardens needed volunteers to teach elementary school students about seeds, I leaped at the chance. Still, I wondered whether kids raised on twenty-first-century technology would find the plants at all interesting.

Clare, our leader, identified the sepals, petals, stamens, and pistil using a model flower as big as her head. The third graders identified the same parts on a flower with petals like a freesia. Then, using a plastic knife, we carefully sliced open the bulbous ovary at the top of the stem and showed the students how to view the contents with a hand lens.

"Oh my," blurted a little boy, "there's a *seed* in there!"

Oh my, indeed. God, You amaze another generation with the mystery of life. —Gail Thorell Schilling

Digging Deeper: Genesis 1:29–31

Thursday, November 2

For the Spirit God gave us does not make us timid, but gives us power.... —2 Timothy 1:7 (NIV)

"To celebrate my birthday, we'll be cross-country skiing from our home to a restaurant. Hope you can join us." I stared at the e-mail from our friends in Crested Butte, Colorado. *That sounds like fun*, I thought. I'd reached the one-year mark since my hip-replacement surgery. But skiing? *I should decline. Or maybe I can drive and meet them at the restaurant.*

I thought about my four-year-old grandson Wyatt's visit several months earlier. We were walking on our property, which contains patches of low-lying cactus. The previous day his sister had stepped on one. Wyatt was afraid he would too, but he didn't want to miss out on the walk, so he'd taken my hand and talked his way through the prickly areas: "You can do this. Be brave. You can do it." Once he'd done it, his smile stretched from ear to ear.

I made the decision to go.

Several weeks later I clicked into my skis. A hefty snowfall had preceded our trek. The air was clear and frigid. Talk and laughter filled it as we joined our friends in preparation for the hour-long ski to dinner. "You can do this," I told myself. "Be brave. You can do it."

I began tentatively and then gained courage. My skis slid over crunching snow. White-robed mountains towered majestically. Brilliant stars punctuated the sky. I felt that God was with me, and my fear disappeared, replaced by exhilaration.

Thank You, God, that with You by my side, I can do it. —Kim Henry

Digging Deeper: Psalm 18:29, Proverbs 3:25–26

Friday, November 3

Rejoice in the Lord alway: and again I say, Rejoice. —Philippians 4:4 (KJV)

When I am tempted to grouse, I think of Pumpkin, our family Chihuahua, a rescue dog. He was smart and charming. If you said, "That baby can dance!" Pumpkin would stand on his two hind legs and hop. If you said, "Look at him smile!" Pumpkin would bare his teeth in a canine version of a grin. Each year we adored him more, and he loved us in return.

One night, even though he was getting up in age, Pumpkin followed me as I made my way to my third-floor bedroom. I was happy to have his company. However, I was roused from my sleep by the gentle sound of a trickling stream. *Ah . . .* My sigh soon turned to an alarmed gasp. "Pumpkin!" I stumbled angrily to the bathroom for a basin of hot water, cleanser, and a scrub brush.

In the moonlight, with his head bowed, Pumpkin looked like a mortified bed wetter. Suddenly, a thought came to me: *Be grateful that you have a dog to clean up after, a dog who loves you.*

I sighed again and then whispered, "It's okay, boy. Mama loves you."

When I finished cleaning up, I nuzzled my dog. Soon we were both back to sleep.

Lord, thank You for Your many blessings and for reminding me to be grateful. —Sharon Foster

Digging Deeper: 1 Chronicles 16:10, Ephesians 5:18–20, Colossians 3:15

Saturday, November 4

Let all bitterness and wrath and anger and clamor and slander be put away from you, along with all malice. Be kind to one another, tenderhearted, forgiving one another, as God in Christ forgave you. —Ephesians 4:31–32 (ESV)

"I was hurt," I said. "I sat at the table and waited. I wanted to be pursued."

My friend Kim sipped her coffee. I'd been telling her about a miscommunication that had happened between my husband and me the night before. Lonny had texted: *I miss you. Date tonight after boys' basketball practice? 9:00?* I'd been missing him too. We'd been running wild with things for our sons. We needed the time alone.

But that evening our plans fell apart. Lonny forgot to stop by the store after work, and dinner was delayed. Basketball practice went late too. The little boys were surly and fought during baths. By nine o'clock I was on a short fuse, and Lonny went upstairs to wrangle the boys into bed. He never came back down.

"Why didn't you just go upstairs and tell him that you wanted to go?" Kim asked.

"I told you. I wanted to know that our time together mattered to him."

Kim looked at me in a way that made me squirm. "I'm sorry," she said, "but you didn't have a date because you were being stubborn."

I opened my mouth to refute Kim's comment. I'd just wanted to feel valued, to hold an important place in the crazy pace of the day. But then something washed over me like a healing salve, comforting the wounded edges, making my heart clean. "Lonny's a good guy," I said. "He loves me well."

Kim just nodded. She didn't need to say anything else. Her words had already brought understanding and truth to my soul.

Lord, help me to assume the best of others. Amen.
—Shawnelle Eliasen

Digging Deeper: Proverbs 11:27, 15:13; Ephesians 4:29

Sunday, November 5

And the Lord...said, Write the vision, and make it plain.... —Habakkuk 2:2 (KJV)

I did hear a Voice once. I was in despair. It was the nether reaches of the night. No one is up at that hour for any good reason. I was up because I was terrified and broken and helpless and lost. The bedroom door was closed and the windows were closed and everyone else was asleep in their rooms, but a Voice spoke to me. It was so clear and crisp that I looked out the window to see if someone was there.

I am a little uncomfortable sharing the exact words, so I will paraphrase. The Voice told me to lose the urge to edit and control and repair and fix and understand what was happening in the house.

The Voice was gentle and calm but firm about this. It brooked no argument, so I did not argue. I listened long for more, but there was no more.

It was enough. Something loosed in me, and I surrendered to whatever was going to be. I came to realize slowly that all I could do was be patient and gentle and open, and so that is what I tried to be over the next two years as things went the way they went.

I know this sounds mysterious and mystical, but it wasn't. It was stunning and real and frightening, and it might well have saved my family from shattering. It doesn't make sense, so I'll just tell you that a Voice spoke to me and I heard it and I suspect you know what I mean.

Dear Lord, as *You* know very well indeed, there are more things beyond our ken than we will ever know. But because we cannot explain them does not mean that they are not so and not gifts of extraordinary, immeasurable grace. Thank You. —Brian Doyle

Digging Deeper: 1 John 4:1

Monday, November 6

Don't get involved in foolish, ignorant arguments that only start fights. —2 Timothy 2:23 (NLT)

I typed an offhand response to a friend's Facebook post but shouldn't have. Her remark was political in nature and I try to avoid political disputes, but my comment had seemed harmless enough. Someone else thought otherwise. A woman I'd never met decided to point out how foolish my comment was. My response to try to diffuse the situation served only to further ruffle her feathers. *Argh!* Why had I gotten myself into this ridiculous argument? I was offended, indignant, and angry.

At five feet four inches, I've never been physically imposing, but with words I can be dangerous. *Oh, she has no idea whom she's dealing with!* I thought, dozens of scathing responses rushing into my brain. Which one would serve best to put this stranger in her place? I had so many zingers it was hard to choose. Then I made the hardest choice of all: I deleted all of my comments and left the conversation.

It bothered me to think that the woman would conclude she'd scared me off, that she'd "won." But it troubled me more to think that I was so prideful I worried about it at all.

Maybe I need to spend less time working on my comebacks and more time working on my heart.

**Lord, give me more wisdom and less pride.
Help me to put my energy into things
that really matter.** —Ginger Rue

Digging Deeper: Ecclesiastes 7:25, James 3:6

Tuesday, November 7

"Fear not. . . ." —Isaiah 41:10 (NKJV)

It was a somber crowd that gathered together after the polls had closed. We were waiting to hear the results of a bond renewal election. Passage would mean additional funds to finance much-needed programs. Voting it down would mean budget cuts and layoffs. Employees were doing their best to stay upbeat, but the tension was apparent.

My boss rose to speak. In a voice heavy with emotion he said, "I realize I have a choice. I could be a person full of fear or a person full of faith." He looked around at the crowd. "Whatever the outcome, I'm choosing to be a person full of faith. We are going to be okay, no matter what."

I was standing with coworkers, and Monica turned to me. "I sure needed to hear that," she said. "I'm waiting to hear the results of some medical tests. I want to have that kind of faith, too, but I'm just so afraid."

"I know how you feel," Sarah said. "I struggle with fear every day. I wake up with the 'what ifs' swirling in my head! What if my husband loses his job? What if my son doesn't get his scholarship? So, every day I have to pray to *not* be afraid."

"Every day?" I asked.

"Every day," Sarah answered. She smiled. "Did you know that 'Do not fear' is written in the Bible 365 times?"

"Really?" Monica said, surprised.

"Yes," Sarah replied. "So that's a daily reminder from God to live each day without fear."

Lord, may my faith always be bigger than my fear.
—Melody Bonnette Swang

Digging Deeper: Deuteronomy 31:6, Psalm 27:1

Wednesday, November 8

"No one after lighting a lamp hides it under a jar, or puts it under a bed, but puts it on a lampstand, so that those who enter may see the light."
—Luke 8:16 (NRSV)

The grocer was offering shoppers the chance to buy a small box of food to be donated to needy families for Thanksgiving. The boxes were stacked at the checkout area, and for an extra five dollars above their own order, folks could contribute a box to the huge bin that was in the center of the store. It was a very big deal, with clerks making a point of carrying over each box to the large container every time someone donated.

I don't like very big deals, especially when it comes to charity. I'm a firm believer in Jesus's admonition not to let the right hand know what the left hand is doing when giving alms. So when the clerk asked me if I wanted to contribute, I said sure.

But when she asked me to sign the box, I smiled uncomfortably. "Sign the box?"

The box had a few printed lines where the contributor could write a message and sign his or her name. I grimaced and shook my head.

She picked up the marker and wrote in large, looping script: "Happy Thanksgiving! Enjoy!"

After she strode over to toss my box into the bin, I slunk out of the store, ashamed that I'd lost the chance to lend a bit of humanity to my gift.

Generous God, keep me from letting my own hang-ups get in the way of doing Your work. Amen.
—Marci Alborghetti

Digging Deeper: Matthew 5:47, 10:42

Thursday, November 9

"You have made known to me the paths of life; you will fill me with joy in your presence." —Acts 2:28 (NIV)

It had only been one week since we'd lost our eight-year-old golden retriever, Millie, to cancer. My wife and I had never gone much longer than that without a dog. The night of Millie's death, I told Julee I sensed there was a dog out there waiting to be loved by us. She felt it too.

The dog in question was a six-month-old female, older than any puppy we'd ever gotten, and absolutely beautiful. Julee was on the floor with the pup in an instant. The dog's eyes shone like melted chocolate, and her coat was the color of the inside of a banana peel. "Give the woman the money," Julee whispered. "Let's get her out of here."

"I'd like to see the mother," I said to the professional breeder. She brought in the dog's mother, who acted like she hadn't had exercise in a long time. Mom and pup cavorted briefly while I completed the transaction. But before I did, I lifted the puppy up— all forty-two pounds of her—looked into her shining brown eyes, and caught my breath. I heard a distinct voice in my head say, *I've been waiting for you.*

We put the puppy on the leash and collar we'd brought, quickly collected all of her official papers, and practically ran out of the door. Julee jumped into the rear seat. The puppy didn't look back. She'd never been in a car but flew right up on Julee's lap and snuggled sweetly, as if she had finally found her family.

Father, You lead us down a path whose destination only You know, and we are rewarded by our faith. You have brought so many blessings to our lives, some of them with tails and eyes like melted chocolate. That's why we named this one Grace.
—Edward Grinnan

Digging Deeper: Psalm 107:8–9

Friday, November 10

One night the Lord spoke to Paul in a vision and told him, "Don't be afraid! Speak out! Don't quit! For I am with you and no one can harm you...."
—Acts 18:9–10 (TLB)

During World War II, my dad was a fighter pilot in the South Pacific. His older brother, my uncle Francis, flew over the Himalayas in the China-Burma-India theater. Both of them flew hundreds of miles over uncharted terrain that encompassed rugged mountains, formidable jungles, unpredictable weather, numerous fatalities, leaky gas barrels, and exposure to enemy aircraft fire.

One time I asked Dad, "How did you survive up there in those small planes when you were under fire? Weren't you scared?"

Dad answered, "Did you ever hear the phrase 'By a wing and a prayer'? Well, it's the best way to describe how we did it. We hoped the planes would hold up long enough, so we could get back to the primitive airstrips. And we prayed like our lives depended on it. That's where lifelong faith comes into play."

I've experienced fear a number of times (waiting for a diagnosis or crossing a bridge), and it always amazes me how a sincere, heartfelt prayer can calm me during scary times. It's as if the Holy Spirit soothes the trembling in my brain, allowing me to continue my journey in comfort.

Knowing how important faith was to my dad and to Uncle Francis, I now have no doubt how they both survived. Prayer saw them through, just as it sees each one of us through.

Heavenly Father, thank You for the calm that comes into my heart, mind, and soul whenever I step into a fearful place and think of You. —Patricia Lorenz

Digging Deeper: Psalm 56:1–7, Mark 6:50–51

Saturday, November 11

Whoever protects their master will be honored. —Proverbs 27:18 (NIV)

I'd never given a thought to doing anything to celebrate Veterans Day. Then my husband, Gordon, started his own Veterans Day tradition—taking out our two sons to a restaurant for lunch because all three had served in the military. Gordon and Chris served in the US Army and Jeff in the US Air Force.

One day I asked Chris what he thought about these yearly lunches and he said, "Dad tells the waitress we're all veterans. It's a good day because people always thank us for our service. We feel appreciated and connected to everyone who has served."

Chris's comment helped me to realize that I was missing out on the perfect opportunity to express my appreciation to those who have served. I decided to start a Veterans Day tradition of my own: sending e-mails of thanks to all of the veterans I know. I sat down right then and made my list. It's never too late to say thank you.

Dear Father, thank You so much for those who have served in our military. May I not be silent when it comes to thanking them. Amen.
—Karen Barber

Digging Deeper: Psalm 5:11, Proverbs 13:13

Sunday, November 12

And he shall send his angels with a great sound of a trumpet, and they shall gather together.…
—Matthew 24:31 (KJV)

"You know, Mom, trumpets are the loudest instruments," Solomon says. I'm making dinner in the kitchen just off the dining room/music room, and for the last twenty minutes I've been enduring the relentless repetition of the first few bars of the *Rocky* theme.

"I believe it," I answer. Solomon has been playing trumpet for four years now, and we're over the hump on ear-piercing wrong notes. Most of the time I'm in awe that he can create such beautiful music, though there are still moments when I wish he'd chosen something smaller, softer, like the flute or clarinet.

Solomon loves that *his* instrument is mentioned in the Bible. His eyes light up and a smile comes across his lips whenever he spots *trumpet*, as if it were placed there for him. My understanding of certain Scripture has transformed too. I nod in agreement the way only a mom of a trumpet player can when I come across verses that speak about the trumpet's strength, the way it signifies an alarm of war, a call to assemble, or a symbol of the beginning of deliverance, as in when "the great trumpet will be blown" (Isaiah 27:13, NKJV).

I'm finishing dinner when Solomon moves on to playing a trumpet concerto. In seconds, I feel my mood lift with the music, pure and peaceful, filling every nook of my spirit with heavenly sound.

Dear Lord, thank You for the many ways Your Word grows with our lives and in our hearts.
—Sabra Ciancanelli

Digging Deeper: Psalm 119:105, 2 Timothy 3:16–17

Monday, November 13

And my God will meet all your needs according
to the riches of his glory in Christ Jesus.
—Philippians 4:19 (NIV)

I spotted an envelope from a federal credit union
I'd never heard of and assumed it was junk mail.
I opened it to find a check for $843.00 and a
letter stating that I was receiving my portion of the
remaining balance in an account belonging to my
mother, who had passed away.

While assisting my sisters in managing our mother's
estate, I hadn't seen any documentation on this credit
union. I called one sister to get to the bottom of it.

She had received a duplicate letter and payment
and had called our other sister to inquire about
it. She'd reminded her of my mother's savings
account that she'd opened to contribute to her
grandchildren's education funds. Over several years
she had put away twenty-five dollars here, fifty
dollars there.

My eyes watered as I surveyed the check with new
understanding. Just the week before I'd been poring
over documents, trying to secure financial aid for my
son Kalin, a high school senior. Our savings weren't
much to speak of. I'd fretted, complained to my
husband, and finally prayed, asking God to provide

for Kalin's college education and for the faith to believe He would.

The check I held in my hand wouldn't cover even one semester. Yet it was God's reminder that He would provide. It was a reminder that He'd used my mother during her last years on earth to sacrifice for my children's sake. It was a reminder that my parents' love for education had created a legacy for my children. It was a reminder for me to never lose faith.

Lord, thank You for supplying all of my family's needs. May I learn to trust in Your gracious provision.
—Carla Hendricks

Digging Deeper: Matthew 6:25–34,
2 Corinthians 9:8

Tuesday, November 14

"Martha, Martha," the Lord answered, "you are worried and upset about many things, but few things are needed—or indeed only one...."
—Luke 10:41–42 (NIV)

This was new territory for me, appearing on a TV show. Anticipating the close-up camera shots, I'd resolutely stopped biting my fingernails to the quick. I'd scheduled a haircut. And for a week I'd been fussing about what I'd wear. Friends offered contradictory advice: "Bright but not red." "No, red is good." "That navy cotton dress—dark…"

The day before I boarded a plane to get to the out-of-state studio, I got a professional manicure. As for my attire: *I'll keep my options open,* I thought as I layered four potential outfits and three pairs of shoes into my carry-on. By the time I zipped it shut, it was heavy, laden with clothing, packed with stress.

At the airport gate, to brush up on the content of my presentation, I opened the book about hospitality that I'd be discussing. Right off the bat, a bold-faced chapter title grabbed my attention: "The Pressure of Perfect." *Yes, that's the name of my tension.* And then another, quoting Jesus's kind reproach to His harried hostess: "Martha, Martha." The admonition turned to a personal "Evelyn, Evelyn," spotlighting my preoccupation with my appearance more than with my message.

What to wear for the interview? The next morning I chose quickly and calmly: red and black; reliable pumps.

And later? "I liked your smile and comfortable presence," viewers noted—the intended welcome of my refocused heart.

Lord, when I'm preoccupied with self-centered details, give me a new, broader perspective on what's important. —Evelyn Bence

Digging Deeper: Philippians 4:4–9

A man's heart plans his way, but the Lord directs his steps. —Proverbs 16:9 (NKJV)

The lights flickered off, on, off, on, and then off… for good. Our family was plunged into darkness. Heavy winds had toppled a tree and pulled down some power wires in our mountainous area.

The blackout could not have come at a worse time. We had a four-hour drive set for 2:00 a.m. to catch a flight. It wasn't just the overnight commute that worried us. We were also prepping our home for an open house. That final rush of cleaning, polishing, arranging, and perfecting was suddenly interrupted by pitch-blackness.

Really, God?

My wife, Margi, and I looked at each other in the dim lighting. For us, no power also meant no water. No water meant no showers. After a day of cleaning and packing, the loss of a well-deserved shower hit us hard.

That's when our kids got hold of their flashlights, and the games began. Running, chasing each other, startling one another in the darkness—a cloud of disappointment dissipated in an atmosphere of fun. They held lights as we made the beds, washed the counters, cleaned the sinks. Perfectionism became "good-enoughism."

We loaded our car and began our trip early—at 11:30 p.m. We figured we could drive till we were tired and then find a hotel. At least we'd get a shower.

Wise Father, when plans go haywire, inspire me to trust that You have something better in store.
—Bill Giovannetti

Digging Deeper: Isaiah 55:8–9

Thursday, November 16

For he shall give his angels charge over thee, to keep thee in all thy ways. —Psalm 91:11 (KJV)

The sun wasn't even up when I got the e-mail saying school was canceled. I let the boys sleep and tried to get some work done. I was knee-deep in a problem when I heard Henry yell, "Yippee!" from his bedroom.

Looking out the window, I noticed the ground was completely covered with fresh, powdery snow. Solomon groaned, but I could tell from his smile he was thrilled to have the day off too.

Henry couldn't wait. He put on his snow pants and boots and ventured out in the cold without having cereal. I kept working, smiling now and then when the splat of a snowball would hit my office window.

Tony made grilled cheese sandwiches, and I went downstairs, surprised that it was already lunchtime. The boys were on the couch. Henry's mittens and boots were drying by the fire. His cheeks were still rosy from outdoors.

"Like your angel?" he asked. I didn't know what he was talking about, so I shrugged. "I made it for you, Mommy. Outside your window. You didn't see it?"

He ran upstairs, and I followed him to my office. Perfectly placed, just outside the window facing my desk, was my snow angel.

Dear Lord, thank You for the reminders that no matter what challenges I face, it's important to look up now and then, to see blessings right in view.
—Sabra Ciancanelli

Digging Deeper: Psalm 103:20, Hebrews 1:14

Friday, November 17

"Have faith in God." —Mark 11:22 (NLT)

It's 2:45 a.m. I make a fist and pound my pillow into shape, but it's no use. Sleep escapes me. Friends think ranch life is carefree and pastoral. It's anything but. Road disputes. Water disputes. Grazing restrictions...

I switch on the light and open my Bible. Israelites enslaved in Egypt. *Nah, not uplifting.* My thumb chooses another spot. Then another. The Israelites keep sinning. The prophets keep warning of total dispersal; only remnants survive. I sigh and close the book. Turmoil has been going on since the dawn of time and doubtless will continue until the end of time. I feel worse.

"Life would be so much better without all the stresses we put on ourselves and each other," I grumble.

The reply was unexpected: *I got them through that. I can get you through this. Believe Me. Trust Me. Follow Me.*

I reconsider the depressing Bible scenes. Though facing seemingly impossible odds, God's people didn't quit. I glance at the clock and feel a thrill. It's 3:16 a.m. I am reminded of John 3:16: "For God so loved the world."

I grab a piece of paper and scribble down ideas for the problems I can do something about. I add notes in the margins about the blessings God bestows on me. At that moment, I turn worry into worship. Peace surrounds me, and I drift off to sleep.

Life will never be easy, Lord, but You are there, just as You have been since the dawn of time and will continue to be until the end of time. —Erika Bentsen

Digging Deeper: Deuteronomy 30:9–10; Psalms 22:8, 32:10

Freely ye have received, freely give.
—Matthew 10:8 (KJV)

It was a cold day in Nashville, Tennessee. I was meeting my mother for lunch. Her mother, my grandmother Bebe, had died just a few months before, and today would have been her birthday. In addition to the generous life Bebe had enjoyed, she was the person who had most inspired us to live like Jesus.

"Brock, you can't outgive the Lord," I could almost hear her say as I got out of my car and threw on my warm overcoat. I was looking ahead to my mother and her loving smile. Even in her sadness, it was clear she chose living in joy, as Bebe would have wanted.

"Brock, did you see that poor homeless man? He must be freezing!" I hadn't, but it was just like her to put something like that first. Mom and I had a great visit regaling ourselves with the many "Bebe-isms" that meant so much to us.

Lunch almost finished, she motioned to our waiter. "Can we get a cheeseburger and fries to go?" She looked at me, eyes dancing. "A birthday present for Bebe."

As we walked out, my mom made her way to the homeless man. "My mother went to heaven a few months ago, and today is her birthday. We'd like to celebrate with you."

The man got a big smile on his face and wrapped his arms around my mother. "Miss, I knew there was something special about you when I saw you walking by!"

He was right. Happy birthday, Bebe!

Father, we celebrate Your saints by giving freely.
—Brock Kidd

Digging Deeper: Deuteronomy 15:7–8,
Proverbs 21:25–26

Sunday, November 19

Abide in Me, and I in you.... —John 15:4 (NAS)

Sometimes my most meaningful moments of prayer have little to do with words I speak or emotions I express to God. Rather they have much to do with remembering and obeying a word Jesus frequently used: *abide*.

When I was a seminary student, a New Testament professor explained that the Greek word translated as *abide* means to lean back and put down your full weight on an object. It is like lying on a bed or sitting in a chair.

There are some days when I am so perplexed, frustrated, or anxious that I cannot express myself in words. I do not know how to pray. In these moments, I have a favorite reclining chair that I sit in. I prop up my feet, kick back, close my eyes, and sink into silence. I often fall asleep. In so doing, I allow myself to abide in the Lord—to put down my full weight. Often, when I awake, my life is in better perspective. I am aware that I have been in the calming presence of God.

When the apostles were crossing the Sea of Galilee and encountered a storm that threatened to sink their small boat, they grew terrified. While they were fighting the waves, Jesus was asleep at the stern. He was not overcome with fear; He was abiding in the protection of His Father.

There is a time to talk to God with words and emotion. There are other times to abide in God and simply rest in His loving presence.

Father, may I abide in Your care, knowing that You will support me through all crises. Amen.
—Scott Walker

Digging Deeper: Psalm 55:22,
Mark 4:35–41, 1 Peter 5:7

Monday, November 20

With praise and thanksgiving they sang to the Lord.... —Ezra 3:11 (NIV)

"Are you happy?" my son asked, aware of how much mileage I have put in looking at apartments. The day we found our new place, I'd logged over sixteen thousand steps in one afternoon.

"I feel like...," I began and then paused to identify exactly what it was that I felt. Apartment hunting in New York City is insane. We'd been looking for that rarest of residences: an affordable three-bedroom in a building that accepts dogs, within walking distance of our current home. Something bigger than the nine-hundred square feet we'd been shown at one place and cleaner than the filth-encrusted lobby we'd seen at another. A space without a long list of complaints of noise, vermin, or building code violations.

We carried a flash drive with copies of tax returns, IDs, bank statements, W2s, a picture of the dog— for we knew that if we found a livable apartment, we'd need to act instantly.

"I feel the way you feel after a brutal winter with lots of snow and it's the first day you can go outside in the spring, wearing just a jacket," I told my son. Relieved, lightweight, free or, put another way, thankful.

My heart doesn't open wide with gratitude very often, so when it does—when my soul sings with a resounding *yes!*—I try to make a mental note of it so I can hum it at other times. The new apartment added another tune to my repertoire.

Lord Jesus, teach me to sing songs of
thankfulness and praise. —Julia Attaway

Digging Deeper: Psalm 95:1, 2 Corinthians 1:20

**Join us for our Thanksgiving Day of Prayer. Find
out more at guideposts.org/ourprayer.**

Tuesday, November 21

How can we thank God enough...?
—1 Thessalonians 3:9 (NIV)

I couldn't remember visiting her in the hospital. It's
such an automatic thing to call on a friend recovering
from surgery. But months after she came home,
I received a card. "I was remembering again your
kindness to me when I was hospitalized. Your visit
lifted my spirits and, I'm sure, had much to do with
my recovery. I just want to say thank you again."

Thank you again. I'm sure this gracious woman
had thanked me at the time but how much more
this meant! I kept her card on the refrigerator door
for weeks.

There's power in "thank you," not at the expected
time but out of the blue. What if I were to practice
the Second Thank-You?

The response when I actually do this is out of
proportion to the effort it takes. On my list was

the man who found my key and brought it to my apartment. "I've viewed strangers more kindly ever since," I wrote him months later. He wrote back that he'd sent copies of my letter to every grandchild. In July, I phoned the woman who led carolers through our apartment building last December. "I'd almost decided not to try it again this year," she said. "You've changed my mind!"

It's a strange thing too. As I write down the nice things people do, there are more and more of them to record.

Father, have I thanked You a second time for all You've done for me today? —Elizabeth Sherrill

Digging Deeper: 1 Chronicles 29:13,
1 Thessalonians 3:12

Wednesday, November 22

But as for me, I am poor and needy; may the Lord think of me. You are my help and my deliverer; you are my God, do not delay. —Psalm 40:17 (NIV)

I pleaded with God to help me settle into my new home. "This is so hard. I need Your help." I tried all kinds of petitions. Still, God seemed silent and, frankly, not very helpful.

Then I looked at what I was doing. I prayed, and then I sat down in my cozy chair to knit. Or

I escaped into a book. It was months, and I hadn't finished unpacking our boxes yet. *I'll get to it*, I promised myself. But I hadn't put anything on the walls or painted a room to freshen it up and make it feel like our home.

I was not committed to being in our new location. And if I wasn't willing to help, how could I expect God to do all the heavy lifting? I wanted Him to make my new house a home and my new community a neighborhood. I wanted a magic fix, when the process of settling in takes time as well as my participation.

I began to take my prayers more seriously. I asked for a different way to see settling in. I needed the discipline to unpack and not escape into a book or knitting. My prayers changed into: "Give me discipline to work for an hour unpacking. Grant me energy to do the hard things, like finding a new church. Help keep me calm when I get frustrated with how long it takes to do everything! Help me sustain an attitude of trust in You."

Most of all I remembered to say: "Thank You for being here with me wherever I live. Help me continue to make this house our new home."

Dear Father, help me put a little elbow grease into my prayers. Amen. —Lisa Bogart

Digging Deeper: Colossians 4:2,
1 Thessalonians 5:16–18, Hebrews 10:22–23

Thursday, November 23

**He who sows bountifully will also reap bountifully.
—2 Corinthians 9:6 (NKJV)**

"I just don't think I can do the traditional Thanksgiving dinner for the family this year," my wife said. "I'm tired. My joints hurt. My eyes are bad, and I make so many mistakes."

I felt bad for her, but I didn't know what to say.

The next day the phone rang. It was our granddaughter Hannah, a senior at the University of Missouri. She sounded excited. "I want to fix Thanksgiving dinner for everyone this year at my place!"

Sharon and I locked eyes. "Can she cook?" I asked.

"Oh yes. But can we get everyone into her little apartment?"

Not to worry. Hannah produced a feast. We piled our plates high and perched wherever we could find a spot. It was a wild and hilarious day. Even Eddie, her dog, enjoyed it.

On the way home, I said to Sharon, "You know what? You are reaping what you have sown."

"What's that supposed to mean?"

"Well, you taught your daughter and granddaughter to cook. Now you are reaping a harvest."

She said nothing but thought about it.

"This meal is just the beginning," I went on. "Who knows what amazing things your grand ones will do in years to come? It's the law of the garden. You have been sowing good seeds all your life. Now it's time for a harvest of happiness."

I could tell by the gleam in her eyes that I had finally found the right thing to say. God's law of sowing and reaping gives us hope for our September years.

I thank You, Lord, for the harvest that comes late in life, just when we need it most. —Daniel Schantz

Digging Deeper: Psalm 126:5–6, Galatians 6:9

Friday, November 24

Do nothing from selfish ambition or conceit, but in humility regard others as better than yourselves. —Philippians 2:3 (NRSV)

"I appreciate you."

During a business trip to Little Rock, Arkansas, I kept hearing that phrase over and over. I was having breakfast with my colleague Ken, and I thanked the server. He responded, "I appreciate you."

Ken said to a cashier, "Thank you for your wonderful service." She replied, "I appreciate you."

Maybe all food-service personnel are trained to reply to customers this way, I thought.

At our hotel, Ken noticed an older woman on her knees, working hard to clean the floor. As we walked by, Ken paused and said, "Thank you for your service." She looked up at him and said, "I appreciate you."

My nephew's girlfriend is from the area, so I asked her, "Do people always say, 'I appreciate you' in response to 'Thanks'?"

"Yes, all the time. It is an expression we're taught to say."

William James, an American psychologist and philosopher, wrote, "In every person from the cradle to the grave, there is a deep craving to be appreciated." Try saying those three life-giving words: *I appreciate you.* I guarantee it feels good to say and to hear.

Lord, I appreciate You. —Pablo Diaz

Digging Deeper: Mark 14:3–6, Romans 12:10

Saturday, November 25

O Lord my God, you are very great. You are clothed with honor and majesty, wrapped in light as with a garment.... —Psalm 104:1–2 (NRSV)

It's before sunrise in Central Park, near the end of my morning run. This was the same route I'd run the day before. And the day before that. An icy

New York City winter had rendered most paths too slippery, so I ran another loop around the ring road.

Since moving back here from San Jose, California, I'd felt unexpectedly cooped up. I missed the big skies, the landscape of the West. I missed the wild hills near our house, where running routes were infinitely varied and mornings felt fresh as creation itself.

I knew I was being irrational, ungrateful. In San Jose, I'd missed the hustle of the big city. Was I turning into one of those perpetually dissatisfied people?

The sun emerged from some clouds and cast a pale, wintry light on the skyline west of the park. The light reminded me of something. Suddenly, I remembered feeling homesick a few days earlier, especially for California mountains—symbols in our family of a whole outdoor way of life.

Be in the mountains in the city, a Voice said.

That light reflecting off the apartment buildings was exactly like early morning light at an alpine campsite, when the sun begins to crest the peaks, illuminating high places before reaching the basins.

The skyline was its own mountain range. And God was as present here as He was in the mountains. All I had to do to see Him was to stop complaining and give thanks for this wild, fresh morning here in the heart of the city.

"Thank You," I said. The light gathered strength as I ran the last mile home.

Gratefulness gives me eyes to see You, Lord. Help me to be thankful today. —Jim Hinch

Digging Deeper: Psalm 50:14–15

Sunday, November 26

"See, I am coming soon. . . . I am the Alpha and the Omega, the first and the last, the beginning and the end." —Revelation 22:12–13 (NRSV)

"Daddy, let me find it." I handed my well-worn pocket version of the New Testament and Psalms to Timothy. His small fingers thumbed through the pages for a passage in Revelation he'd learned in Sunday school. "This!" he said triumphantly. Then he read in a firm, clear voice, "'I am the Alpha and the Omega, the first and the last, the beginning and the end.' That's my favorite verse."

"Why do you like it?" I asked. Was it because it mirrored the challenge of remembering what letters went first in his spelling words, like the *e* or the *i* in *receive* or *neighbor*? Or maybe it was the dawning awareness of who was first and who was last in school tests and playground contests.

"It's just so big," he said. We got off the subway, and as we walked to his school I made a little speech about how Jesus had come and would come back and that we were in this period of both celebrating His coming and awaiting His return, that He was both in time and outside of time, a little like a sci-fi movie. "And we pray for His kingdom on earth to come as we prepare for Christmas."

Timothy walked in silence for a moment and then said, "But He's here now and He's everything. The Alpha, the Omega, the beginning, and the end."

"Yes," I said, "exactly."

"Bye, Daddy," he said, running to catch up with some friends. It made me think I would be running to catch up with *him* for the rest of his life.

Jesus is here now. Why didn't I put it that way? The beginning and end and everything in between.

Dear Lord, we await Your coming like we await the arrival of a best friend who is already here.
—Rick Hamlin

Digging Deeper: Psalm 118:21–22

Monday, November 27

Let us then approach God's throne of grace with confidence, so that we may receive mercy and find grace to help us in our time of need.
—Hebrews 4:16 (NIV)

I called my mom, sobbing, on the way to the hospital. "Mom," I choked out as my daughter wailed in the backseat, "Olivia broke her leg."

Two weeks before, I had stared down the barrel at a pinkeye diagnosis for my toddler, thinking about the drops I'd have to give her daily while I was thirty-nine weeks pregnant. "Lord," I prayed, "anything but pinkeye. I can't handle pinkeye, a toddler who touches everything, and a newborn!"

Turns out, my daughter didn't have pinkeye. Instead, a few weeks later when my newborn was one week old, Olivia broke her leg jumping on the bed.

As I drove to the hospital, racked with emotions, my mom calmed me. "Ashley," she said, "she's breathing. Her heart is beating. All the major parts are working. If her leg is broken, we'll deal with it. Just breathe. God's got this." I took deep breaths, settling down before I arrived at the ER.

An hour later, I headed home with a sleepy toddler and a diagnosis: Olivia had indeed broken her leg. I remembered my fear-racked prayer from weeks before. *I didn't think I could handle pinkeye. How am I going to handle a newborn and a toddler in a cast?*

I couldn't. I had to depend on the help of family, friends and, most of all, God.

God, forgive me when I put limits on Your power.
Remind me always that You are sovereign.
—Ashley Kappel

Digging Deeper: Exodus 23:25,
James 5:15–16

Tuesday, November 28

"You intended to harm me, but God intended it for good to accomplish what is now being done...."
—Genesis 50:20 (NIV)

I laid my son on the operating table and watched him giggle through the anesthesia mask. In a matter of seconds, Tyler's eyes closed. My full-of-life little boy was about to have his first surgery. Although it was a routine tonsillectomy, watching him lie motionless on that table was the hardest thing to see.

I walked down the corridor. *He'll be fine*, I thought to myself. *And God is going to use this*. I didn't just mean that Tyler would breathe easier after the surgery; God was doing more.

In the waiting room sat my ex-husband. After a year of no communication, he had recently come back into our sons' lives. Brandon and Tyler had spent time with him over the last few months, but this was my first time seeing him. We didn't speak much, but we did talk when we absolutely had to. And after the surgery, we went in to comfort our son. It was the first time in a long time that we both were in the same room with him.

Tyler was delirious with pain, but as my ex-husband and I both worked together to make our son comfortable and I saw him snuggled in his father's arms, I was grateful that God turns moments of pain into opportunities for something greater.

Lord, thank You for turning even the hardest circumstances into something better.
—Karen Valentin

Digging Deeper: Romans 8:28

Wednesday, November 29

Then Joab fell to the ground on his face and bowed himself, and thanked the king....
—2 Samuel 14:22 (NKJV)

I needed to write thank-you notes, but I kept putting it off. I don't have a computer, so all my messages are handwritten or typed.

I can still hear my mother telling me, "Always have an attitude of gratitude." She helped me write thank-you notes before I started school. I, too, had my girls write them as small children. (I never managed it with my boys.) Frequently, I run across notes from my daughters to my mother: "Dear Goge, I love my new pink sweater. It's the best. So are you. I love you. Julie." "Dear Goge, your present was just what I wanted. How did you know? Love, Jennifer." There were misspelled words, but that didn't matter.

I delayed attending to my notes because I'd become comfortable in my recliner. After all, I'm old and my joints hurt, especially my hands. I have little energy. *I'll do it tomorrow*, I told myself.

Satisfied with my excuses, I picked up the newspaper. I've always read the want ads since I was fresh out of college and searching for a job in Atlanta. They are like short stories: items for sale, puppies and kittens that need homes, families who want to buy a house...

I sat straight up when I read, "Thank you to the person who found my bracelet in the parking lot and turned it in. I'm so grateful to have it back."

I didn't wait another moment. I got up, selected a note card, and picked up a pen. "Dear Sara..."

Father, thank You for the Cross, my salvation, home, husband, children, grandchildren, beloved pets, cherished friends.... —Marion Bond West

Digging Deeper: Luke 17:15–19,
1 Thessalonians 1:2

Thursday, November 30

Above all, carry the shield of faith...and
the sword of the Spirit, which is God's word.
—Ephesians 6:16–17 (CEB)

Last November my husband, Don, and I attended
our grandson David's commissioning as a second
lieutenant in the US Marine Corps. My family has
a history of military service. My father was a World
War II pilot who spent months in a prison camp
after his plane was shot down. My brother Mike, a
career Marine, was in the Gulf War, and Don served
a two-year stint in the US Army.

I'm proud of their service, but I had mixed
feelings about David's joining the Marines. With
American troops serving throughout the world, there
is a strong possibility he will be in dangerous areas
and situations. Thinking about long deployments,
separation from family and friends, and extreme risks
faced by military personnel made it hard for me to
concentrate on the ceremony.

Then my brother presented a Mameluk sword
to David, which has been given to Marine officers
since 1825, in recognition and memory of the 1805
Battle of Derne, Tripoli, in North Africa. It was the first
American battle on foreign soil. As the presentation
ended, someone softly repeated the Marine motto:
Semper fidelis (always faithful).

David is a Marine and a man of faith. Along with his sword, he has "put on God's armor" (Ephesians 6:11, CEB) and placed his trust and confidence in Jesus Christ, Who is always faithful. That's where my trust and confidence must be as well.

Mighty One, You are "our shield and defender, the ancient of days, pavilioned in splendor, and girded with praise" (Robert Grant, 1833). —Penney Schwab

Digging Deeper: Psalm 28:7–8, Hosea 2:18, Romans 8:35–38

IN GOD'S HANDS

1 _____

2 _____

3 _____

4 _____

5 _____

6 _____

7 _____

8 _____

9 _____

10 _____

11 _____

12 _____

13 _____

14 _____

15 _____

16 _____

17 _____

18 _____

19 _____

20 _____

21 _____

22 _____

23 _____

24 _____

25 _____

26 _____

27 _____

28 _____

29 _____

30 _____

DECEMBER

"Glory to God in the highest heaven, and on earth peace to those on whom his favor rests."

—Luke 2:14 (NIV)

Friday, December 1

Sing to the Lord with grateful praise....
—Psalm 147:7 (NIV)

I am tired today. Very, very tired. Up all night with our brand-new puppy. Shoehorned on to a rush-hour subway that moved at the same speed I walk. Bombarded the minute I stepped into the office by meeting reminders, well-meaning colleagues with questions they could easily answer for themselves, a croaking chorus of coughing, and a screen full of e-mails. And it was only 9:00 a.m.

Then I thought about my wife, Julee, cursing her lupus but climbing out of bed and into the shower because she had promised to have breakfast with a friend who needed a shoulder to cry on. I thought about my puppy, Gracie, bravely holding her bodily functions until she got two feet outside our apartment building. I considered all those commuters crammed onto the subway car. Who among them felt beaten down for one reason or another that I would never know?

I glanced at my desk, messy but full of things I wanted to do. I surveyed my colleagues, who made me look a lot better at my job than I actually am, people I loved spending my days with.

I am tired today. Very, very tired. Yet not so tired I can't manage to see the blessings all around me, gifts that I will never tire of.

I live a full life, Lord, that can sometimes
feel too full. Let me never be too weary to see
Your abundant blessings all around me.
—Edward Grinnan

Digging Deeper: Psalm 138, Jonah 2:9

Saturday, December 2

"People look at the outward appearance, but the
Lord looks at the heart." —1 Samuel 16:7 (NIV)

I was making a quick run to the grocery store when,
from across the produce department, I caught sight
of my friend Ginny. No, wait, that couldn't be
Ginny. Ginny is a grandmother, and this woman
appeared much younger. I took a closer look. Yep,
that was Ginny wearing a pink ball cap and not a
stitch of makeup. Seeing her is always a treat. She's
forever smiling and full of kindness. I went over for a
hug and a chat before I rushed off to my next errand.

Later that evening, I was still thinking about
Ginny's smooth, unlined skin. How had I never
noticed it before? I'd always thought she was lovely,
but how many women could look gorgeous, makeup-
free? I sent Ginny a message asking about her skin-care
regimen. Whatever she was using, I wanted to try it.

Ginny gave some credit to her faithful use of
sunscreen, but her real secret was "I care more about

inner beauty, and that happens only when I spend time with Jesus and am not thinking about myself."

It made perfect sense. I hadn't noticed Ginny's skin before because her true beauty was in her sweet nature, her positive outlook, her genuine love for other people. Ginny was radiant because she radiated the joy of the Lord.

Lord, let me be beautiful in Your sight. —Ginger Rue

> **Digging Deeper:** Proverbs 31:30,
> Luke 11:36, 1 Peter 3:3–4

First Sunday in Advent, December 3
THE WORD AMONG US
Celebrating the Word

He said, I am the voice of one crying in the wilderness, Make straight the way of the Lord.... —John 1:23 (KJV)

I was expected to sing a solo at Riverside Church. I had to step out from the choir and stand at the foot of the steps facing the congregation, the organist and choir director behind me. I was all of twenty-four years old and had never felt more alone. *Good thing I have a robe on,* I thought. *They won't be able to see my knees shaking.*

The text was about John the Baptist and how he prepared the way for Jesus's coming. I'd learned it so well I hardly needed to follow the score, but I kept thinking of a friend's advice: "The notes aren't a problem, Rick. They sound great. Just sing them with more passion. Act as though you mean what you're singing."

I did as my friend suggested and sang with all my heart. I thought of John and the role he played, baptizing Jesus, making it clear that he was not the Christ, not even worthy to tie His shoes. I thought of how we were all still working, some two thousand years later, in this church and countless others, making a home in our hearts for Christ. The words of Scripture came alive. "I am the voice of one crying in the wilderness," I sang John's words. "Make straight the way of the Lord."

Did my knees tremble? Of course. But the text and the music gave me courage. They still do.

Lord, as we sing Your praise in carols and songs, we come to know Your story and You. —Rick Hamlin

Digging Deeper: John 1:1

Monday, December 4

BEAUTY FROM ASHES
Just One Friend
A true friend is closer than your own family.
—Proverbs 18:24 (CEV)

From what I understand about divorce, the steps that lead to healing are similar to the five stages of loss and grief: denial and isolation, anger, bargaining, depression, acceptance.

I've grieved over loved ones who've died, but I've never been divorced and couldn't identify with how my daughter Katie was feeling. She sounded dejected. Often, I didn't know how to respond. Sometimes I asked too many questions.

She phoned after her first Divorce Recovery class. A local church offered the thirteen-week series free of charge. "How was it?" I asked, hoping for good news.

"It was okay. I didn't talk much. Probably won't go back."

"Is it hard to go alone?"

"Sort of. I really want to put everything behind me and move on."

"Want me to go with you?"

"No, thanks. I need to figure this out by myself."

Lord, I can't help Katie. Will You send her a friend? Someone who's a little further down the path of healing, who understands what I don't and can encourage her?

The next week, Katie dropped out of Divorce Recovery.

Just one friend, Lord.

Weeks later, Katie called. "Mom, you'll never believe it, but my coworker is going through a divorce too! She surprised me with lunch and reminded me to eat even though I'm not hungry. I can be honest with her. Nothing shocks her. Sometimes we laugh about stuff. Next Monday night's her birthday. Guess where we're going? Divorce Recovery!"

> **Lord, sometimes all we need is just one friend who's been there and cares enough to listen. Thank You for sending that friend to my daughter.**
> —Julie Garmon

Digging Deeper: John 15:12–15, Romans 12:10

Tuesday, December 5

And when they were come into the house, they saw the young child with Mary his mother, and fell down, and worshipped him: and when they had opened their treasures, they presented unto him gifts; gold, and frankincense and myrrh.
—Matthew 2:11 (KJV)

There is a grocery store I sometimes visit that has the most fragrant oranges. They are large and brightly colored. I love smelling them almost as much as I enjoy tasting their sticky sweetness. I press them to my nose, breathe in, and I think of holidays and family.

At Christmastime, my father chopped the vegetables for whatever delicious dish my mother was preparing, especially for her potato salad and dressing. My mother baked the turkey and made cakes, pies, and macaroni and cheese. The warm savory smells made our stomachs rumble.

My father, however, filled the house with the sweet joyous smells of Christmas: fruitcake, peppermint, walnuts, apples, and oranges. His eyes twinkled as he stuffed our stockings with candy canes, nuts, and fruit. Counting down the days until Christmas, while my mother played carols on the piano, my father, brothers, and I munched on navel oranges and cracked walnuts.

Those are the aromas that still signal Christmas to me. The last several years since my father's been gone, I've missed those smells.

Standing in the store, the memories and the sweet citrus fragrance inspire me. I grab a bag of oranges and then head for the candy canes. I can pick up the mantle, follow in my father's footsteps, and create lasting sweet Christmas memories for those I love.

Lord, thank You for the joys of the Christmas season. Thank You for treasured recollections. Thank You for new life, new hope, and new memories. —Sharon Foster

Digging Deeper: 2 Kings 2:13–14, Proverbs 27:9, Song of Solomon 4:6

Sing to the Lord a new song....
—Isaiah 42:10 (NIV)

My neighbor signs up with a charitable organization
that finds anonymous donors who provide
Christmas gifts for children. For several years I've
worked behind the scenes with the charity to be the
secret Santa for my neighbor's daughter with special
needs—buying a coat, a no-reading-required game,
a scooter... On Christmas mornings the family
has invited me over. Nobody has recognized the
clandestine satisfaction behind my smile.

This December again, with great anticipation,
I shopped carefully for this girl. With advance
permission, I delivered to the agency a large bag: a
classy cardigan, a hat, a family game, a read-aloud
book. But someone at the charity dropped the ball.
Yesterday my neighbor asked me to help wrap the
gifts she'd received for her daughter—fine, worthy
toys and clothes, but not the ones I'd picked out.
The packages I'd earmarked "especially for..." had
been given to a stranger's child.

My exclamations—"Oh, what a nice shirt!" "Oh,
look at this!"—belied a deep disappointment that
had found and drawn out a lifetime of Christmas
hopes unmet, anticipations unfulfilled. It's as if I was
remembering every snowless Christmas, unanswered

Santa letter, holiday away from home, too-silent night.

I wallowed in sadness until I finally turned on a radio station that plays carols. As I listened, the Spirit amplified lines as personally as I'd chosen distinct gifts: "No more let…sorrows grow" and "The hopes…of all the years are met."

As the festive music continued, I was able to imagine upcoming happy Christmas scenes: a girl I've never met sporting a new cardigan; my young neighbor opening a stranger's gifts as I sit nearby and cheer.

God of hope, I give my disappointments to You, resting in the wonders of Your Christmas love.
—Evelyn Bence

Digging Deeper: Psalm 96

Thursday, December 7

Have we not all one father?… —Malachi 2:10 (KJV)

The star of Christmas can be elusive. But I do believe it hangs out in the night sky, waiting. And we, like unsure shepherds, must find it and follow.

"Our group wants to have dinner together," my husband announces. "I volunteered our house, if that's okay with you." He smiles, knowing I'm always ready for a party.

The group David is referring to is the Family of Abraham. It is a gathering of Muslims, Jews, and Christians who come together to find common ground, promote understanding, and encourage peace.

I choose to cook the meal and ask everyone to bring a traditional dessert. I study the dietary restrictions of the different faiths and decide that my turkey roll-ups will be perfect. I plan the seating, rearranging the living room, so we can set up extra tables. I haul out the china.

I hesitate, looking around: the Christmas tree, the crèche... The house is decorated to the hilt. I hope no one will be offended.

The people arrive: Jewish friends, Christians, a rabbi, a couple of ministers, an imam, and several women dressed in Muslim attire. The decorations attract enthusiastic interest. Then dinner is served, and everyone mingles at the tables. The highlight comes as guests explain the traditions behind their desserts.

It is then, amid laughter and conversation, that I recognize the coveted star shining brightly inside our home. It shines from the beautiful faces of a people bound together by love. As it was for the shepherds long ago, the star is a sign, a promise, a hope of a new world coming.

Father, we are all Your children, the seeds
of Abraham, looking up, claiming Your peace.
—Pam Kidd

Digging Deeper: *Genesis 17:4, Galatians 3:29*

Friday, December 8

Your love has given me great joy and encouragement, because you, brother, have refreshed the hearts of the Lord's people. —Philemon 1:7 (NIV)

The cleaning frenzy started with a book on organizing. The author claimed you should go through your things and only keep what brings you joy. *So simple!* I thought.

When I put the theory to the test and actually began looking around at the things in our house and asking myself if I loved them, if they made me smile, I was amazed at how much stuff I was keeping for all the wrong reasons.

I discovered an entire desk drawer of things that made me feel bad. Letters and mementos from upsetting experiences—like the hospital band from my appendectomy or a letter I wrote when I was angry. There were weird things that, for the life of me, I had no idea why I had been dragging around—boxes that remained taped and unopened from our move years ago.

In one month's time I shredded lots of things, donated a ton, and felt a tangible weight shift. The more I cleaned around me, the more I started to apply the same principle to my thoughts. When a negative, nagging worry would arise, I'd think, *Nope, not happening*, and replace it with a prayer of praise for something that would bring me joy.

Dear God, when I let go of the things that bring me down, I feel my spirit rise closer to You.
—Sabra Ciancanelli

Digging Deeper: Psalm 16:9, Proverbs 17:3

Saturday, December 9

Every man shall give as he is able....
—**Deuteronomy 16:17** (KJV)

When the calendar turned to December, a stranger appeared at my front door. "My mother-in-law has had this for years and we thought you might enjoy it," the young man said, handing me a timeworn black-and-white photo. "It's a picture of your cabin when it was first built."

When the snow scene was photographed at the turn of the twentieth century, there were no other homes in the area, just some towering pine trees like the ones that had been used to construct my log cabin. I was positively enchanted with this glimpse into the time when my dear little home was first loved, and I put the gift to use on a Christmas wreath. Every year when I unpack it, I'm reminded of the thoughtfulness of folks who didn't even know my name. But the thing that impresses me most is that an object of no use to them brought me extreme joy.

Ever since, I've been on the lookout for items past their prime that might brighten someone else's spirit. Maybe you, too, possess something that would delight another individual. I promise: you will be the one who is most blessed.

Truly, some of the best things in life are free, Lord. Teach me to be more aware of them.
—Roberta Messner

Digging Deeper: Deuteronomy 15:10, Proverbs 3:27, Matthew 6:3–4

Second Sunday in Advent, December 10

THE WORD AMONG US
Spreading the Word

Therefore, the Lord will give you a sign. The young woman is pregnant and is about to give birth to a son, and she will name him Immanuel.
—Isaiah 7:14 (CEB)

I don't know where Mom got the energy or found the time back then. There were four of us kids, two girls and two boys, and somehow in the midst of running errands and taking care of us while Dad worked, she mailed out a hundred Christmas cards. There was usually a family picture and her heartfelt greeting in red ink.

I remember our posing for those photos: on the backyard swing set, in our little sailboat at the reservoir, all dressed for Thanksgiving dinner. Once we had a photo shoot at church, the girls in dresses, we boys in coats and ties, our shaggy mutt, Andy, wagging his tail exuberantly, too distracted to look at the camera.

Christmas cards were a holy ritual and, to tell you the truth, I wondered if they were really worth it. We'd get stacks of them, and they'd sit in a bowl on the kitchen counter, waiting to get thrown out with all the wrapping paper and ribbons sometime in January. Why all that effort?

Then, just the other day, I got a letter from an old friend. "I found these, and thought you might want them." Inside were two family Christmas-card photos from days gone by. There I was in my first coat and tie with a tail-wagging dog. In another I was just a toddler on a blanket, squinting up at a camera.

It's taken me a few decades, but I've come to treasure this tradition: preparing for the coming of the Lord by wishing the very best to our loved ones with squinting grins and red pen and distracted dogs.

May we spread the good news the heavens declared: the Lord has come! —Rick Hamlin

Digging Deeper: Romans 15:12–13

Monday, December 11

Mary treasured up all these things and pondered them in her heart. —Luke 2:19 (NIV)

It's my favorite time of the year. The kids are tucked in bed, my husband is in the basement, finishing up some work, and I'm sitting in the living room in total darkness except for the glow of the Christmas tree lights. Everything, even the scattered toys left out after an evening of fun, looks more magical when bathed in that twinkling glow.

I spent the previous week running through my to-do list: pick up the tree, get stamps, drop off donations, make the grocery list, decorate cookies. I felt accomplished but empty. The one thing I'd forgotten to put on my list? Prepare my heart to celebrate the birth of Jesus.

So here I sit, just me and the Christmas tree, as I open my heart to the magic of the season. For me, a working mom of two, preparing my heart means taking God's words literally: be still.

A few years ago, I added this personal preparation to my holiday routine. Yes, we still hang stockings, send Christmas letters, and sing our hearts out to favorite carols, but I now get one hour alone, with my lights and the Nativity, to dwell on the gift God sent the world.

As my life has changed, so has that hour. As a newlywed, I focused on being less material. As a new mom, I thought of Mary's journey. Was she anxious? In days she'd meet not only her son, but also the Savior of the world.

Join me this year in letting the dishes sit and the phone go unanswered. Instead, take an hour—or even a minute—to breathe in the spirit of the season and simply believe.

Come, Lord Jesus! My heart is open and ready to celebrate Your birth! —Ashley Kappel

Digging Deeper: Psalm 46:10, Matthew 1:21

Tuesday, December 12

For from his fullness we have all received, grace upon grace. —John 1:16 (ESV)

"You seem a little huffy about it," Caroline said. "That's because I *am* huffy about it," I replied. I had just told my friend about a hurtful message I had received from my sister.

"I hear you," she said, slipping seamlessly into her life-coach hat, "and based on the other information you've told me, there may be some underlying issues coming into play that she has not dealt with."

"Well, she's gonna learn today!" I said, allowing my ears full license to emit smoke if they could find a way to do so.

"I'm just saying maybe you should apply a little more grace," Caroline offered.

Grace. There was that word again! It seemed to be popping up everywhere recently. I was exhausted and running on fumes at the end of my seminary career. I was fresh out of grace. Anyone expecting grace from me would simply have to wait until my next shipment arrived in about six to eight weeks.

But my sister was on the outside looking in and did not see all of my work and stress. She was surprised when my grace was not like God's—it was not abundant. Yet, as I am called to be a reflection of God's love and light, what do I do when I am at the end of a rapidly unraveling rope? Venting gets me only so far. Patience with myself along with prayer gets me a lot further.

God, You know I am tired. Fill the gap between where I end and others begin. Help me to be a reflection of You and Your unending grace. Amen.
—Natalie Perkins

Digging Deeper: Isaiah 40:31, 2 Timothy 4:22, James 4:6

"Every branch in me that does not bear fruit he
takes away, and every branch that does bear
fruit he prunes, that it may bear more fruit."
—John 15:2 (ESV)

"Don't worry, Gail. We'll wait until you go home
to prune the papaya. You don't have to watch!"
Dana, my sister-in-law, knows how I cringe at the
process.

I had spent my first winter in Florida, yet still
could not take in the rampant jungle-like growth
and what seemed like severe pruning to control it.
Plants like the magenta bougainvillea, for example,
could triple in size within months. Sure, I knew that
pruning was necessary to remove diseased or broken
limbs on bushes and trees. Hadn't I often thinned
a dormant lilac to encourage growth? But to hack
off healthy limbs that were already leafing out and
producing fruit? No way!

Dana reassured me that the pruned papaya limbs
would become stronger and less likely to break while
forcing fruit to grow instead of foliage. I knew she
was right because a dozen papayas ripened on her
kitchen counter. Still...

So I reflect upon the times I've been thriving
when *wham!*—a dizzying change, a sudden loss,
chops off part of my routine. Can loss actually make

me stronger and more productive, like Dana's papaya tree?

I consider the severed relationship that taught me to forgive more than I thought possible; the financial reversal that taught me to trust God's infinite providence; the medical scares that taught me gratitude for the health that I do have. I doubt I'll ever eagerly embrace loss or pain, but like the pruned papaya tree, I can trust the process and keep growing.

Creator God, I have faith in the bewildering and uncomfortable ways You shape my life.
—Gail Thorell Schilling

Digging Deeper: Hebrews 12:6

Thursday, December 14

She is like the merchant ships, she brings her food from afar. —Proverbs 31:14 (NKJV)

Some women dread grocery shopping, but it's the watershed of my wife's week. To her, it's an adventure. She starts on Wednesday, working out menus, poring over newspaper ads, clipping coupons. On Thursday, she starts her shopping day with breakfast at her favorite food shop, savoring a cinnamon biscuit while reading her P. D. James mystery novel. All the while she keeps one ear tuned to a table of retired males, whose favorite discussion topic is "The Government." They always seem to know what's going on in the community, and she learns a lot.

Sharon works the aisles of the grocery store like a marketplace missionary, encouraging everyone she meets. "Are you a new employee here? I love your shoes, but I'll bet your feet get tired from all this standing."

Back home, she unloads her treasures and entertains me with stories of her escapade.

"Did you know Moberly is getting a new factory?"

"Oh, really? Are you hinting that I need a job?"

"Oh, and there was this guy in the store, talking to his dog on his cell phone! Can you believe it?"

"*Hmm*, a digital dog whisperer."

She holds up a glass jar. "I got these expensive peaches just for you. Anything to keep my husband happy."

"You are a sweetheart!"

Like the godly woman of Proverbs 31, Sharon serves her family and her community. By her enthusiasm for others, she has transformed a duty into a delight. Now, if only I could find her kind of enthusiasm for mowing the lawn.

Father, help me find ways to make my work a service to others. —Daniel Schantz

Digging Deeper: Matthew 25:40, Romans 15:13

Friday, December 15

You keep track of all my sorrows. You have collected all my tears in your bottle. You have recorded each one in your book. —Psalm 56:8 (NLT)

My family celebrated my college graduation with dinner at my favorite restaurant. When the plates were cleared and the bill was on the table, my dad passed me a small box wrapped in blue-striped paper.

I held it to my ear, and the ticking told me what was inside. I peeled back the paper to find my great-grandfather's pocket watch. It was smooth and worn from the pockets of three generations of Eliasen men. When I was little, my dad would let me hold it. He had promised me that when I was all grown up, he would pass it on to me. I had waited for years for this day.

My dad's voice broke my reverie. "Let me show you how to wind it."

I passed him the watch. It clicked as he turned the stem on top. Then I heard a snap. The sound was harsh, metallic, and made even more prominent by the silence that followed.

I looked at Dad's face. I could tell that he felt awful. He wanted to give me something wonderful and good, probably even more than I wanted to receive it. I reached across the table and put my hand on his. "It's okay, Dad. Thanks."

I didn't want the watch to break. It was unfortunate and sad. But my dad loves me, fully and completely, and that night he hurt for me. That was more valuable than the pocket watch.

Lord, thank You that I don't have to go through life's troubles alone. —Logan Eliasen

Digging Deeper: Psalm 34:18, Revelation 7:16–17

Saturday, December 16

The Lord is not slow about his promise, as some think of slowness, but is patient with you, not wanting any to perish.... —2 Peter 3:9 (NRSV)

To learn patience, take a crosstown bus in rush-hour Manhattan. Cars surge into jammed intersections, jockeying for position. No one goes anywhere.

Thanks be to God, my daughter and I have C. S. Lewis's The Chronicles of Narnia. No matter how slow or crowded the bus, no matter how loud the conversations around us, we settle into a seat at the back and read his books together.

Even before I had children, I dreamed of when I would get to read them the Narnia books, which were my favorites as a child. However, that dream had not featured this noisy, crawling crosstown bus. Frances got home from gymnastics too late for relaxed, cozy bedtime reading; we did our reading while in transit. Sometimes I had to raise my voice to be heard. Sometimes other kids leaned in, drawn by the story. Always our stop came too soon, right in the middle of a good part.

"I wish we could keep reading!" Frances declared as we stepped from the bus. I did too. Together, in the story, we were in another world that, without my knowing, had started me down my own long, meandering road toward God.

Unlike me, Frances is growing up in church. But a relationship with God is a lifelong thing, one she ultimately will have to work out for herself. That, too, will require patience—from me and from her.

You are so patient with me as I make my stumbling way toward You, God. Help me to take a few more steps today. —Jim Hinch

Digging Deeper: Proverbs 6:20–22

Third Sunday in Advent, December 17

THE WORD AMONG US
Living the Word
And Mary said, "My soul magnifies the Lord."
—Luke 1:46 (RSV)

She was one of the shyer kids in the Sunday school class. Smart but awkward and not one to raise her hand. I don't know who asked her to read the long passage of poetry in Luke, known as the Magnificat, but I'm sure I was not the only parishioner who was surprised to hear her small, wavering voice from the back of the church: "My soul magnifies the Lord" (Luke 1:46, RSV).

We turned our heads. "I think she's going to do it from memory," I whispered to my wife.

Indeed, the girl continued, her voice growing a little steadier as she walked down the center aisle: "And my spirit rejoices in God my Savior, for he has regarded the low estate of his handmaiden" (Luke 1:47–48, RSV).

Mary would have been about her age, I thought, maybe one of the shyer, more awkward children in her village. What an odd choice for God to make, just like the choice of this girl's reciting Mary's words. In fact, I'd always considered the Magnificat too sophisticated to be believably the expression of a teenage mother in Galilee.

No longer. "He has shown strength with his arm, he has scattered the proud in the imagination of their hearts" (Luke 1:51, RSV), the sixth grader continued boldly, transformed in our eyes as Mary was transformed, as we all are when we answer God's call, no matter how impossible it might seem.

She finished in the front of the church, looking confidently at all of us. Then she made a *phew!* expression, ran to the pew to sit with her mom, and looked every bit the thirteen-year-old she was. But I would never see her with the same eyes. She was Mary, capable of great things.

Lord, in the pageants and Christmas plays of the season, we see Your hands at work.
—Rick Hamlin

Digging Deeper: Luke 1:26–33

Monday, December 18

First of all, then, I urge that supplications, prayers, intercessions, and thanksgivings be made for all people. —1 Timothy 2:1 (ESV)

"How are things?" I asked a colleague who stopped by my office to drop off paperwork.

"Not good," he replied. "My sister's cancer has returned. I'm sad and angry. I can't even find the words to pray."

"Then let me say your prayers for you," I blurted. He looked surprised, and I was too. Mark and I weren't close. He and I had served on committees together and never saw eye to eye.

"I'll say prayers for you, Mark," I said again, "until you can."

"Well, *um*, okay," he replied a bit awkwardly.

So every day I prayed: "Comfort Mark's sister, Lord, and comfort Mark too. Give them a faith that reminds them that even in their sadness and confusion they can look to You for peace and acceptance and understanding. Amen."

I received an e-mail from Mark about one month later: "I'm praying again. When my words couldn't come, though, thank you for yours. Would love to stop by. Lunch, maybe? God bless."

"Sure!" I responded. "How about Friday? Looking forward to catching up. Take care."

I smiled. Our exchange read like it was from two old friends.

Thank You, Lord, for prayer that changes things. But even more than that, thank You for prayer that changes me. —Melody Bonnette Swang

Digging Deeper: Ephesians 6:18, Philippians 1:9–11

Tuesday, December 19

"As for me, I would seek God, and to God would I commit my cause, who does great things and unsearchable, marvelous things without number." —Job 5:8–9 (ESV)

Do I have a story for you! What does one do when meeting a moose on a path in the woods?

The path was long and winding over rocks and half-ruined stone walls. But I knew my way. I came to know it over a decade of walking most mornings. Bear scat, snowy owls, raccoons, red foxes, and wild turkeys were almost to be expected.

I was out by myself, trying to clear my head. I was worried about a friend who had explained how he thought his son might have leukemia. More tests had to be run, but it didn't look good.

I hiked up the mountain, higher than usual, not even thinking much about the path, its creatures, tracks in the snow, all the things I usually enjoyed. Until, suddenly, I heard what could only be described as a snort. I lifted my head, stopped looking at my shoes. Standing fifteen feet in front of me was a moose. Not a cute moose; they are never cute. This moose seemed to be twice my height and was staring at me.

What I did next was ridiculous. I flopped onto the ground and a few seconds later thought, *Wait a minute! Maybe this is what I'm supposed to do if I meet a bear, not a moose!*

So I jumped up and ran and, thereafter, I have looked up while walking—even when talking with God, desperately seeking help from His grace.

Today, God, I am praying to You with my eyes wide open. —Jon Sweeney

Digging Deeper: Colossians 4:2–3

PRODIGAL HOMECOMING
Joyful Memories
Remember the days of old....
—Deuteronomy 32:7 (KJV)

Jeremy helps us put up the Christmas tree now. It's not just a tradition. We need his strength and height. I enjoy hanging decorations on the tree after the hard part is accomplished by my energetic son.

From a cardboard box that contained decorations, I pulled out a small, wooden, green circle, held it, stared at it, seeming unable to release the handmade ornament. I quickly added up the years. Forty.

"What's that, Mom?" Jeremy leaned over my shoulder.

When I could speak, I explained, "It's your brother's thumbprint from when you two were in second grade."

Jeremy picked up on my mood and reached for the ornament, studied it for a moment, and then hung it on the tree. Happily, he asked, "Remember when all six of us cut down a Christmas tree? Daddy insisted that year. [His father had died in 1983.] Man, what fun!

"And remember the year it snowed unexpectedly? Daddy said we should all bundle up and walk to the store like he had to as a child in Virginia. Remember the *crunch, crunch* of our feet and how Jon seemed to be leading us?

"Remember the year Daddy took us to the movies on Christmas Day to see *Chariots of Fire*?

"Remember the Christmas we got our bicycles? Red for me, blue for Jon, and we took off riding down the street yelling, '*Yahoo!*'"

Jeremy had done much more than help me with holiday decorations. He'd lined my heart with the joy of memories.

Father, I marvel at the healing power of memories. Help Jon remember too. —Marion Bond West

Digging Deeper: Esther 9:28, Proverbs 17:17

Thursday, December 21

"For God so loved the world that he gave his only Son, so that everyone who believes in him may not perish but may have eternal life." —John 3:16 (NRSV)

The above Scripture passage is one I've heard in many contexts, most often during Christmas and Easter. It has the power to both thrill me with joy when I consider that depth of love and chill me with horror at the price our Lord paid for that love. It is no less than the beginning and end of all the Gospels.

Yet, by virtue of the fact that it is God's love, I cannot fully grasp it. It is so far beyond any love I can conceive, much less understand. Perhaps because it is hard for me to comprehend such love, it is equally difficult for me to believe that I could be its subject. *How can God love me that much?*

During Christmas Eve Mass, televised from the Vatican, I heard Pope Francis's explanation. It wasn't just that God so loved the world that He gave His only Son, he suggested, but that God took the glorious, extraordinary step of becoming like us, to meet us where we live, to share our fears, angers, and vulnerabilities, and to show us, in the midst of our limited humanity, what love could look like. If only we could recognize and accept it.

If only I can.

God, in Christmas You made the extraordinary ordinary so that we could experience You as love— purified, personified, realized. Amen.
—Marci Alborghetti

Digging Deeper: Luke 1:67–79, 2:25–35

Friday, December 22

Always let him lead you, and he will clear the road for you to follow. —Proverbs 3:6 (CEV)

While living in Argentina, my wife, Pat, and I decided to adopt a child. Through our church, we found an adoption organization in Buenos Aires where we attended a two-day orientation. But we were pulled from the program near the end of it because we were foreigners who were not affiliated with the church they served.

Deeply disappointed, we drove home. "Lord, lead us to a child who needs a home," we prayed.

At work the next day, I shared our experience with my manager, Ed. "Just tell everyone you know that you want to adopt a child," he said.

The next day, the telephone operator, Lena, said she had heard we wanted to adopt and asked if she could help us. "Yes, thank you," I said, doubting she could really do anything.

A few days later, Lena called again. Her friend, a social worker, was looking for a home to place a child. Lena had arranged for us to meet with the social worker and a little boy. That meeting was the start of a one-year process that included many hurdles and a few major roadblocks, but also many people who came into our lives just when we needed their help. Only God could have worked out all of the crazy details, starting with Lena, to "clear the road" for us.

On Christmas Eve, just a couple of months after we'd prayed to be led to the right child, we received our greatest precious blessing—our son, Johnny.

Dear God, thank You for being so fully present in the activities of our lives. Give us eyes and ears to recognize those You use to bless us along our way! Amen. —John Dilworth

Saturday, December 23

"Stand ready and be prepared...."
—Jeremiah 46:14 (RSV)

At 10:00 a.m., every December 24, our family
gathers around the radio to hear the service of
Nine Lessons and Carols, broadcast each year from
Kings College Chapel in Cambridge, England.
The moment I like best comes at the beginning.
The hymn is always the same, the first stanza sung
unaccompanied in the high treble of a twelve-year-
old boy. "Once in royal David's city stood a lowly
cattle shed...." The flawless voice spellbinds millions
of us listening around the globe.

How nervous that boy must have been, I'd always
think, *during the many weeks of preparation!* How
could he sleep at night knowing that the all-important
first moments would depend on him alone?

I got the answer to my question from a graduate
of Kings College. No boy lies awake with the weight
of performance on him alone. As the choristers line
up outside the sanctuary on Christmas Eve in their
black-and-white robes—fourteen men, sixteen boys—
the choirmaster scans the waiting faces. Seconds

before the procession begins, he points a finger at one of the youngsters. "You!" And that child launches into the hymn he and the others have practiced so often. There's no time for butterflies, not a second for self-consciousness.

What an image, I thought, *of what the church should be!* Each of us equipped, prepared, ready, and waiting for the moment that he or she is tapped to fill a need in the kingdom.

Show me how to prepare, Father, for those times when a quiet voice tells me, "You!" — Elizabeth Sherrill

Digging Deeper: Romans 12:6–7, 1 Peter 4:10

Christmas Eve, Fourth Sunday in Advent, December 24

THE WORD AMONG US
The Word with Us
The Word became flesh and made his home among us.... —John 1:14 (CEB)

I'm usually slow to get into a deck-the-halls mood. One of our sons might remember an ornament he created in the third grade, and I'll rummage through the Christmas box on the top shelf of our hall closet and take out a crayon-scribbled star to hang from a doorjamb. The electric candles make it to the windows the third week of Advent. The twinkling lights have to wait until we get a tree, and sometimes if we jet across the country to be with family, we'll skip the tree altogether. But the crèche goes up first.

I put Mary and Joseph on the living room table, the wooden shepherds and their sheep in the back, an angel or two at the side. William, our older son, was always a stickler for detail, so we weren't allowed to put out the wise men until January 6, when their visit to the newborn king is celebrated. So I put the gift-bearing kings on the piano across the room, symbolic of their voyage. The only piece that stays in the box is the baby in the manger, so the space on the table stays empty, waiting for the birth.

Christmas Eve, whether we're rushing to the airport or dashing back from church, I reach into the box for the missing piece, small but never hard to find. I dust it off and put Jesus right where He belongs, the Child Who changed the world. It's always satisfying, the wait well worth it, like asking yourself, "What am I missing in my life?" and finding the answer wrapped in tissue paper, sitting in a box at the top of a closet, ready to be rediscovered.

Jesus, we know You are always there, just waiting to be found. —Rick Hamlin

Digging Deeper: Jeremiah 29:13

Christmas, Monday, December 25

THE WORD AMONG US: Loving the Word
If we love each other, God remains in us and his love is made perfect in us. —1 John 4:12 (CEB)

The presents all have to be opened, and we do it one person at a time, one present at a time, starting with the youngest and working our way to the oldest, until we go back around the circle and continue the ritual until finally all packages are opened and every giver is thanked.

It takes a while. Our family keeps expanding. Nieces and nephews get married and then have children, and even if everybody's not there, at our last family Christmas gathering we were eighteen.

"Hurry up!" someone will say. "Who's next?" Nudged, one of us will open the tantalizing box in our lap, reread the card, and exclaim how perfect the gift is. But all of us grown-ups have figured out by now, it's not the presents that count. It's the opportunity to be together, the sublime wonder of it, all of us crammed into Mom's living room, on floor, couch, stool, and chair, next to the tree with ornaments that go back generations, talking, laughing, listening, loving one another, held fast through the accumulation of memories. When we were kids, we wanted to open the presents as quickly as we could. Now we linger.

Some two thousand years ago wise men brought gold, frankincense, and myrrh to the Christ Child, and because of their gifts, we give to each other at Christmastime. But the biggest gift of all is the love we share, a reflection of the love God has shown us.

"Dinner's going to get cold," someone says.

"Merry Christmas!" we say, gathering up scraps of wrapping paper. "Let's eat!"

Love, Lord, is the gift You gave and the gift we give, honoring You. —Rick Hamlin

Digging Deeper: Romans 13:10, 1 Corinthians 13:13

Tuesday, December 26

**"For whoever does the will of my Father in heaven is my brother and sister and mother."
—Matthew 12:50 (ESV)**

Many couples spend Christmas Eve with one side of the family and Christmas Day with the other. That doesn't work well for Emily and me since our families live two thousand miles apart!

When we got married, we decided we would alternate Christmases between my home state of New Jersey and hers, Texas. This was her year, and I felt a little trepidation because it was my first Christmas away from my parents, brother, and grandparents. The trip went well…at first. The Christmas Eve party was fun, and Emily and I made out well from the Yankee Swap. I missed my family on Christmas Day, but I got to talk to them plenty.

Then Emily and I got the flu. We were staying with her dad, Mark, lying in bed all day in the guest room. It was bad enough being sick, but relying on someone else's parent was worse. I felt embarrassed to be seen that way, like I should be pretending to be healthier than I was. But Mark just kept on taking care of us. He cooked for us, arranged doctor appointments, and made sure we had everything we needed.

As I got better, I began to feel more comfortable and stopped thinking that I was away from "my family," as if my immediate one was all I had. I had two families now.

Thank You, God, for allowing me to see Your love through more and more people. —Sam Adriance

Digging Deeper: Proverbs 17:22

Wednesday, December 27

PARENTING ANEW
Superhero to the Rescue
The Lord is my rock, my fortress and my deliverer.… —Psalm 18:2 (NIV)

Today, the responsibility of raising my grandson, Logan, was heavy on my mind, as I wondered how long my husband, Chuck, and I could manage this challenge, which was going on two years. My quiet reverie was broken as first Chuck, then Logan, joined me.

"I'm here to protect you!" Logan announced, stomping into the kitchen. Wearing a red cape, mask, armbands, and belt, he carried a foam shield and sword.

"So what's your name?" Chuck tried to keep a straight face.

"Super Logan Anthony Batman Big!" Logan crossed his arms in classic superhero form.

"Would you like to escort me to the grocery store, Super Logan Anthony Batman Big? I could use some protection."

"Yes!" My superhero strode out the back door.

At the store, Logan stood guard at the automatic door, keeping it open until I entered, and then preceded me down the aisles, a serious threat to any villains. Customers and store employees smiled, playing along. "Hello, Superman!" "Hi, Captain America!" Logan proudly corrected them with his official name.

Back in the car, I told him that I appreciated having a superhero looking out for me. Removing his mask, he said, "I'm really Logan Anthony Lyttle.

I'm not really Super Logan Anthony Batman Big, but everybody thought I was!"

"You still did an excellent job protecting me," I assured him.

Logan was only pretending to be a superhero, and his wish to protect me was heartwarming. But Chuck and I really do have a superhero: God, Who protects all of us, even our little superhero Logan.

Thank You, God, for being our rock, fortress, and deliverer. —Marilyn Turk

Digging Deeper: Psalm 5:11

Thursday, December 28

But I trust in you, Lord; I say, "You are my God." —**Psalm 31:14** (NIV)

"Climbing," my son says as he looks up at the rock-climbing wall towering sixty feet above his head.

"Climb on," I respond, letting him know I'm ready as well. The two of us are connected by a long rope that loops through the top of the wall. One end is tied to my climbing belt and the other is tied to his. Brandon starts his ascent, and I gather the rope's slack as he goes higher and higher.

"Take!" he yells, alerting me to hold tight as he lets go of the wall to hang in midair. He shakes out his arms and plans his next moves.

My friend who watches him climb for the first time is amazed and terrified as Brandon reaches the top. "Aren't you afraid for him, going up that high?"

"No," I say, "because I control the rope that holds him. I know he's okay."

She shakes her head, still baffled. "But he's so high! How is he not afraid?"

I look at my little boy dangling sixty feet over my head. "Because he knows I won't let him fall."

Thank You, Lord, for being a God I can trust with my whole life. Help me to always stay connected to You.
—Karen Valentin

Digging Deeper: Psalms 9:10, 25:2

Friday, December 29

There are "friends" who pretend to be friends, but there is a friend who sticks closer than a brother.
—Proverbs 18:24 (TLB)

Brenda is Jewish; I'm Christian. Since 2004, we've been the best of friends, often sharing each other's traditions. I've learned to *kvell*, *kvetch*, and *kibitz* with gusto. Brenda taught me how to make matzo ball soup and matzo brei (eggs and crushed matzo, fried up like French toast...yummy!).

Brenda and her husband, Paul, often invite my husband, Jack, and me to their house for Passover dinner. Some years they've come to our home for Easter and Christmas. Brenda took me to a synagogue for an art show one year. On our cruise to Spain and Italy, where 90 percent of the people are Catholic, we took them to more than one dozen cathedrals and churches. They were as impressed by the beauty of the artwork and architecture as we were. Brenda teaches me fun words like *meshuganah* (crazy) and *ferklempt* (overcome). Once, I even gave her a Jesus needlepoint.

One year Brenda taught me about Yom Kippur, the Jewish Day of Atonement, which happens ten days after Rosh Hashanah, the Jewish New Year. During the time between the two holidays, God is writing in the Book of Life. Then, on Yom Kippur, Jews fast and pray to atone for their sins. That year I decided to fast with Brenda. She lasted for twelve hours and I made it for nineteen hours, which only added to our delight in sharing each other's beliefs.

Over the years I've come to see that although Brenda and I are different in many ways, what binds us is respect for each other's faith.

God, some call You "Yahweh," others call You "Lord."
Help me to respect the beliefs of others and to grow
in my own faith as they grow in theirs.
—Patricia Lorenz

Digging Deeper: Proverbs 17:17, 27:10;
Philippians 3:12–14

Great is his faithfulness; his loving-kindness
begins afresh each day.
—Lamentations 3:23 (TLB)

My husband and I had a wonderful time at our
grandson Caden's hockey tournament in Denver. We
saw four matches; then ate a fabulous pizza lunch
with the team and spent time visiting. We said our
good-byes on the night of December 30 and went to
our hotel to pack for an early-morning trip back to
Copeland, Kansas. We were hosting a small dinner
party on New Year's Eve.

By daylight, however, Don was sick with the
flu. There was no way we could drive home. We
couldn't even make it to Caden's house. I hurried to
the front desk to ask about keeping our room. "I'm
afraid we're fully booked for New Year's," the clerk
said, "but I'll check." To her surprise and my relief,
the room was still available. When I explained that
Don was ill, the clerk gave me a lower rate than the
holiday price. I called our friends, who promised to
pray for us and check back later to see how we were
getting along.

It had snowed all night, and the roads were icy.
Although I dislike driving in bad weather, I made
it to a nearby shopping center where I bought
medicine and electrolyte drinks for Don, plus

crackers and microwavable soup for me. Don slept; I read and watched TV. When the ball dropped in Times Square—10:00 p.m. our time—I rang out the old year with a prayer.

Late New Year's morning, Don was well enough to travel. I drove, and we made it home safely. It wasn't the celebration we had planned. But we ended the old year and started the new one at peace and with a sense of joy.

Thank You, Lord, for being the One in charge of our life circumstances. —Penney Schwab

Digging Deeper: Psalm 32:7–8, Philippians 4:6–7, James 4:14–15

Sunday, December 31

"We must work the works of Him who sent Me as long as it is day; night is coming when no one can work." —John 9:4 (NAS)

This year I will turn sixty-five years old, the fabled time of retirement for my generation. It brings mixed feelings. I do not plan to retire anytime soon. I am having too much fun teaching and working with college students. But what does it mean to retire? When is it time to furl the sails and rest in a safe harbor? Does such a time exist?

T. S. Eliot writes in his poem "East Coker": "Old men ought to be explorers." I think Eliot is correct. As we grow older, the desire for further exploration and contribution should grow stronger. Consider for a moment that in 1900, the average life expectancy of an American was only forty-seven. Yet, over four hundred years before, Christopher Columbus set sail to discover the New World when he was forty-two. And Ferdinand Magellan ventured forth to find a western passage to the "Spice Islands" when he was forty-one. Most important, Jesus left Nazareth to engage in His public ministry at thirty when the life expectancy of a Galilean peasant was thirty-five. They believed that "old men ought to be explorers."

The most significant contributions are often in the last major chapters of life. Mother Teresa toiled for years in the extreme poverty of Calcutta, India, before becoming a symbol of servanthood in her last decades. And former President Jimmy Carter is making some of his most important contributions to international diplomacy, world peace, and human rights—decades after leaving the White House.

For all of us, our best years stretch before us, even unto eternity.

Father, may we never drop anchor before our voyage is through. —Scott Walker

Digging Deeper: Joel 2:28, Acts 2:17

IN GOD'S HANDS

1 _____

2 _____

3 _____

4 _____

5 _____

6 _____

7 _____

8 _____

9 _____

10 _____

11 _____

12 _____

13 _____

14 _____

15 _____

16 _____

17 _____

18 _____

19 _____

20 _____

21 _____

22 _____

23 _____

24 _____

25 _____

26 _____

27 _____

28 _____

29 _____

30 _____

31 _____

After graduating from law school in the spring and taking the bar exam, **Sam Adriance** of New Haven, Connecticut, finally entered the working world, where he serves as a judicial law clerk to a federal judge. His wife of nearly three years, Emily, also started a new job, working for a network of schools, and they and their cat, Crookshanks, welcomed a new kitten, Stitch, into their home. Through all of the changes, they do their best not to worry too much, to trust that there is a plan for their lives—and they can't wait to see what exciting developments next year has in store!

Marci Alborghetti of New London, Connecticut, has spent a lot of time this past year trying to loosen her own grip and release so many things into God's hands. A bad fall, complete with a broken clavicle and rib, in the middle of the summer, her favorite season, hastened the process. This journey is, at times, almost as painful for her as the bruises and broken bones were, but God is helping/healing her along, little by little. His greatest gift to her continues to be her husband, Charlie, whose love, attention, and good humor have been unwavering even as he struggles to grasp the notion that Marci is, indeed, breakable!

"Occasionally it occurs to me that I've been given an unusual number of trials in recent years," writes **Julia Attaway** of New York City. "Yet one thing I'm learning is that whether or not I remember to place my life in God's hands, I am held there anyway." When she's struggling, Julia finds comfort in the image of herself writhing—small but safe—in the wounded palm of Christ. "Stresses and distresses are less acute when I remember that our life on earth isn't the whole story. It helps immensely to hold tight to Romans 8:18 (NIV): 'I consider that our present sufferings are not worth comparing with the glory that will be revealed in us.'"

"Lately we've experienced the truth that our family is always in God's hands as we supported our son during a rough time in his life," writes **Karen Barber** of Alpharetta, Georgia. "Thankfully, our son is doing much better now. And we are too. At first I prayed for a quick fix. Then over time I changed my prayer to 'Lord, teach us how to live well.' Part of living well meant believing that God would help take care of things back home while I embarked on a weeklong spiritual pilgrimage to Assisi, Italy, with my friend Mary Lou Carney. Things were just fine while I was gone, and I came back with a greater understanding of our God, Who has kept countless generations in His capable hands."

Evelyn Bence of Arlington, Virginia, writes, "My typical week is punctuated by interruptions: clients asking for quick turnarounds or neighbors looking for attention. But when I try to summarize my past year as a whole, I see a rather quiet workaday life: maintaining professional, home, and church responsibilities; occasionally hosting dinner guests; a quick trip to Florida to promote *Room at My Table*; a summer and then holiday sojourn to visit my out-of-town family. At every turn I've clung fast to the fact that I'm held securely in God's hands."

Erika Bentsen of Sprague River, Oregon, writes, "My new husband is teaching me how to run a line truck, so I can build fences and set poles with equipment. I love it! I used to do all this work by hand—it's no surprise my back broke down. Now I'm learning to work smarter, not harder." BlueDog has taken moving into a new home in stride. "Randy's dog was pretty jealous at first, but now they're great friends. I am so blessed. Trusting God to help me through the rough spots has really brought me closer to Him. When life gets tough, He is my rest. I can feel the strength and love in His hands."

"This was a year with a Keith-shaped hole in my life," says **Rhoda Blecker** of Bellingham, Washington. "I've kept busy. I teach at a community college, do spiritual direction, edit books, give sermons, do research, and keep my home in good shape. I see friends fairly often, and I take care of my pets Anjin and L.E. But, through it all, there's a melancholy that comes and goes, and I'm taken by surprise by certain pieces of music and things people say. What keeps me going is the conviction that God wants me here for a reason, even if I don't know what it is, and that, at last, my husband and I will be together again."

"Moving to New York from California was a shock to the system," writes **Lisa Bogart** of Scarsdale, New York. "We've been here two years now, and it's finally beginning to feel like home. I found a part-time job at a little yarn shop. I love it, and it has helped me to connect with the community and to make some friends. And the discount on yarn is a lovely fringe benefit. I continue to knit every day. The time I spend with needles in hand is my favorite part of the day. It gives me the quiet to recharge when things get hectic. And I think I'm finally quiet enough for God to reach me then. I reflect and pray as well as make gifts for loved ones and charities. Knitting is my cure for a bad day."

Sabra Ciancanelli says, "So many times this year I felt blessed to be in God's hands. Like the night our dog wiggled out of his leash and disappeared into the darkness. For an agonizing hour I searched, calling his name and praying. Under a starry sky Soda's furry face appeared in the eye of my flashlight, galloping toward me at full speed, out of the woods and into my arms. Or the day my son Solomon was onstage playing his trumpet at a jazz festival, and I couldn't find him among the band members. I worried something must have happened until I realized he was right in front of me, just not so little anymore." Sabra lives in Tivoli, New York, with her husband, two sons, three cats, and a dog, who, thankfully, hasn't run away since.

 **Mark Collins** of Pittsburgh, Pennsylvania, says, "It's been a year of serious wins and serious losses. We lost my aunt (age 100) and then my 94-year-old dad, and some losses are simply too great for words. Meanwhile, our oldest daughter has come to grips with crippling health issues and has learned to thrive through modern medicine and her own iron will. We rejoice like the parents of prodigal offspring. Also, after taking off a decade, I finished another book of essays and poems called *Wayward Tracks*, featuring some of my devotions from *Daily Guideposts*. Rereading what I've just written here makes my head snap back from emotional whiplash."

 "Elba and I appreciate our new status as empty nesters," writes **Pablo Diaz** of Carmel, New York. "We do look forward to Christine and Paul visiting us with their significant others and traveling to destinations such as Spain and Mexico. We enjoy the cultures, people, traditions, and especially the food! I continue writing my weekly blog, 'Life, Faith and Prayer.' At this time in our lives, many things remain in the hands of God: the health of our parents, the futures of our children, and accomplishing our unfinished dreams. One of the most valuable spiritual insights I learned long

ago is that God will not reveal His plans to us, but we discover them along our journey of faith. I continue trusting that our lives are in God's caring, loving presence."

"Concluding the first year of retirement, I find myself busy and enjoying opportunities for volunteer work through our church, mentoring small businesses, and leading a prison ministry," writes **John Dilworth** of North Canton, Ohio. "My wife, Pat, and I love spending time with our son, Johnny, wherever he is stationed in the Air Force. We also enjoy visiting our family and friends in Florida and the Carolinas, especially during the cold months. Retirement has given me time for reflection and seeing God's work in places along my path that I had missed before."

Brian Doyle is the editor of *Portland Magazine* at the University of Portland in Oregon. Of late he is happily, madly, puzzledly writing novels, which are totally great examples of being in the capacious hands of the Coherence, because "Who knows what is going on in my novels? Not me," he writes. "All the kids are in college, the dog has learned to read almost at a second-grade level, I remain exhilarated and confused after twenty-eight years of marriage, and I have a new novel called *Chicago*. You tell me what it's about."

"I thought this past year would be a slow one," writes **Logan Eliasen** of Port Byron, Illinois. "The plan was to wrap up the last few credits of my theology degree and take some time to recoup before I hurtled into law school. I think my breathing space disappeared somewhere in the midst of job interviews, college applications, and standardized tests. I'm so grateful that I can rest easy in God's hands because mine are constantly full. I can't believe how much has happened in a year! It's reassuring to look back and see how God has held me steady in familiar ways. It's exciting to know He's stretching me in new ones too."

Shawnelle Eliasen of Port Byron, Illinois, writes, "I'm learning about the peace of God's presence. The Lord is with me in times of joy, but He's there in tough times too. In fact, I think this may be when I'm most aware of His presence—when hope in Him is all I have, and I know that it's perfectly, gracefully, enough." She, her husband, Lonny, and their five sons live in an old

Victorian near the banks of the Mississippi River. She home-teaches her three youngest and finds life to be wild, sweet, and full. "No matter what my circumstance, I'm taking confidence in knowing that the situation, and we, are in God's hands—and they are loving, kind, and good."

"Every year I'm reminded of what a joy it is to be part of the *Daily Guideposts* family," writes **Sharon Foster** of Durham, North Carolina. "Your letters, e-mails, and invitations always come at the right moment. My children are doing well: Chase sang twice at the Lyric Opera in Chicago, and Lanea navigated the storms and calm waters of her nonprofit organization. I'm putting the final touches on one of my novels, *Abraham's Well*, in preparation for its republication. It has long been my hope that somehow my books would help feed hungry people. So I'm thrilled to be partnering with World Church Service's Crop Hunger Walk for a special edition. You can read a good book *and* help feed the hungry!"

Katie Ganshert of Bettendorf, Iowa, graduated from the University of Wisconsin in Madison with a degree in education and worked as a fifth-grade teacher for several years before staying home to write full-time. She lives with her family of four, which is a huge praise, considering how long they fought and prayed to bring their daughter home from the Democratic Republic of Congo. When Katie's not busy penning novels, she enjoys having coffee with friends, reading great literature, studying the Bible, eating copious amounts of dark chocolate, and resting in God's hands.

"It seems that God gave me my one-word theme for this year: *simple*—the opposite of *worrywart*," writes **Julie Garmon** of Monroe, Georgia. "Intrigued with the idea, I wondered if I could possibly change. I'm discovering that prayer is a lot less complicated than I thought. These days, I talk out loud to my heavenly Daddy. Sometimes I even get up and dance. In pursuing simplicity, I discovered three truths: becoming simple means letting go of all grudges and worries; people who live simply laugh a lot; to live simply means to leave every single thing in God's big, strong, supremely capable hands."

"This past year has been full of changes," writes **Bill Giovannetti** of Santa Rosa, California. "My daughter, Josie, and son, JD, who were homeschooled, entered public high school. They're thriving, and we couldn't be more proud. Margi, my wife, has joined the staff of our church and gave the commencement address at Simpson University, where she continues to serve as adjunct professor of business law. Every day I feel the comfort of being safely held in God's hands."

"This has been a year of joy and heartbreak," says **Edward Grinnan** of New York, New York. He and his wife, Julee, lost their beloved 8-year-old golden retriever to cancer. "I wrote many devotions and blogs about Millie because she taught me so many lessons. I think that's why God sent her to us. The heartache of loving dogs the way Julee and I do is that you outlive all but the last one." Their new golden retriever puppy is helping them overcome their grief. "She's as sweet as Millie but different in so many ways. I can't wait to see which lessons she has been sent to teach me. That's why we named her Grace."

"We have relished seeing our now-grown sons thrive on two continents," writes **Rick Hamlin** of New York, New York. "William continues working in Silicon Valley, and Timothy spent the year doing mission work in South Africa, living with a group of Benedictine monks, working in their elementary school. My wife Carol Wallace's latest book is *Ben Hur*, which came out in conjunction with the new movie version. The original novel was written by her great-great-grandfather, Lew Wallace, and she has produced a new version, faithful to the original but more readable for a twenty-first-century audience. As always, we put all that we do and our future in God's hands."

Carla Hendricks learned to abide in God's hands more than ever before as she endured a tumultuous time in her family: her parents' deaths, exactly three weeks apart, and a relocation from Conway, Arkansas, to Franklin, Tennessee. This season of personal loss matured her faith, rooted in God's "righteous right hand" (Isaiah 41:10), and led her to her new role as communications director at New Hope Academy, a school dedicated to uplifting underprivileged youth. Carla enjoys blogging, volunteering in foster-care ministry, and spending time with her husband, Anthony, and their four children, Kalin, Christian, Joelle, and Jada.

"It seems like my husband, David, and I were away from home this year almost as much as we were home," writes **Kim Henry** of Elizabeth, Colorado. "We traveled to fifteen countries and had the joy of visits with our children and grandchildren. I love the adventure of travel, but I am blissfully content right now to soak in the grandeur of our Colorado skies, to take long walks with our dogs, and to return to my favorite part of the day—sunrise, coffee, and my quiet time with God each morning."

 "We moved again. Back to New York City. In fact, back to the same church-owned house we lived in the last time we were here," writes **Jim Hinch**. "Kate is now leading the Episcopal church where she was formerly a junior priest. We remain divided in our loyalties. Good friends, good schools, and the incomparable saltiness of New York are in the East. Family, the mountains, and big skies are in the West. God is everywhere, so we are content to follow His lead and do the work He provides for us."

 "We live in such a quickly changing world, and how our faith adapts amid those changing realities helps to sustain us," says **Jeff Japinga** of Holland, Michigan. Jeff left his seminary deanship to become an executive for sixty-plus Presbyterian churches in Minnesota's Twin Cities and western Wisconsin, where he gets to help church leaders envision and do vital ministry in their own communities—and learn how to play hockey on the side! He has the

privilege of walking alongside his children, Mark and Annie, as they move through graduate-school programs into their chosen professions. "A lot in life has changed, but this one thing certainly hasn't: the faithfulness of God's presence, no matter what the circumstances in which we find ourselves."

 With an infant and a toddler running around, **Ashley Kappel** of Birmingham, Alabama, has officially given up on perfection and is embracing the wonderfulness of chaos. By day, she works as a senior editor at Time Inc. By night, she savors every minute with Olivia, James, and her husband, Brian. Favorite phrases this year include "No licking the wall"; "That doesn't go in the toilet"; and "Don't bite your brother, even if you are a lion." In her free time, Ashley volunteers and enjoys lazy walks with her golden retriever, Colby.

 "God continues to bless us in wonderful ways," writes **Brock Kidd** of Nashville, Tennessee. "My wife, Corinne, and I have stepped up our involvement with the Martha O'Bryan Center, our city's oldest nonprofit organization." Brock took on the role of chairman of a start-up school with the mission of serving kids in need, and he continues to enjoy his career as an investment adviser. "Our children keep

right on amazing me, with Harrison now in high school, and Mary Katherine, 4, and Ella Grace, 3, seemingly attached at the hip!"

"David and I are busy, happy, and involved in worthwhile activities," writes **Pam Kidd** of Nashville, Tennessee. "Our children, Brock and Keri, live within five miles of us. Why then does an unnamed burden shadow me? Is it right to be happy when refugees longing for freedom perish at sea? When mothers cry for children gunned down on our streets? When people not far away are lonely, homeless, hungry? I don't have an answer, except this one: in the midst of the good life, a part of me stands ready to say yes to whatever opportunity God puts in my path. Welcome the stranger, feed the hungry, comfort the afflicted, be kind, spread love. As long as my yeses keep coming, my happiness grows deeper as my burden grows lighter."

Patty Kirk of Westville, Oklahoma, was promoted to full professor at John Brown University. Her daughter Charlotte passed her qualifying exams for the PhD. Before starting grad school, Patty's other daughter Lulu claimed her high school graduation present: a trip to France. Though neither could drive a stick shift, Patty and Lulu rented a

Fiat, figuring they'd learn as they went. They did—not just how to keep the car from lurching, then stalling in the terrifying roundabouts at virtually every intersection, but also how to get along under the stresses of traveling.

"We opened the year with my husband's back surgery and closed it with his foot surgery," writes **Carol Knapp** of Priest River, Idaho. "God has us in His hands. A joyous event led us on a road trip to Texas to celebrate the birth of our nineteenth grandchild, Sarai Ruth, named for my mother, Ruth. Traveling to Minnesota for our son-in-law Brett's graduation from veterinary medicine school was the occasion for my first cross-country train ride! Our daughter Tamara and family relocated to our area after many years in Alaska. We are loving life back in our 'roots' country, living on a forested mountainside in a shared home. It's a wonderful exchange of hospitality and generations working together."

"I celebrated a birthday with a zero in it, and our family, ages 2 to 72, gathered at a house on a lake in the mountains for a week of chaotic fun," writes **Carol Kuykendall** of Boulder, Colorado. "The get-together was made more meaningful because of the memories of my last zero birthday, when my husband and I were diagnosed with advanced cancers, which affected our whole family. Reflecting back over that decade, we can see how God held us in His hands, strengthening our faith as we trusted His promises. Since then, Lynn and I have found many opportunities to walk alongside others who are navigating the cancer journey. God's gifts of life and family, perspective and purpose, give us much to celebrate this year."

 **Patricia Lorenz** of Largo, Florida, writes, "Both stepping out in faith and putting my trust in God's hands have carried me through many adventures, travels, and experiences. One of my greatest adventures has been marrying Jack in my 60s. This year we celebrate our fifth wedding anniversary. Last year my fourteenth book, *57 Steps to Paradise: Finding Love in Midlife and Beyond*, was published. Of course I have Jack to thank for the sweet ending to that book. Ten children and twenty grandchildren certainly make life sizzle. I hope our adventures last a lifetime."

 **Debbie Macomber**, a No. 1 *New York Times* best-selling author, is proud to be given the moniker "America's Christmas storyteller." She and her husband, Wayne, live in Port Orchard, Washington. They have four children and ten

grandchildren. The latest addition is Mason Dale, named after his uncle Dale who died in 2011. Debbie considers herself abundantly blessed and continues to serve on the Guideposts National Advisory Cabinet.

 **Erin MacPherson** finds time to write amid the whirlwind of soccer practice, swim meets, and freezer-meal parties with the women of her church. But by placing herself—and her crazy schedule—in God's hands, she has found the peace and joy that come even in those whirlwind seasons of life. She and her husband, Cameron, live in Austin, Texas, with their three grade-school kids, thrilled to spend their days lounging in the sunshine instead of shoveling snow. Erin blogs at erinmacpherson.com.

 "I've been scribbling in little books ever since I started writing for *Guideposts* way back in 1990," says **Roberta Messner** of Huntington, West Virginia. "It's the most productive spiritual practice I have ever engaged in, next to reading Scripture." The thing that struck her was how many of God's provisions arrived just in time ("manna for the moment"). As she confronts retirement from her thirty-eight-year nursing career

with the Veterans Administration, that thought brings her considerable comfort. "I know I will face many challenges as I age, yet I know that God will be with me at the precise moment I need Him."

Discovering treasures in God's hands was the focus of **Rebecca Ondov's** year. She loves horseback riding and hiking in the mountains that rim her valley. "I might leave my home in Hamilton, Montana, burdened down by life. But after investing a couple of hours admiring God's creation, I come out with a fresh outlook—and with a new collection of pinecones and a rock or two, and Sunrise, my golden retriever, nearly always packs out a stick." Rebecca is excited for the opportunities God has given her with the release of *My Horse Diary for Girls* and appreciates it when her readers send her a friend request on Facebook.

Natalie Perkins of New York, New York, graduated from Union Theological Seminary and won the Karen Ziegler Feminist Preaching Prize for her class. She is now working on several creative projects that aim to marry art and spirituality, including a podcast with the Westar Institute in its Young Leaders in Religion

Forum. Natalie is traveling to churches around the country, speaking on extracanonical texts, and continues to perform with the USO Show Troupe. You can follow her on Twitter @divadoesdiviniT or on Facebook at Diva Does Divinity.

Ginger Rue of Tuscaloosa, Alabama, is debuting a book series for elementary grades, about a nine-year-old girl named Aleca Zamm who can stop time just by saying her own name. "I think we've all, at some point, wished we could make time stand still. I feel it more than ever now that my children are growing up. I'd love to be able to set a pause button and hold them close just a little while longer!" The theme "In God's hands" hit home for Ginger when she taught her oldest how to drive. "I have to remind myself that God loves my daughter even more than I do and to trust that He will take care of her."

A cloud has hung over **Daniel Schantz** of Moberly, Missouri, for over a year, since his son-in-law lost his job as fleet manager in Kansas City. The job search has taken a toll on his son-in-law, and the loss of income has made life difficult. On the bright side, Dan's daughter Teresa is qualifying herself for paralegal work, which will help with finances and also give her something to do when her boys graduate from their homeschooling soon. "Dozens of friends have offered prayers, job leads, and references, and their support is so comforting. It's hard to watch our children suffer, but we have lived long enough to know that God's hands are at work, even when we don't see it."

Gail Thorell Schilling of Concord, New Hampshire, relied on the security of God's hands during her convalescence after breaking her kneecap. "My daughter Trina and her husband, Steve, took me in for the first week until I could navigate the stairs to my apartment. My daughter Tess lugged groceries and cleaned. My granddaughter Hannah took out the trash. Family and friends ferried me to school, church, and shopping—with lots of cozy conversations along the way." By Christmas, Gail was crutch-free to enjoy all four of her children and their families for the first time in sixteen years!

Penney Schwab of Copeland, Kansas, writes, "Our children have entered middle age and I wonder, *How did the time pass so quickly?* The year's highlights were a family reunion and grandson Ryan's wedding to Paige. Grandson David is a Marine Corps officer. Mark, Caleb, and Olivia are college students. Caden plays hockey and is active in 4-H club. Our little church was without a pastor for several months, and we realized how blessed we are with a church family who works together to sustain worship services, mission giving, and community activities."

Elizabeth Sherrill and her husband, John, of Hingham, Massachusetts, spent a lot of time this year in Nashville, Tennessee, as their son, a country songwriter, pioneered a new kind of recording. With the family gathered around the kitchen table, John Scott played the guitar, sang, and spun real-life yarns while his wife, Raena, sons, Peter and Spencer, John, and Elizabeth chimed in with stories of their own. "Of course we retold family favorites. But the surprise was how many great stories we'd never shared!"

Melody Bonnette Swang of Mandeville, Louisiana, recalls telling the hospice nurse who helped her care for her terminally ill husband that she just wanted it to be three years down the road so she'd be past the enormous grief she knew was coming. "Now, as I reflect back over the years, I'm so grateful for God's mercy, which carried me through those dark days." Today, Melody has many reasons to smile again—her church, her job producing shows for a local TV station, her four children and eleven grandchildren, and now an unexpected relationship. "I ran into an old friend whom I've known for over forty years, and we've talked every day since. I've learned through the years to trust God's perfect timing in my life."

Jon Sweeney moved from the Midwest back to northern New England (Montpelier, Vermont), changed jobs, graduated a child from college, and took his 4-year-old every day to preschool. Jon's popular history, *The Pope Who Quit*, was a History Book Club selection and optioned by HBO. A screenplay is currently in development.

"It's so different from when I was young," writes **Stephanie Thompson** of Edmond, Oklahoma. "I rarely studied and went to ballet class once a week." But daughter, Micah, has several hours of homework each evening, varsity sports practice after school, and club volleyball practice twice a week. Stephanie admits that being a parent of a teen is exhausting and sometimes overwhelming. Thank goodness that she and Michael don't have to do it alone. "We ask for wisdom daily and look for God to lead us. After all, Micah is His daughter too. She's in His hands."

 **Marilyn Turk** of Niceville, Florida, writes, "My husband, Chuck, and I thought we'd enjoy our time in retirement being footloose and fancy-free. But God had other plans for us. We started over in the role of parenting when our grandson came to live with us. Now our days are organized around Logan's lively schedule: school, sports, and Scouts. The challenge of raising a young child can be especially daunting at this stage of our lives, but we know that God has given us this ministry and is leading us through. During this time, God has also blessed my being part of *Daily Guideposts*, something I've always dreamed of."

 "I'm in disbelief as I open the box that's just been delivered," writes **Karen Valentin** of New York City. "It's been one year since I left my job. 'You're crazy!' was the consensus at the outset. I didn't know what the future held, but there was a fierce sense that I was meant to take the step. I wanted to spend more time with my children and nurture their talents. I also wanted to nurture my own. I was in God's hands. He created me to be the

artist and mother I longed to be, and I was confident He'd lead me there. I hold my memoir in my hands, *The Mother God Made Me to Be*, and I'm filled with gratitude. God has brought me here, and I can't wait to see what's next."

"Beth and I recently experienced the birth of our first grandchild, Alice Rushton Walker," writes **Scott Walker** of Macon, Georgia. "Generations flow together, and we glimpse the promise of the future. I visited Port-au-Prince, Haiti, to plan for Mercer University graduates to go there to teach English and to work in public-health clinics through the program Service First. Two young women will be our initial volunteers, and I ask you to pray for them. I published a new biography, *To Make a Difference*, which tells the story of a couple who discovers that their greatest joy is giving their wealth to worthy causes. I always learn the most from the lives and stories of other people. This is the Guideposts way!"

"My husband, Gene, suddenly lost the ability to speak," writes **Marion Bond West** of Watkinsville, Georgia. "My son Jon continued denying his long-standing addictions and remained homeless. Jon's twin, Jeremy, stopped taking prescription medications for bipolar disorder and began a perilous concoction of drugs. God promised in Isaiah 41:10 (NAS): 'Do not fear, for I am with you. Do not anxiously look about you, for I am your God. . . . Surely I will help you, surely I will uphold you with My righteous right hand.' Remaining steadfast in God's hand, I am shielded from fear."

SCRIPTURE REFERENCE INDEX

AUTHORS, TITLES, AND
SUBJECTS INDEX

A NOTE FROM THE EDITORS

We hope you enjoyed *Daily Guideposts 2017*, created by the Books and Inspirational Media Division of Guideposts, a nonprofit organization that touches millions of lives every day through products and services that inspire, encourage, help you grow in your faith, and celebrate God's love.

Thank you for making a difference with your purchase of this book, which helps fund our many outreach programs to military personnel, prisons, hospitals, nursing homes, and educational institutions.

We also create many useful and uplifting online resources. Visit Guideposts.org to read true stories of hope and inspiration, access OurPrayer network, sign up for free newsletters, download free e-books, join our Facebook community, and follow our stimulating blogs. To delve more deeply into *Daily Guideposts*, visit DailyGuideposts.org.

You may purchase the 2018 edition of *Daily Guideposts* anytime after July 2017. To order, visit Guideposts.org/DG2018, call (800) 932-2145, or write to Guideposts, PO Box 5815, Harlan, Iowa 51593.

Don't miss Daily Guideposts 2018!

We look forward to spending
another year with you.

Sharing *Daily Guideposts* with family and friends is
a wonderful way to nurture your relationships
with those you love.

Shop online at Guideposts.org/DG2018

DAILY
GUIDEPOSTS

A community of *friends* that accompanies
you on a path to a greater *connection*
with God, lifts your *spirits*, and reminds
you of all that is *precious* in life . . .
every day of the year.

 DailyGuideposts 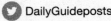 DailyGuideposts